Psychological Anthropology & Education

Psychological Anthropology & Education

A DELINEATION OF A FIELD OF INQUIRY

Charles Harrington

AMS PRESS
New York, NY

082167 12896

Library of Congress Cataloging in Publication Data

Harrington, Charles Christopher.
  Psychological anthropology and education.

  Bibliography: p.
  1. Ethnopsychology.   2. Educational anthropology.
  3. Personality and culture.   4. Ethnopsychology—
  Abstracts.   5. Educational anthropology—Abstracts.
  6. Personality and culture—Abstracts.   I. Title.
  GN502.H37   155.8   78-18943
  ISBN 0-404-16012-3

MANUFACTURED
IN THE UNITED STATES OF AMERICA

for Giselle

Foreword

In 1972 the National Academy of Education appointed a select committee of anthropologists to consider the role of anthropology in American education. Specifically, the committee was charged to explore ways by which the sometimes tenuous relationship of anthropological discipline to the domain of education could be improved; to promote and advocate the value of anthropological perspectives among educators; and to encourage anthropologists, long steeped in research outside the United States, to direct their studies toward an understanding and resolution of problems in American education.

To aid in its deliberations, six working papers on specific issues in educational anthropology were commissioned by the committee. One of these, on the state of psychological anthropology, was ably provided by Professor Charles Harrington of Teachers College, Columbia University. On a theoretical "school" of inquiry, this theme is of such obvious importance to educational research that the Committee called for a thorough and impartial review from an active practitioner of the specialization. Manifestly, psychological anthropology, a methodologically rigorous descendent of culture and personality studies of the past, is ideally suited to the systematic study of education, particularly in unraveling cross-cultural variations of learning processes, in delineating different patterns of socialization or enculturation, and in exploring the complex educational problems that follow in the wake of social change. As Janet Dolgin and I have stressed elsewhere, considerable differences exist—from society to society and from culture to culture—in the forms through which teaching and learning occur. From birth to maturity, individuals are socialized as members of particular groups. This is a process by which the patterns of group membership are appropriated and internalized as individuals become social actors in specific parts of specific social orders. Perhaps more importantly in these days of turmoil, individuals learn how to perceive their social world, their relation to it, and the means by which that world can be changed so that changes are, if not applauded, at least regarded as "real," "sane," or "appropriate." Psychological anthropology, in its assessments of such convoluted phenomena as ethnic stereotyping, psycho-cultural impact of migration, non-formal education, curricula, or educational institutions, has increasingly investigated the context in which individuals are socialized. And, as emphasized in the final report of the Committee to the National Academy of Education, psychological anthropologists have brought to such politically sensitive research—and thus to policy makers—a valuable corrective: the tendency of anthropology, given its cross-cultural stance, to question basic principles that other disciplines most often take for granted.

The working paper on psychological anthropology presented by Professor Harrington to the Committee was later augmented and refined for this volume. It now offers not only an incisive review of past accomplishment and failure in the specialization, but also a charting of the future, wherein a dynamic psychological anthropology can operate in the broad area of education. In this publication, the author provides full assessments of three distinctive subjects, each germane, if not central, to the concerns of psychological anthropologists involved in educational research—that is, perception and cognition, socialization, and culture contact. For each he maps historical dimensions, research trajectories, weaknesses, and strengths, and for each he offers annotations of a broad selection of the extant literature.

I am more than pleased to welcome this field-defining contribution to the social sciences and education. I would like to express my appreciation to Professor Harrington for having undertaken this important, demanding task and bringing it to fruition.

Lambros Comitas
Chairman, Committee on Anthropology and Education
National Academy of Education

Acknowledgments

In producing this document, I have benefitted from the collaboration of my colleagues in the anthropology and education program at Teachers College, Columbia University. I must also thank John Whiting, not only for the influence he has had on my ideas, but also for his collaboration in the production of Harrington and Whiting (1972) from which sections of Part II are derived. In addition, I owe a debt to a long collaboration with Peter Gumpert; in many areas it is difficult to tell where my thoughts end and his begin. Part One incorporates material from the jointly authored Gumpert and Harrington (1972). Sections of Part III were published previously in the *IRCD Bulletin*, and sections of Part IV were published in the *Teachers College Record*. When this document was originally prepared for the National Academy of Education in 1975 I decided that it would be useful to have annotated those items that my bibliographic search had identified as relevant to the work but which I had decided not to discuss in the text. In this way the reader of that report could put my material in context, to better assess what biases had led me to emphasize and to leave out. I am grateful to Elizabeth Sklar for providing the abstracts, which are complementary to the text which precedes them and thus limited in their intent. I owe a strong debt to a most conscientious, dedicated, and long-suffering assistant, Barbara Frankfurt, who has been able to translate scribble into prose, and remain calm in the face of untold obstacles and variations in temperament. The manuscript benefitted from readings by Jonas Soltis, Giselle Harrington, and Peter Gumpert. The preparation of the manuscript was partially subsidized by the National Academy of Education's Committee on Anthropology and Education, Lambros Comitas, Chairman, and the ERIC Clearinghouse on Urban Education, Edmund W. Gordon, Director.

Ancram, New York
April, 1979

Contents

Psychological Anthropology & Education

A DELINEATION OF A FIELD OF INQUIRY

Introduction

The goal of this book is to review current approaches and findings in psychological anthropology in such a way as to demonstrate what I perceive to be their relevance and importance to an adequate anthropology of education.

In meeting this goal, of necessity, I must abstract from the vast material generated by researchers in psychological anthropology certain topics which I feel are the most directly or immediately relevant to education. What follows does not pretend to be a summary of research in the field of psychological anthropology (see Barnouw 1973), but is limited to that research likely to lead to a psychological anthropology of education.

The field of inquiry known by the rubric psychological anthropology is concerned "with human behavior primarily in terms of the ideas which form the basis of the interrelationship between the individual and his society" (Hsu 1972:6). The field "take[s] it for granted that there is some connection between the make up of a culture and the particular personality (or personalities) of its human carriers . . . . By 'personality' we mean two things. We can mean, first, the sum-total of the overt modes of behavior of an individual, in which we discern some integration and consistence, and which we thus understand to be facets or 'traits' of that totaled patterned entity. Or secondly, we can mean some basic mental make-up underlying the pattern of overt behavior and accounting for it in the sense of a hidden machine or a casually effective set of 'factors' "(Nadel 1951:405). While this broad conceptualization delimits an area of inquiry, it is not helpful in constructing the boundaries of that inquiry. As Hsu has pointed out, since all human behavior is mediated through individual human beings, all human behavior is at once psychological and social in nature (Hsu 1972:5)

As a practical matter we define as psychological anthropology works which fit one of the following descriptions:

1. A work of psychological anthropology is one by an anthropologist who has a good knowledge of psychological concepts or by the member of another discipline who has a good knowledge of anthropological concepts.
2. Any work that deals with the individual as the locus of culture.
3. Any work that gives serious recognition to culture as an independent or dependent variable associated with personality.
4. Any work by an anthropologist which uses psychological concepts or techniques or by a scholar in a psychological discipline which provides directly pertinent data in forms which are useable by anthropologists . . . . [Hsu 1972:2].

The basic theoretical question that psychological anthropology raises is the one which most determines its relevance to the field of education—the question of enculturation. Psychological anthropology as a part of anthropology has a goal of explaining the diversity of human cultures, and how cultures, and hence the diversity, are maintained over time. To the psychological anthropologist the latter explanation lies in the ability of the culture to transmit itself from one generation to another, and, in the process, to grow and incorporate some change.

Surely it should not be necessary to construct arguments for the relevance to education of this branch of anthropology. This issue is not as clear as it might be, however. When anthropologists first became formally involved in the study of education and began to appear on the faculty of schools of education, their *raison d'etre* was often to overcome the tremendous dominance of the psychologists in the field. Thus many anthropologists of education in a sense made their careers, or at least justified their existences, by researching and behaving differently from psychologists. As a result, a curious imbalance has occurred within the field of anthropology and education. Because psychological anthropology (or culture and personality as Levine, 1973, still prefers) was associated, at least to some, with psychology and psychiatry, anthropology-and-education scholars tended to ignore it and even to respond as if it were pretty much in the "enemy's" camp. That this trend continues to the present is evidenced by the fact that the recent Burnett (1974) bibliography of anthropology and education, commissioned by the Anthropology and Education Committee of the National Academy of Education and published under the sponsorship of the Council on Anthropology and Education of the American Anthropological Association, specifically excludes studies from psychological anthropology, at the same time acknowledging their possible significance.

It seems to me very likely that in linking their attitude toward psychology to psychological anthropology, anthropologists of education have (some might think in a very literal sense) thrown the baby out with the bath water. Accordingly, this book reviews the literature of psychological anthropology, hoping to make it useable to students of education, while at the same time arguing its relevance to that inquiry. The general point is that no study of education can reasonably ignore the cross-cultural studies of learning process, socialization and social change of psychological anthropology. These are essential, indeed major, components of any anthropology and education.

Psychological anthropology, because it is embedded within anthropology, has three contributions to the study of education which it shares with the rest of the discipline and which, taken together, form the basic orientations for the studies which produce the substantive results to be discussed in detail below. These three orientations have to do with the definition of education, method, and cross-cultural comparison.

Education

Anthropological definitions of education have consistently marked a point of departure between anthropology and other disciplines. Anthropologists have taken very broad views of education. They have insisted that education not be confused with the narrower concept of "schooling." By defining education as encompassing both formal (or directed) as well as informal learning, the anthropological conceptualization of education has become quite nearly "everything that happens to a person throughout his lifetime," while definitions used by educators have occasionally been so narrow as to be limited to what a child learns through the formal curriculum in school. While several historians of education have, in recent years, argued that a definition of education which includes more than just schooling is essential (see e.g., Cremin 1970), it is still a defensible position that anthropology in general, and psychological anthropology in particular, have early on taken a broad view of education (see e.g., Whiting 1941), while those professionally concerned with education have taken more narrow views.

Method

A second hallmark of anthropological approaches (and hence of a psychological anthropology of education) is the methodology brought to bear on the problems being researched. Social and psychological anthropology both share a dedication to the variety of techniques subsumed under the label *participant observation*. However, within that shared orientation, each has developed more specific, more specialized, ancillary methods in response to the problems each has chosen to solve. In particular, psychological anthropology has emphasized the importance of the systematic observation and recording of data, the use of adaptations of psychological techniques of personality measurement, projective testing, and experimental design to learn about individuals, and the analysis of "cultural products" as clues to learning and cognition. In addition to these methods, which are relevant to the concerns of this paper

as techniques available to observe and assess educational outcomes, and which are reviewed in Barnouw (1973), a part of
the field has been concerned with producing what for our purposes we might call "narratives of education," or more traditionally, "life histories." These (more or less auto-) biograpical
materials provide vivid descriptions of growing up through
adulthood in societies with and without formal schooling, and
are especially relevant materials to those interested in education in its broadest sense. While the heyday of "life history"
production was in the 30s and 40s, autobiographies continue to
appear (e.g., Spradley 1969). An important development of the
50s and 60s, however, was the appearance of records of family
histories which enabled the reader to compare descriptions of
events from the point of view of various family participants.
The pioneer and really sole artisan of these family
autobiographies was, of course, Oscar Lewis; and while the ex-
pense and enormity of his undertakings have discouraged im-
itators, his works remain a legacy for those who would seek to
understand the details of family interpersonal dynamics and
their place in the socialization of children (Lewis 1951, 1961,
1965, 1969). However, narratives in general are out of fashion.
They are, after all, secondary data, subject to the whims of
recall and having dangers akin to those of the self-report
methods of other disciplines (for a bibliography of life histories,
sec Langness 1965). The hallmark of psychological anthropologists of the present is the generation of primary data,
either by observation or through systematic elicitation.

Cross-Cultural Comparison

The third anthropological orientation is that we insist on examining educational phenomena in a cross-cultural framework, as part of an anthropological commitment to the study of
what Chase calls "contemporary man," everyone alive on
earth. As such, we are not content with what so much of main-

stream psychology, especially experimental psychology, often seems to be: the psychology of 100 undergraduates at a large midwestern university. While many psychologists have become aware of the necessity of broadening their subject base, the mainstream of the discipline is still culture bound. Similarly, while studies of our own society do occur in anthropology, the mainstream of the discipline almost excludes such study. Psychologists have tended to view the cross-cultural method as one by which certain assumptions about personality development may be tested. Anthropologists, on the other hand, are more likely to focus on the shared aspects of human behavior and to use such studies as tests of hypotheses concerning the way in which elements of a culture can be integrated by underlying psychological processes.

•   •   •

The three anthropological orientations described above are implicit or explicit in a vast amount of substantive findings which are relevant to an informed inquiry into education. Much of it has appeared, however, in professional disciplinary journals and in forms not easily accessible to those other than fellow specialists conducting similar kinds of research. It is our purpose here to synthesize substantive material together into a coherent and integrated form, so as to make its relevance to educational inquiry apparent. In organizing the material I have delimited three major areas of inquiry as deserving of top priority for this report. Each is closely linked to each of the others, and some of our classifications of particular studies may appear arbitrary. My intent in setting up the three areas is not to enshrine each as a separate area of inquiry, but merely to represent an organizational tool whereby the vast amount of material we need to examine can be handled. The three areas for which psychological anthropology offers substantive findings are: perception and cognition, socialization, and social change.

In examining the relevance of psychological anthropology to the study of education, I have chosen to begin the substantive review of the literature with an examination of studies of perception and cognition. There are good reasons for this. First, examining the learning process itself, we must be concerned with what individuals learn with, and for the purposes of this book, that means their perceptual equipment; i.e., what they can be aware of which is a precondition of learning. Secondly, what do they do with their perceptions? We shall use the word cognition to refer to the structure of thought processes. Taken together, perception and cognition describe how people experience their world and think about it.

The term, "socialization," to denote the process by which culture is transmitted from one generation to the next, gained favor in the 1930s. One use of the term described the socialization process as "an account of how a new person is added to the group and becomes an adult capable of meeting the traditional expectations of his society" (Dollard 1935). While the term acquired formal acceptance in the 1954 review article by Child, anthropologists in particular have been unhappy with the term's emphasis on social roles and behavior to the exclusion of beliefs, values, and other cognitive aspects of culture. Alternate terms proposed have included "culturalization" (Kluckhohn 1939) and "enculturation" (Herskovits 1948). In this report the term "socialization" is often used as a synonym of the term "enculturation" in its broadest sense. This is the sense in which "socialization" is used by Hartley and Hartley, "as learning to be a member of a group. It means perceiving what is considered to be correct and essential in a group; accepting these precepts as right, good, and necessary; and learning to behave in congruence with them. This progress includes ways of thinking, or feeling as well as ways of behaving, and it covers attitudes towards one's self as well as attitudes and behavior towards other people" (Hartley and Hartley 1952:206). Psychological anthropology views socialization as a learning process essential to the structure and continuation of every human, and more recently non-human-primate, society (see Poirier 1973).

While discussing socialization, cultures are treated as stable from generation to generation. In our discussion of social change we shall examine psychological anthropological studies of acculturation, especially in studies of migration and ethnicity within the United States. We now examine the three areas in order.

The reader is cautioned that the discussions are selective, and that the materials are embedded in a fuller set of materials arranged at the end of the book as an annotated bibliography (where works already discussed in the text are omitted). Our selections are made with our purpose in mind: the delineation of a field of inquiry for psychological anthropology and education. Implicit in that commitment is a presentation of what the field could and should be, not simply a report of what it is.

I

Perception and Cognition

Students of education have long understood that knowledge about how children and adults experience and think about their world is as important to their discipline as is knowledge of how people learn. The study of perception and cognition is considered fundamental to education: first, because these processes are assumed to be biological givens, universally employed by humans in all human groups; and second, because one must know how people perceive and think in order to understand what one can teach them and how to do it efficiently.

In relying primarily on psychologists for basic knowledge about perception and cognition, educators have been led astray in certain crucial respects. First of all, they have adopted explanations and theories of perceiving and thinking that were based on psychologists' culture-bound interpretations of these data. Second, they have adopted measurement techniques based on culturally restricted assumptions and, employing them, have reached erroneous (not to mention racist) conclusions about the functioning of members of groups other than their own. Psychological anthropologists, in contrast, have searched both for cross-cultural uniformities and differences in studying perception and cognition, with the goal of developing more universally applicable theories which would be useful in understanding education in its narrow sense, as well as other aspects of enculturation.

The literature reviewed in this section is roughly divided into subsections concerned with "perceptual" processes and "cognitive" processes respectively. It is important to point out that this division is a completely arbitrary one, since the two terms actually refer to two inseparable aspects of a single process; for humans, at any rate, there are no perceptual processes in which cognitive processes do not play a part and no cognitive processes that do not also involve some aspects of perception. One additional caveat is perhaps in order here. The substantive findings presented below represent only tentative and incomplete answers to the fundamental questions they address. Frequently they merely suggest reformulations of old questions, and it is these questions that we consider vital.

Perception

The importance of studies of perception can perhaps best be made clear by examining one of the first researches in the field: the now famous Torres Straits Expedition reports of W. H. R. Rivers (Rivers 1901). While the susceptibility of the subjects to optical illusions may seem a trivial subject for study, the idea that impelled the Rivers research was embedded in late 19th century thought, which dichotomized savages from civilized peoples, and which consistently searched for explanations—often racist—of why the subjects of travelers' reports had not advanced to "the higher stages of civilization" (Malinowski 1948:70). For the psychologists of the time, one explanation for the arrested development of the culture of the savages was "faulty equipment." That is, an inability to perceive as accurately as the European. In the section on cognition, we shall of course encounter the same argument, but there the suspect organ will be the brain, and the issue intellect.

Rivers set out to test comparatively the perceptual equipment of the savages with samples of European subjects, using optical illusion as an operationalization of perceptual ability: the more susceptible, the more inferior the equipment. Of course, whatever his findings, the idea—and its underlying but thickly veiled racism—has continued into the present. For example, in a prestigious review of the literature on cross-cultural measurement of perceptual and motor skills, Provins, Bell, Biensheuvel, and Adiseshiah (1968) argue that the evaluation of perceptual skills in different cultural groups is important as a way of determining the "ease" with which a primitive group may accept technological advancement, or be absorbed into a technologically more sophisticated society. The important thing about Rivers' results was the fact that differences between Western and non-Western peoples existed in both directions; i.e., that the non-Western peoples seem to be less subject to one illusion while more subject to another. Obviously, the failure to find differences that are consistent in direction eliminates any simple explanation of the existing differences, including the view, prevalent during the 19th century, that since "primitive" peoples are less well endowed intellectually than "civilized" peoples, the former ought to be more easily duped by illusions and therefore consistently more subject to them. The suggestion in Rivers' data that the "primitives might actually be less subject to the Muller-Lyer illusion is embarrassing to any such hypothesis" (Segall, Campbell, Herskovits 1966:64). Explanations of Rivers' findings had to recognize the significance of experience in the formation of inference habits that affect perception. In 1966 Segall, Campbell, and Herskovits reported on an attempt to test the ideas raised by Rivers' research in a comparative study of illusion susceptibility in sixteen cultures. They conclude:

> Perception is an aspect of human behavior, and as such is subject to many of the same influences that shape other aspects of behavior. In particular, each individual's experiences combine in a complex fashion to determine his reaction to a given stimulus situation. To the extent that certain classes of experiences are more likely to occur in some cultures than in others, differences in behavior across cultures, including differences in perceptual tendencies, can be great enough even to surpass the ever-present individual differences within cultural groupings.
>
> We have reported here a study that revealed significant differences across cultures in susceptibility to several geometric, or optical illusions. It should be stressed that these differences are not "racial" differences. They are differences produced by the same kinds of factors that are responsible for individual dif-

ference in illusion susceptibility, namely, differences in experience. The findings we have reported, and the findings of
others we have reviewed, point to the conclusion that to a
substantial extent we learn to perceive; that in spite of the
phenomenally absolute character of our perceptions, they are
determined by perceptual inference habits; and that various inference habits are differentially likely in different societies. For
all mankind, the basic process of perception is the same; only
the contents differ and these differ only because they reflect different perceptual habits (Segall, Campbell, and Herskovits
1966:213-214).

Segall, Campbell, and Herskovits's accounts are not un-
challenged. Jahoda (1966) points out that the simple ecological
interpretation of "carpenteredness" led him to predict incor-
rectly differences between the Lobi and Dagomba, on the one
hand, and the Ashanti on the other (all in Ghana), in susceptibility to Muller-Lyer and Horizontal-Vertical perceptions.
Further, groups with the same ecology have been found to
show differing responses (based on data from Morgan 1959,
Reuning 1959, and Mundy-Castle and Nelson 1962). Jahoda
and Stacey (1970) reported a comparison of Ghanian students
and Scottish students, suggesting formal education, not
ecology, as the critical variable. Other variables linked to illusion susceptibility are age (Walters 1942, Piaget and Morf 1956
[for Horizontal-Vertical]) and "sophisticated environment"
(Werner and Wapner 1955). However, Dawson, Young, and
Choi (1973) have found support for the position that a
carpentered world also contributes to the variance in illusion
susceptibility.

The Segall, Campbell, and Herskovits work still remains
definitive, however, because of its scope and rigor. Failures to
replicate its results in retesting any one group for comparison
are not as worrisome for their analysis as would be a new cross-
cultural study, like theirs, in which effects of formal education
as well as environment could be tested. It is also interesting

that the criticisms of Segall, Campbell, and Herskovits come only from psychologists with other theoretical axes to grind and not from anthropology.

In addition to the "carpentered world" effect of the environment on perception, travelers and anthropologists have commented more informally on the impact of a physical environment on perception. Filmmaker Robert Flaherty ("Nanook of the North," "Moana," "Man of Aran," etc.) tells vividly of being on hunts with Nanook when Nanook would navigate through the snow by signs that he, Flaherty, could not "see." Clearly, immersion in an environment can enable a person to see differences so subtle that they are missed by a novice (e.g., degrees of packedness of snow, in the Flaherty case), or form automatic habits of visual inference, which may be totally missed by the visitor who does not comprehend their significance; e.g., during a blizzard, the direction of fur on one's parka (if the wind is consistent) can tell relative direction (Carpenter, Varley, and Flaherty 1959).

This, and the "carpentered world" hypothesis, focus upon informal, experimental learning. The inferences we learn to make by being a part of a particular physical scene become established over time. Psychologists have also been fascinated with the effects of exposure to two-dimensional representation on visual differences. Specifically Hudson (1960) raised the question of the difficulty of perceiving three dimensions from two-dimensional representations, like drawings and pictures, for people unaccustomed to such phenomena. Anthropologists had noted these phenomena for years but Hudson (1960) presented a detailed examination of the problem, which was followed up by several researchers (e.g., Mundy-Castle and Nelson 1962; Dawson 1963; Vernon 1965; Deregowski 1968, 1969; Deregowski and Byth 1970; Hudson 1962; and Mundy-Castle 1966). Hudson (1967) summarizes this research and explicitly deals with its relevance to education. He offers the following rare commentary on educational planners:

We take it very much for granted that methods which are only moderately successful in our own cultures will prove equally, if not highly, successful in an alien culture. We fall into the error of thinking of the black man's mind as a *tabula rasa,* which we have only to fill with the benefits of our cultural experience in order to promote whatever objectives we have in mind. We forget or ignore the fact that the black man possessses his own indigenous culture.

Is it rational for us to shut our eyes to the role that culture plays in education and in the assimilation and association of new concepts and practices? We do not ignore cultural and environmental differences among the national populations of Europe. Why should we do so in Africa? Even in such a limited field as that of pictorial perception, the facts, once we become aware of them, illustrate the gravity and extensiveness of our irrationality (Hudson 1967).

Kilbride (1971) and Kilbride and Robbins (1969) provide strong evidence for the position that for pictorial depth perception, visual perception skills are largely learned and significantly related to relative amounts of exposure to Western culture. Their data are from the Baganda of Uganda. At another level of study, Child (1968) examined judgments of the relative aesthetic quality of paintings by expert judges of several societies, and concluded that there was some generality to aesthetic principles. Ekman and Friesen (1971), Ekman, Sorenson, and Friesen (1969), and Cuceloglu (1967) argue for a similar cross-cultural universality in emotion attributed to facial expressions.

The physical environment's effect on perception is often seen as mediated by language, to which effect on perception we now turn. Human languages provide their speakers with sets of categories into which experiences are classified. Snow is important to Eskimos; they distinguish types, ergo they are said to perceive snow differently than peoples who are not familiar enough with it to require more than one category. Linguists are perfectly familiar with the inability of speakers of languages to "hear" sounds which are not phonemically distinctive in their own tongue. Thus, English speakers often do not "hear" aspiration, etc. Many researchers have investigated the categorization of a color, a particularly fascinating area in which to study classification, since objectively color is one continuum which can be arbitrarily divided into categories. This research has not produced much that I would consider directly relevant to educational inquiry, but a couple of observations are in order. Kellaghan's (1968) study of color categorization in African children, using the Weigl-Goldstein-Scheerer color form sorting test and other instruments, found Irish subjects performing better than their Nigerian (Yoruba) contemporaries. However, their data suggest that lack of familiarity with test materials could account for the supposed "deficits" in the Yoruba subjects, a finding which again emphasizes the learned aspects of category perception. More recently, Adams and Osgood (1973) presented data from a 23 culture semantic differential study of the affective or feeling correlates of certain colors. Their findings are of relevance to educational inquiry and even to the design of education facilities, since they suggest that there are strong "universal trends" in the attribution of affective domains to colors. A detailed review of the colors and their affective attributes is beyond our scope here, but we do feel obligated to enter one demurrer. The consistency of their "cross-cultural results" may be due not so much to the universality of the attributions under study, but rather to the instruments they used, which require subjects who could read and write! We shall return to this point below in our discussion of cognition.

Recently, Levi-Strauss has emphasized the importance of classification, and the linkages to perception are easy to see from some of his examples.

> The Hanunoo classify all forms of the local avifauna into seventy-five categories... [they] distinguish about a dozen kinds of snakes...sixty-odd types of fish...more than a dozen... types of fresh and salt water crustaceans...a similar number

of... types of arachnids and myriapods.... The thousands of insect forms present are grouped by the Hanunoo into a hundred and eight categories, including thirteen for ants and termites.... Salt water mollusks... of more than sixty classes are recognized by the Hanunoo, while terrestrial and fresh water types number more than twenty-five....Four distinct types of bloodsucking leeches are distinguished...altogether 461 animal types are recorded....The acute observation of the pygmies and their awareness of the inter-relationships between the plant and animal life... is strikingly pointed out by their discussions of the living habits of bats. The *tididin* lives on the dry leaves of palms, the *dikidik* on the underside of the leaves of the wild banana, the *litlit* in bamboo clumps, the *kolumboy* in holes in trees, the *konanaba* in dark thickets, and so forth. In this manner, the Pinatubo Negritos can distinguish the habits of more than fifteen species of bats. Of course, the classification of bats, as well as of insects, birds, animals, fish and plants, is determined primarily by their actual physical differences and/or similarities...

Even a child can frequently identify the kind of tree from which a tiny wood fragment has come and, furthermore, the sex of that tree, as defined by Kabiran notions of plant sex, by observing the appearances of its wood and bark, its smell, its hardness, and similar characteristics. Fish and shellfish by the dozen are known by individually distinctive terms, and their separate features and habits, as well as the sexual differences within each type, are well recognized (Levi-Strauss 1966).

Durkheim and Mauss (1903) is an obvious source of many of Levi-Strauss' ideas. Their conclusion that classification systems were not innate (or indeed psychologically derived), but were instead products of society (or culture) is fundamental to the notion that humans classify as they are taught to classify, not as a result of innate patterning. Today we might say that the capacity and psychological processing provide limits within which classification systems are learned. Further, Levi-Strauss's position is sympathetic to earlier positions of various schools in linguistics (e.g. Lee 1950) that reality is codified, and grasped through language, and that classification systems and therefore world view (perceptions) vary from language to language.

Not only does long term exposure to environment and language affect perception, but experimental psychologists have been able to demonstrate the short-term exposure to group pressure can also bring about changes in perception. A remarkable series of experimental studies by Asch (1956), which stimulated a large number of studies of "conformity" by other social psychologists, argued that information provided by a majority of other people about the attributes of an object was frequently taken into account by observers of the object, even when that information contradicted the evidence of the person's own senses. Although there is considerable evidence (e.g., Deutsch and Gerard, 1955) to suggest that some apparent "conformity" to majority perception may represent mere surface responses to emotional factors such as fear of group disapproval, it remains clear that the judgments of others are, under certain conditions, used as information by observers in categorizing ambiguous stimuli. Moscovici et al. (1969) and Biener (1972), for example, have demonstrated that observers' thresholds for labelling colors can be influenced by the color judgments that are radically different from those of the experimental subject and of other members of the observing groups. It is not clear from the evidence whether these effects are transitory or whether they exert long-term influence on the category boundaries of the experimental subject; but it is not difficult to infer that repeated exposure to these effects would indeed have long-term consequences.

Evidence of more indirect forms of social role influence upon perception is seen in the work of Munroe, Munroe, and Daniels, and of Herman Witkin and his colleagues. Munroe, Munroe, and Daniels (1969), in a replication of an experiment by Bruner and Goodman, have shown that the size of the father's landholdings in Kenya was related to the perception by children seven to thirteen years old of the size of a series of coins. The poorer the father, the larger the child reported the size of the coin to be. The explanation given is of relative

deprivation sort: Coins are more important to children of
poorer parents, and this importance is projected to perception
of size. What is important here is not so much the explanation
as the further evidence that social role affects perception.
Socialization to certain roles in society other than social class
has also been shown to have perceptual consequences. Recent
studies of field dependency made in the United States (Witkin,
et al., 1962) offer within-culture evidence that perceptual style
correlates with social role. In the field dependency test, in
which a vertical line is projected upon a shifting background,
women, more often than men, are fooled into thinking the line
is no longer vertical. This field dependence is paralleled in the
woman's role by her greater socio-emotional competence and
her greater concern with others' feelings.

Further investigations into field dependency cross-culturally,
including its associations with behavior and with biology as
well, seem especially promising. For example, Berry (1966)
found field dependency differences between men and women to
be culturally determined. Eskimo women are not treated as
dependent; Temne men exercise strong control over their
wives. Temne women show strong field dependency when
compared with Temne men. Eskimo women show no differences in field dependency from Eskimo men. MacArthur
(1967) replicated Berry's findings for Eskimos. Socialization
into the requirements of a social role, then, can be seen as actually influencing perception, which of course thereby reinforces future role learning. Irving (1970) provides additional
evidence from a study of Dutch people, Mexicans, and U.S.
blacks that social role prescriptions affect field dependence
perceptions; Wober's (1967) review of the African literature is
consistent with this interpretation. The demonstrated association of perceptual skills with social role prescriptions has enormous consequences for educators in two ways: (1) showing a
self-training effect (i.e., the more a person is socialized the
more likely he is to be channeled to learn particular skills and
less likely to learn others); (2) because of the latter, there is a
built-in resistance to later learning which requires different

perceptual habits. For example, in social movements whose aim is a redefinition of sex role behaviors, are men less able to learn socio-emotional roles because they are less field dependent? Are women by the same token less likely to achieve instrumental success? While one would not argue that perceptual habits can alone account for such behavior, the existence of an effect on learning is reasonably inferred from the available evidence.

By stressing the cumulative nature of the socialization experience and the concurrent blinding to other options that takes place, Endleman (1967) properly describes the process of socialization as one in which culture shows one the world, but makes one blind and deaf to worlds revealed by other perceptual skills. Adler and Harrington (1970) have applied the point of view represented by these studies from the psychological anthropology of perception in constructing their model of how political socialization takes place.

The studies above are important to educators in several respects. They demonstrate, in the first place, that the content of perception is culturally determined and culturally learned, and argue strongly against assumptions of biological differences between people of different cultures as accounting for differences in perception. Second, they suggest that certain perceptual styles, emphases, and skills—certain aspects of the perceptual process—are also culturally influenced and not biologically determined. Third, the studies can be seen to demonstrate that it is important for the student of education to understand how these cultural factors operate to influence the content and process of perception; clearly, such an understanding can be helpful to educators in a variey of ways. Finally, many of the studies provide specific information about the content and process of perception in particular cultures, and suggest research techniques whereby such information can be gained about still other cultures and subcultures, members of which are encountered by educators in their work.

Cognition

The difficulty with the study of cognition is that it cannot be studied directly, because we cannot observe what actually goes on inside someone else's head. All we can study are responses to stimuli provided, inferring but not directly demonstrating the existence of cognitive structures. This particular axiom was forgotten for a while in a rush of enthusiasm over componential analysis in the late 50s and 60s, but Burling and others have more recently provided a corrective, and simple-minded equation of analytic models and psychologically "real" models (Schneider 1965) now seem to be more rare. Ardener (1971) has performed a valuable service by putting the entire problem into historical context (a history was often ignored or even denied by writers in the 60s), rehearsing the problems of the linguistic analogy upon which so much anthropological research into cognition is based, and fully dealing with the problems of the indeterminacy of psychological reality.

Cross-cultural research in cognitive development is, of course, a large field, and one in which numbers of psychologists have worked. Indeed, of all the literature reviewed here, the perception and cognition literature is the most dominated by psychologists, and when anthropologists are included, they generally are part of an inter-disciplinary team. One of the differences between the two disciplines, psychology and anthropology, is important in understanding this literature: that the two disciplines have differing usages of the term "cross-cultural."

Put simply, for the psychologists a comparison of English and French children is called cross-cultural research; for the anthropologist, in most usages, it would not be. The anthropologist is likely to apply the term "cross-cultural research" to research that as been carried out across several cultures, and in which non-western cultures form a major group. The English-French study alluded to above would, for most anthropologists, not include sufficient representation of the world's diversity to be cross cultural, and secondly, would be interpreted as a comparative study of groups within the Western European culture area.

It seems most fruitful to make a detailed analysis of cognitive issues as they occur in the study of one particular aspect of cognition most relevant to educators: intelligence or intellectual functioning. Anthropology and psychology have, during the past hundred years, developed a number of assumptions about the relationship between culture and thinking which are frequently quite divergent. The assumptions in turn affect how each discipline explains apparent differences in the thinking of people of different cultures.

There is an anecdote sometimes told in introductory anthropology courses, concerning an educational psychologist who sets out for Australia to test the intelligence of the aborigines. He expects to be able to account for their "backwardness" by showing that their intelligence is not up to standard. He arrives in Australia with IQ tests under his arm, rents a Land Rover, and sets out across the outback to find his subjects. As he drives through the desert, his Land Rover fails him. His supply of water runs low, and he sets out on foot in growing desperation; eventually he collapses in the barren land. Two passing aborigines come upon him shortly thereafter. Scooping sand not two feet from where the psychologist's head lies, they expose a spring and give him water. Revived, he signals that he is hungry, and one of the aborigines throws a stone, kills a rabbit, and feeds the psychologist.

The point of the story, of course, is that the Western educational psychologist very visibly failed an aboriginal intelligence test. Anthropologists have long taken the point of view that coping with the exigencies of the physical and social environments of any culture demands the full range of mental abilities that humans possess. As Wallace (1962:355) has said:

> To suppose that the "primitive" is *unable* to think rationally, for instance, would lead to the expectation that the primitive hunter would perform the following feat of cerebration with

suicidal consequences: A rabbit has four legs. That animal has four legs. Therefore, that animal is a rabbit.

Further, the anthropologist who studies an unfamiliar culture typically has enormous difficulty mastering the intricacies of its members' daily functioning, and feels woefully ignorant and unintelligent while attempting to do so. It is not surprising, therefore, that the anthropologist can only understand the concept of "intelligence" as relating to an individual's ability to perform in a particular cultural setting. From this point of view, intelligence tests as we know them measure success at performing tasks in ways associated with a Western European lifestyle—particularly that of the American middle class.

But those from other cultures (or subcultures) who do not perform well on such culture-bound tests are often labeled cognitively or culturally deprived by non-anthropologists. Psychologist George Miller (1971) says:

> Every culture has its myths. One of our most persistent is that non-literate people possess something we like to call a "primitive mentality" [because it is] different from and [therefore] inferior to our own . . . . The same stereotype is likely to be applied to ethnic minorities living in the West.

Anthropologists have long jousted with these twin ethnocentrisms: that cultures different from Western civilization are inferior, and that "primitive" cultures (e.g., those with hunter-gatherer economies) are the result of an inferior mentality among their members. The point of view of modern anthropologists, based on their experience with these other cultures, has emphasized the cognitive unity of mankind —which means, essentially, that thought processes (such as logic) do not differ from culture to culture. What differs, according to this doctrine, is content (what is thought about), situation (the conditions that elicit the thinking), and the premises that are accepted as true or binding. The cognitive unity idea has not always been accepted among anthropologists, however. Boas (1911) turned anthropologists away from a very different position. That earlier position, which was patterned after Darwin's and Huxley's biological propositions, posited that complex, civilized societies evolved from primitive ones in a systematic way. Furthermore, just as the young of a species presumably pass through the species' evolutionary history during development, the minds of children in civilized societies also pass through primitive stages in mental development, which reflect the mental capacities and strategies of adults in primitive societies. Differences in material and religious culture, then, imply differences in thinking; primitive man was illogical or, as the French Levy-Bruhl (1923) put it, "prelogical" rather than logical, concrete rather than abstract, and so on. Current thought, as most recently formulated by Levi-Strauss, is quite different. As Cole, *et al.* (1971) interpret it, all men seek to make nature accessible to rational inquiry. "Both Western and non-Western strategies seek objective knowledge of the universe; both proceed by ordering, classifying, and systematizing information; both create coherent systems."

Psychologists, too, have been fascinated by evolutionary metaphors. The idea that the history of the human species can be seen in the development of civilized children enjoyed enormous popularity around the turn of the century. Furthermore, it was widely believed that primitive men had primitive minds. The primitive child, in one writer's summary of the literature as of 1928, was thought to be precocious until puberty, when his perspicacity came to a dead halt. This arrested mental development, as it was called, had been attributed to a variety of factors: sexual excesses and alcoholism, biological inferiority, and the culture's inability to provide the resources which make further development possible. Although the first of these explanations for assumed cognitive deficiencies has passed out of the psychological literature, the latter two—biological and cultural inferiority—remain as alternative accounts of the reasons underlying the mental deficiencies that are still assumed by some psychologists to exist among people of certain cultures. The resistance to change of this assumption is in part due to the rise to prominence of a subdiscipline within psychology which has had a continuing concern with the measurement of intellectual functioning.

The intelligence testing movement began around the turn of this century when school officials in Paris asked Alfred Binet to produce a test which would identify dull children, because they could not trust teachers to make unbiased assessments. Work on existing and new intelligence tests is still going on, and many of the psychologists who have been involved with the refinements of these instruments are highly respected in the profession. The standardized tests of intelligence are now used not only to predict school and vocational performance, but also in psychodiagnostic work. Some of the basic issues involved in intelligence testing, however, remain unresolved. There is scholarly disagreement, for example, about whether the term "intelligence" should be taken as having a psychological reality—as representing some characteristic of the brain—or whether it should be taken merely as a convenient abstraction, a mathematical entity which describes certain interrelated behaviors. The second view is the more cautious and perhaps the more common one among psychologists working in this field. Some of these researchers, however, along with most laymen, do view the general factor that is common to performance on several subtests of standard intelligence tests as if it were ". . . *a capacity* [emphasis ours] for abstract reasoning and problem solving." The quote is from Arthur Jensen's controversial 1969 paper, but Jensen is far from alone in his view. For example, D. Wechsler (1944:3), who developed the most commonly used test of adult intelligence, gave this definition: "Intelligence is the aggregate or global capacity of the individual to act purposefully, to think rationally, and to deal effectively with his environment."

We should point out that Jensen and others like him, who use comparisons of IQ scores of "whites and blacks" to show evidence for the genetic origins of intelligence, are talking about neither intelligence nor heredity, but the relationship between two cultural categories: "white and black (or Negro)" are not genetic classifications but cultural ones (Washburn 1963). IQ tests measure performance on skills in a way which successfully elicits them from members of one subculture. Therefore, the relationship shows that those whom a culture classes as "white" appear to do better than those classed as "black" at tasks which the culture trains "whites" to do. What is truly astounding about the Jensen controversy is the relative absence of this anthropological commonplace in the criticisms that followed publication of Jensen's paper. Although Jensen's argument for heritability rests on data other than "white-Negro" comparisons, the main thrust of his paper is the failure of compensatory education programs, and we all know what that means. Intelligence, from this vantage point, is "what intelligence tests test," and it is measurable by these carefully designed standard instruments. Being measurable, it must be a quantity of something which varies from one individual to another and, equally likely, from one group to another.

Note that the reification of the abstract idea "intelligence" is both subtle and easy to make; the ease with which it is accomplished can be traced to the unstated assumption that anything quantifiable and measurable must have a more-or-less physical existence. Certainly anything we have taken so very much trouble to measure reliably and validly must exist, or else why would we have taken so much trouble with it? Furthermore, the intelligence test scores of individuals don't really change very much when they are administered repeatedly to the same individuals; they predict performance on many tasks that are very important to us, and there is evidence that scores vary less within families than among them. All these factors, along with certain politico-ideological considerations, make the reification of the concept virtually inevitable. It is only a small step from reifying "intelligence" to viewing it as a causal factor; the lack of technological progress in a nation or culture, for example, has often been seen as caused by a deficiency in intelligence in its population. The reader will see that such a theoretical position is easily supported by comparing the intelligence test scores of a random sample of individuals drawn from their culture with a sample drawn from ours. The fact that the intelligence tests were made for our culture is easy to forget as soon as one has reified the concept they are supposed to measure.

A great many Americans, for example, accept as valid an ideology of opportunity which posits a causal link between high ability, working hard, and receiving high social and material rewards. People who believe that those in control of social rewards act upon this principle tend to attribute their difficulties in "getting ahead" to their own failings of ability, effort, or both. Intelligence tests and the various related aptitude tests that are replacing them in schools are generally believed to be valid indicators of ability, so that when they are used to assign pupils to different classrooms and different schools, the general view is that assignment has been fair and reasonable. It has been documented that assignment to "slow" classrooms and inferior schools contributes to inferior learning, and tends to lead eventually to placement in inferior social positions—thus perpetuating existing economic differences among subcultures whose members tend to perform differently on the tests. Those who believe that the ideology of opportunity "works" probably wish to believe also that most people have received more or less what their abilities and efforts warrant; they therefore have some stake in believing in the cross-cultural validity of the tests that are used to make school assignments. Explanations of ethnic differences in test scores form particularly striking examples of the process. As Washburn (1963) points out, "...if you look at the literature, you will find that when two groups of Whites differ in their IQ's, the explanation of the difference is immediately sought in schooling, environment, economic position of parents, and so on, but that when Negroes and Whites differ in precisely the same way the difference is said to be genetic."

Once it is established that members of a given culture or subculture are intellectually "deficient," one can begin to inquire into the causes of the deficiency. Arthur Jensen and a number of others have emphasized the role of genetic differences; Philip Vernon and others have pointed to "cultural" causes. Vernon, writing for the Toronto Symposium on Intelligence in 1969, said of cross-cultural intelligence studies:

> One can further argue that members of more backward groups are functioning mentally at Piaget's preoperational, or Bruner's enactive or iconic levels (cf. also H. Werner), and that the intellectual progress of their brighter students will approximate more to the Western type of operational and symbolic thought. Hence, it is not so unfair as might appear at first sight to test them with the kinds of tests that we apply to younger Western children. We should, though, do our best to ensure that the extrinsic, fortuitous handicaps that I have listed above are minimized—so that the testees do not fail the tests merely because they do not grasp what the problems are, or because the setting is unfamiliar or disturbing.
>
> Another cogent justification is that such peoples provide much more extreme examples of various cultural handicaps than any we are likely to meet within Western nations. Thus, we can hope to advance our knowledge of the effects of different kinds of conditions on different abilities, particularly if we apply a range of varied tests to a number of contrasted groups. Obviously the chain of causation will be extremely complex; one can never be sure which of many cultural conditions is responsible for any particular deficit in abilities. But as studies of this kind accumulate, our inferences will become more soundly based, and we should be able to do more to help backward peoples to progress by diagnosing the underlying causes of their *retardation* [emphasis added] (Vernon 1969:108).

The first paragraph of the quotation from Professor Vernon's paper alludes to the fact that psychologists have long been aware that standard intelligence tests are "culture-bound" for a variety of reasons, most notably language differences. The response of some intelligence testers has been to design so-called "culture-free" or "culture- reduced" tests which do not rely upon verbal accomplishment or fact acquisition (e.g., Cattell 1968). As Vernon has pointed out, however, the more the test-maker has succeeded in reducing cultural content, the less effectively are the tests able to predict the skills and accomplishments valued in the criterion culture; furthermore, these non-verbal tests are themselves often very much culture-bound.

We should emphasize that Professor Vernon is a highly regarded, thoughtful, knowledgeable scholar. He is well aware of the fact that the intelligence notion has outgrown its usefulness to the psychological theoretician, that the intelligence test does not measure any single thing, that it does not measure innate or potential ability, and that it gives us no clue about the nature of the learning and reasoning processes of interest to cognitive psychologists. We have quoted extensively from his discussion to demonstrate the tenacity, even among scholars, of assumptions that give rise to the position that "backward" societies do not progress because of the mental "deficiencies" of their members.

The psychometricians are not the only group of psychologists who have taken an interest in the study of cognitive functioning. On the contrary, cognitive psychology—the study of thinking and its development—has recently become a strong sub-discipline within psychology. It is convenient for our purposes to divide this group of researchers into two general subgroups, which differ from one another both in method of inquiry and in substantive focus. The first of these subgroups centers about the work of Jean Piaget, and (the reader may be surprised to learn) its work bears, in certain respects, a resemblance to that of the mental measurement group.

Piaget's career as a student of human development began when he worked in Binet's laboratory in Paris on the adaptation of some English reasoning tests for use with French children. His method of investigation has been, like that of the mental measurement psychologists, essentially clinical rather than experimental; it employs standardized situations about which the respondent is queried. His theoretical assumptions about the nature of intelligence are also similar to those we have ascribed to a part of the mental testing group—its essence, for Piaget, lies in the individual's ability to reason. Much of the transcultural research that has been done from Piaget's point of view has involved the standard tasks that identify, in European school children, the various stages of cognitive development that appear in Piaget's theory in a fixed sequence. For the Piagetian cognitive developmentalist who is trying to demonstrate that the sequence of mental development is in fact the same regardless of culture, the methodological strategy is perfectly obvious: One takes the standard tasks, translates them into the foreign language, and administers them to foreign children of various ages. Clement, Sistrunk, and Guenther (1970) studied ratings of pattern preferences in Brazilian Subjects (not tribal) and found results very similar to those previously obtained for the United States. While younger Brazilians showed more variability than comparable U.S. subjects, and the development of equivalency occurred later for Brazilians, pattern preferences were like those in the United States. This is a typical finding; i.e., the stages are validated but the non-original group is found to be "slower" [see also Bovet (1968), Heron and Dowel (1973)]. Dasen (1972) summarizes the "cross cultural" research on Piagetian theory and concludes that the stage theories are verified in most cases, but that the rate of operational development is affected by cultural factors; sometimes, in fact, the concrete operational stage is said not to be reached at all. It is not surprising that one of the things that is commonly reported in these studies is the extent to which the foreign children lag behind European children in age as they move from one developmental stage to another. The parallels between this kind of report and those of cross-cultural intelligence testers are too obvious to detail. The fact that Piaget's theory of the development of mental functioning is biological and, in a certain sense, genetic in nature, adds somewhat to the contribution of this cross-cultural work to the longevity of the "primitive mentality" idea.

Lombardi (1969) sought to investigate the psycholinguistic abilities of Papago Indian school children on the ITPA (Illinois Test of Psycholinguistic Abilities) and found the Papagos to perform significantly lower than the standardized population children on psycholinguistic abilities. The author concludes "a greater emphasis should be placed on remediating the Papago's psycholinguistic abilities and fostering language development before the children enter first grade[!]" and that teachers have not recognized fully enough that they are dealing with children with learning disabilities. Clearly, in this literature when a culture doesn't shape up to Western European norm, remediation is indicated. Kuske (1970) did for the Sioux what Lombardi had done for the Papago, and limiting ourselves to his comparison of "non-mentally handicapped" Sioux with the ITPA normative population, he found the Sioux children's performance significantly inferior on most profiles. St. George (1970) found that Maori have ITPA scores significantly lower than European children, which places them in the same category with the Sioux and Papago as reported above, but he accounted for the difference by emphasizing that "culturally" the European children have "more in common" with the world of the school. Irvine (1970) reviewed experiments involving subjects from various groups in Africa and Great Britain on tests of reasoning (Raven's Progressive Matrices). He concluded that test scores approach Western patterns as groups adopt Western value systems. DeLacey administered classification tests based on the work of Piaget and Inhelder to aborigines with and without extensive contact with European culture, and to European children living in Australia. A small sub-sample of high-contact aborigines performed on a par with the European children, but the others did not. Lloyd (1971) compared children from westernized and educated parents and found that they did better on the Stanford-Binet than the traditional students. The difficulty with all these findings, of course, is that they are subject to self-selection explanations, and that chicken-and-egg problems abound in them. However, they emphasize the role of culture and familiarity with tasks being elicited, but explanations are too often *post hoc*.

The trend of findings is not all in one direction. McManus (1970) found similarities between pre-school children from St. Maarten (Netherlands West Indies) and the United States, and argued that a similarity in problem-solving mediational processes in children from different cultures accounts for the similarities. This too is a typical kind of explanation: All cultures must cope with similar problems. Young *et al.* (1970), comparing "Eskimo" students at Barrow, Alaska, with "Caucasian" children at Pullman, Washington, finds similar relationships for both groups between reading performance, achievement test performance (California Achievement Test), and eyesight (refractive error). It is interesting to note that the more myopic subjects tended to score higher on reading and achievement tests. Here we see a study illuminating how physical disabilities have similar effects "cross culturally." El-Abd (1970) reports an experiment showing that East African students' mental abilities are no different from those of students in the West in flexibility of closure, spatial orientation, verbal comprehension, and word fluency. However, note that the subjects were all boys who had obtained their Higher School Certificate or were now University undergraduates.

The other subgroup of cognitive psychologists has been working in very different ways than have those discussed above. They begin with very different assumptions about intellectual functioning. The research method of choice has been experimental in large part, with emphasis on discovering the nature of the strategies that people use to solve various kinds of simple and more complex problems. Let us illustrate. Suppose, for example, we are told that John is taller than Mary, and that Mary is in turn taller than Bill. When asked whether John or Bill is taller we, like most American adults, immediately choose John. The question of interest is this: How have we gone about making the correct choice; that is, how do we actually think when we solve this simple problem? (After all, even those of us

who are not familiar with the formal mathematics of in-
equalities, or with formal logic, can solve it easily.) Now suppose our speculation (like that of cognitive psychologist Clinton
DeSoto) is that we solve this kind of problem by translating the
"taller than" relations into spatial images, which in our
mind's eye we compare with one another. We may imagine a
line for John which is longer than the line for Mary, and a line
for Bill which is shorter than the line which represents Mary's
tallness. In this view, we compare the John spatial image with
the Bill spatial image and the correct answer is directly obvious. Next we must find a way of demonstrating that our speculation is correct. Our task is to design an experiment whose
outcome bears upon the correctness or incorrectness of our
position. Often such an experiment consists of posing the problem to respondents in different forms, such that some of the
forms would seem likely to interfere with a spatial image
method of solving it, and some would not. If there emerged differences among the forms of presentation in the speed or accuracy with which respondents solved the problems, then our
speculation would have received support.

Experimental cognitive developmentalists often utilize such
research tactics. Many of the theoretical ideas have been influenced by linguistics and psycholinguistics, and they often
look for relationships between the development of language
and thinking strategies in the child. Their experiments,
therefore, are frequently designed to demonstrate aspects of
this assumed relationship. (Readers may be reminded by this
of the Edward Sapir-Benjamin Lee Whorf proposition, which
linked the structure of thinking with the structure of language
and the attempts during the 1950s to develop empirical evidence relevant to this proposition, using as experimental subjects native speakers of different languages.) We wish to point
out that the experimental psychologists who study thinking,
although they have been stimulated and influenced by the work
of Piaget and his followers, have not generally made hierarchi-
cal assumptions like those of Piaget and others about the
development of cognitive functioning. They are more likely to

suggest that so little is known at present about the nature of thinking that grand theories about how thinking develops are premature. The experimental tasks which they use in their research are single-purpose—invented for a particular experiment or series of experiments—and there is no temptation to turn the tasks into standard tests of the adequacy, in some person or group, of one or another kind of mental functioning. It is this methodological style that has been adopted by Cole *et al.* (1971) in their study of learning and thinking among members of a non-Western cultural group.

Theirs was the fortunate combination of anthropological commitments and methods, with the experimental techniques of cognitive psychology, that led to the uncovering of new evidence relating to cultural differences in thinking. The position that the new evidence points to is, for most psychologists, quite radical; instead of explaining why cultural differences in cognitive strategies (or mental deficiencies) exist, it calls into question the assumption that the differences exist in the first place.

Cole, Gay, Glick, and Sharp (1971) follow what they call the "common sense dictum" that people's skills at tasks will differ with the culture's emphasis on such tasks, and argue that these "tests and experiments [are] specially contrived occasions for the manifestation of cognitive skills....Failure...becomes *not an illustration of cultural inferiority...[but rather evidence that the skills] are available but for some reason the content [of the tests] does not trigger their use* ."

The focus of their effort was on the Kpelle people of central Liberia, a group which numbers about 250,000. Liberia was founded early in the 19th century as a haven for freed American slaves; its official language is English, and many of its institutions, including its schools, are American in origin and character. Contact between Americo-Liberians and the Kpelle people was fairly skimpy until World War II. Since then, a network of roads has been built into Kpelle-land, and many Kpelle have abandoned traditional ways and become part of the national economy. The Kpelle, therefore, are a people in

transition. Villages remote from the roads have remained more
or less traditional, with upland rice agriculture as the primary
basis of sustenance. Closer to or on the roads, transition
villages exist in which traditional and non-traditional Kpelle
live side by side. Non-traditional Kpelle are also found in urban centers. Many have graduated from high school and have
attended college. Kpelle school children are generally held in
the first grade until they have mastered enough of the curriculum to continue; their average age in the first grade is nine
and in the second grade twelve. (This fact occasions a
methodological digression. While students of learning and
thinking have increasingly felt that cross-cultural research was
necessary in order that their developmental theory not be
culture-bound, they have more frequently failed to do anything
to make their own research truly cross-cultural. The present
research avoids the chief pitfall of much earlier research—un-
controlled comparison. Since the average age of second-grade
children is twelve and of first-grade children nine, cross-
cultural comparisons which assume the same relationship between age and education in both cultures would be mean-
ingless. But by comparing within the Kpelle groups, Cole, *et al.*
are able to investigate the effect of various factors without intercultural confounding.) The dominant teaching style is rote
learning of a set sequence of facts. Many children drop out of
school after the fourth grade, and most by the seventh grade,
for economic, social, or academic reasons. Many children, particularly in the remote areas, do not attend school at all.

It is important to understand what ''school'' means in this
cultural setting:

> The curriculum in the Liberian school is set by the Department
> of Education and follows very closely the pattern of American
> schools. Textbooks are almost always American, either castoffs
> or new books, and their content is at best marginally relevant to
> the Kpelle child's world. [Since] national examinations...deter-
> mine the content of instruction...the students greatly resent a
> teacher straying from the specific material upon which they will

be examined...The teacher speaks one variety of Liberian English, children speak [other] varieties and the textbooks are written in standard [American] English.

Such practices sometimes lead to absurd extremes:

A child who was asked to recite the multiplication tables for his teacher began "la-di-da-di-da, la-di-da-di-da," at which point the teacher interrupted to ask him what he was saying. He responded that he knew the tune but he did not yet know the words. (Cole *et al.* 1971)

When the child graduates from the sixth grade, he takes a national examination which decides if he may continue his education, usually away from home, and, therefore, away from the traditional culture. Although Cole *et al.* do not make much of this, through these restrictions the school system effectively creates national elites. The break with traditional culture tends to occur among school children if they continue their education beyond the sixth grade. Thus, Kpelle children and adults can be divided by age, literacy, life-style, degree of education, and urbanization, so that the effects of all these factors can be studied without leaving the group of people under study. The fact that the decision to continue or not continue in school is most frequently a non-academic one makes differences due to amount of schooling easier to interpret.

Cole and his colleagues present a brief ethnography of the Kpelle, which provided them with some clues (there could be more for the reader) about what to look for in the investigation of complex forms of Kpelle thinking, and where to look for it. The ethnography also makes clear that asking the traditional adult Kpelle questions is a rather tricky business, since knowledge is considered a source of power and prestige and secrecy is an important factor in daily life; asking someone how he knows the answer to a question can be tantamount to asking him to reveal the secret sources of his information, which he may not do. Traditional Kpelle value clever speech and argumentative skills very highly, and exercise them in presenting and judging disputes in informal and formal settings. Although, in one of the later chapters, the authors have reported a court case as an example of the use of evidence and logic among the traditional Kpelle, most of the study is experimental rather than observational in method, and this may disappoint some anthropologists.

More than sixty studies, in which more than 3,300 persons participated, are reported by the authors, including several which, for various comparative purposes, use as subjects non-Kpelle persons (American school children, Vai adults, and Yucatec Mayan adults). Some of the experiments are concerned with effects of the demographic factors we have described (education, age, etc.) and some with the effects of stimulus characteristics, methods of presentation, and so on. Many of the studies investigate both demographic and other factors simultaneously, in order to detect interactions between them. The studies are concerned with a wide variety of topics within three broad categories: classification of objects, learning and memory, and logic and inference. What is perhaps the most important aspect of these studies is that they were conducted and are reported in series, with the first exploratory study on a problem leading to other studies, sometimes quite a number of them. The approach can be illustrated with a set of experiments on memory, which I believe is important for a number of reasons.

The authors began with a free recall task which was administered to non-literate and educated Kpelle subjects of three age ranges: six- to eight-year olds, ten- to fourteen-year olds, and adults. Half of the subjects in each group worked with a list of twenty objects that was clusterable into categories of objects (utensils, tools, clothing, and food) and half worked with a similar list that was not clusterable. The experimenter read the list of items to be recalled at a rate of two seconds per item, and then the subject was asked to recall the list. Each subject received the same list five times, each time in a different order.

Various measures of performance were used: the number of correctly recalled items, the subjects' tendency to recall the items in the order they had been presented, and the tendency to recall items in clusters (in the case of the clusterable list); the tendency for subjects to recall an item as a function of its serial position in the list was also calculated. The results of the experiment were very puzzling. Recall was not high. It increased slightly with age and education and was sightly greater for the clusterable list, but there was only a slight improvement over the five trials; and unlike the results of corresponding studies done in the United States and similar cultures, there was no relation between the serial position of the word and the recall accuracy associated with it. Furthermore, there was no tendency for subjects to recall clusterable lists in clusters—a result very different from what has been obtained with American or European subjects.

In order to discover whether the relatively poor performances of subjects in the first study was due to the fact that they had to remember lists of words, the authors repeated and extended a portion of the first experiment. Only the clusterable list was used; half the subjects recalled the words as before, and half were silently shown the objects the words named. Further, for half the verbal group and half the object group, the clusterable stimuli were presented next to one another in the list—food items together, tools together, etc. The remaining subjects received the stimuli in random order as in the first study. Ten- to fourteen-year old literate and nonliterate boys were used as subjects. Again results were markedly different from typical American data. Memory was poor in terms of the number of items recalled, and there was little improvement with successive trials. Recall of the items in clusters appeared only when they were presented as objects with the same category items juxtaposed. In this experiment, no differences emerged between educated and nonliterate subjects in total amount recalled, but the educated subjects did manifest a serial-position effect similar to that of American subjects.

Obviously, many factors could have been controlling this exceedingly complex pattern of results. So the authors began to conduct studies to see what was happening, and more particularly, to try to isolate the conditions under which Kpelle subjects would in fact behave like American subjects in the way they recalled lists of words. They began by doing the earlier experiments, using similarly developed lists, with American subjects as well as with Mexican Indian and Vai subjects. The Americans showed an orderly development of free recall learning; by the third grade, they did as well as the Kpelle groups, and older subjects performed far better in amount recalled and with the expected organizational pattern. Why were the Kpelle subjects not improving with trials, and not remembering in clusters? One set of hypotheses was motivational in character: Perhaps one needs to have several years of schooling before free recall begins to be organized in the way it is among Americans. Still other hypotheses led to experiments which varied the way the tasks were presented.

Two experiments were then conducted with Kpelle subjects, in which money was offered as incentive for good recall performance. The results were exactly parallel to those in the earlier experiments. Then urban Kpelle were compared with traditional Kpelle: the former group performed slightly better, but in essence not differently. Then Kpelle high school students were compared with nonliterate age mates in two further studies. The high school group performed much better, and, in fact, performed in ways that were similar to the performances of Americans. Now the authors clearly had a different problem: What influences good recall? To suggest that "schooling" does is, of course, uninformative. Schooling consists, after all, of a great many things. Always mindful of the anthropologist's faith that people everywhere have similar cognitive abilities, the authors phrased their question in this way: "Are there circumstances under which nonliterate, traditional people will manifest some or all of the organizational features of recall produced by the Kpelle high school students and older American groups?"

When they discovered that asking subjects to place the items in a bucket or to sort them into cups had a large effect on both recall and clustering, the authors turned to the work of psychologist George Mandler for their next clues. Mandler points out that remembering involves retrieval as well as storage, and that a rememberer must have retrieval cues in order to recall material. In a new experiment, the authors held the objects presented for recall over four chairs so that each item was said to "belong to" a particular chair. Both objects and words were used (objects held silently for a couple of seconds over the chair to which they "belonged"). For half the subjects, a rule was followed such that all the items that belong to the same categories were associated with a particular chair, and for the other half, the association of item to chair was random. Both literate and nonliterate traditional ten- to fourteen-year olds served as subjects. For both groups, presenting the items in category groupings with the chairs produced data that were very much like American data; recall improved dramatically with trials, and showed strong clustering effects. There then followed a long series of studies. In one of them, which varied the method of presentation and the number of chairs, all experimental conditions produced high recall rates, learning rates, and near-perfect clustering. The authors concluded from this study and others that experimenter differences sometimes have strong effects on recall. The point of the chairs, of course, is that they seemed to serve as retrieval cues for these subjects. It appears that one of the effects of substantial schooling is to train students to use single words as retrieval cues for other words; for nonliterate Kpelle, the retrieval function was served by material objects. The next series of studies investigated among Americans as well as Kpelle the effects of various kinds of verbal cueing for recall. Then the word lists were embedded (in still another group of studies) in narrative stories. The way the words were recalled matched the way in which they were structured in the story.

These studies are by no means complete—they do not solve the puzzles to the complete satisfaction of the authors or other investigators. But, in addition to making some contributions to the general literature on the organization of recall of this kind, they show with great clarity that the nonliterate "primitives" being studied are not intrinsically different from literate Americans in the way they remember. What is striking is that the first few studies were unanimous in suggesting that such differences did indeed exist. It was only the perseverance, faith, and energy of this group of investigators that finally exposed the easy assumptions they might have made about these apparent differences.

Such instances appear several times in Cole *et al.* (1971). Some Kpelle children and adults, for instance, seem to have trouble dealing with certain kinds of apparently simple verbal logic problems, for example:

> "Flumo and Yakpalo always drink cane juice [rum] together. Flumo is drinking cane juice. Is Yakpalo drinking cane juice?" One subject answered "Flumo and Yakpalo drink cane juice together, but the time Flumo was drinking the first one Yakpalo was not there on that day." (p. 188)

Many subjects did not respond to the logical relations contained in the verbal problems, but responded to other things instead. However, when given such problems in groups rather than individually, subjects seemed to have very little difficulty with them; for example:

> "Everyone in the town eats rice. The chief is in the town; therefore, the chief eats rice." The answer was, "Yes, it is true because it is said that *everyone* in the town eats rice. The chief is included in that number." (p. 186)

The authors' report on Kpelle logical thinking during a court case also makes clear that traditional Kpelle use evidence, make inferences, and test conclusions just as we do. Furthermore, a report of the details of play of a highly complex game (similar in some ways to the Japanese game of Go) suggests that good players are fine logical strategists. What is impressive is that the authors did not stop working until they had at least begun to uncover conditions under which their subjects' intellective processing is similar to that of Americans and Europeans. This research strategy is particularly striking when contrasted to that of the cross-cultural intelligence testers, who simply take their homegrown testing kits to the other culture, administer the tests, and report the results: the others are not as smart as we are.

The Cole *et al.* research is meticulous. Further, it is generally bound to some portion of the recent research literature in psychology, and frequently makes contributions to that literature. The book has minor flaws. Experimental procedures are sometimes incompletely described, the numbers of subjects run are often omitted, the tables are frequently poorly labeled, and the data are often only skimpily analyzed; one gets the impression that there is much in this material that remains untapped. In addition, experiments and interpretations of results that are reported are frequently difficult to follow, or simply unsatisfying. The reader is left with the impression that some of the studies were designed without much forethought; the connections among experiments are sometimes rather unclear. Finally, the admittedly unorthodox ethnography is inadequate. The authors did not fully do what they set out to do: to use the ethnography as a guide to experimentation. Too often a standard experimental task is initially given to subjects, and the ethnography is used to explain the results and to think of other possible experiments. Further, the ethnography presented in the book is largely limited to information which the authors use later on in their analyses. This deprives the reader of additional material with which he might be able to construct his own alternative explanations, a hallmark of good ethnography.

The major implication of the work, however, is crucial, speaking to the questions of so-called "cultural inferiority" and "cultural deprivation," terms bandied about so frequently by scholars, educators, and laymen alike. It is possible, and even likely, that the idea of cultural deprivation is a consequence of our misunderstanding, our ignorance, of the way the culture (or subculture) works with respect to the intellectual functioning of its members. In typically ethnocentric fashion, we condemn without expending the energy necessary to understand; our immediate impulse is to strike down these cultural differences, and substitute ours for theirs, as if an instrument had no effect and simply "measured intelligence."

The issues raised by studies reviewed here are of direct concern to educators who desire to understand how learning goes on and how it can be measured. The results are therefore providing an ever deepening foundation for the study of socialization, to which we now turn.

II

Socialization

Socialization is a much broader concept than perception or cognition. The person approaching the study of socialization for the first time enters a superficially simple but actually quite complicated set of theoretical and methodological problems. It is easier to assert that the socialization process is a prerequisite of social life than it is to study it and substantiate how it occurs. The biggest problem is, of course, that while our science has acquired the belief "the child is father to the man," studies which actually examined the same adults when they were children (longitudinal studies) are as extremely expensive as they are extremely rare. In psychology Kagan and Moss (1961) report on the best known attempt, the Fels study, but generally the field of socialization does not rely on fullscale longitudinal studies to demonstrate its basic assumption as much as it relies on common sense belief.

The study of socialization is necessary only to the degree that we believe there is some usefulness in the idea that what happens to an individual when he is a child affects what he does as an adult. Not all behaviors may require this approach; some are "situation specific" and do not obviously require appeal to explanations dealing with personality of individual actors. However, the studies reviewed here aim to assess the usefulness of the socialization approach to various problems of relevance to education.

Some Factors in Socialization

John Honigmann's (1967) "assumption of cumulative influence" stresses the continuous character of a person's life and that prior events influence and limit what a person later becomes. Clearly, however, not all experiences are equally potent predictors of later behavior. Therefore one job for a theory of socialization is to specify (or discover) which experiences are critical and which are not. As one might expect there are various theories of socialization, and each can offer us different accounts of which experiences are more crucial than others. We will return to this below.

The timing of experiences can have an effect independent of the experience itself, and this introduces a variable of order (development) and age. At its most obvious, a lecture on human rights can be expected to have greater impact (so far as a lecture can ever have an impact) on a 13-year old than on a 13-day old. It follows from this that certain learning depends upon the development of the child's ability to learn, and that learning of certain behaviors or processes may occur only if the child has acquired a prior skill or knowledge. Certain ages may be critical for the learning of certain skills, and learning may accelerate at certain ages. A corollary of these points is that what has been learned at any given point can determine (e.g., by screening out certain new ideas) what learning will follow. Thus the processes of perceptual development reviewed above are an important part of socialization (see Adler and Harrington 1970: 16ff, for an explicit use of perception in a socialization model). As we learn to cope appropriately with the options available to us in one culture, we can lose sight of, or lose the ability to conceptualize, options that cannot be in our own culture.

The dimension of time is another factor in socialization. Rautman and Brower (1951) report on a replication of a study done by the same investigators in 1943. The results showed that there was definitely less preoccupation with war themes in 1950 than in 1943. Analysis of the children's TAT story endings showed that the 1950 sample was more inclined to give happy endings than was the 1943 sample. Cultural differences are gross exaggerations of such historical effects of time within a

culture. Culture changes not only the content of what is learned, but beliefs and values, and the ordering of learning itself.

The study of socialization is more than the study of how *individuals* learn particular ways of life, but it is basic to our
understanding of how *societies* perpetuate themselves by making
particular kinds of humans as opposed to others. This is why
the study of socialization is not concerned (as is some of
psychology) with the learning of behavior idiosyncratic to an
individual, but rather those behaviors which are meaningful to
other members of a society, i.e., part of the social process.
Socialization is here conceptualized, not as a filling of an empty
vessel with a pre-set picture of a society, but as a dynamic process by which individuals learn to structure reality, in ways
which enable them to properly sort out and make sense of
diverse stimuli which form their environment, and behave in
ways congruent with others' expectations of them in the social
process. Because a complete "description" of a society is probably never possible, students of socialization processes have
found it increasingly necessary to delimit the field of what is being learned, and rather than studying socialization in general,
to study socialization of particular kinds of role behaviors, e.g.,
sex role socialization and religious socialization.

Students of socialization are sometimes criticized for taking
conservative views of the world by seeing societies as if they
were in equilibrium. Such static models are not, however,
generated by the socialization approach itself, but rather by the
view of society held by the authors. In many cases these views
have indeed been static and oriented toward preservation of the
status quo. However, a socialization approach can be taken independent of such assumptions. If one defines society as made
up of competing factions in competition for scarce resources,
and in a constant state of flux, socialization would need to account for how people learned to participate in such competing
systems. Doing what is right and proper in such a society is to
compete successfully by local rules. Such societies pose problems for neophytes of dealing with fluidity as certainly as

static societal conceptions pose problems of how to conform. Conformity is not embedded in a socialization framework, but in the 'what' or the conception of society that is to be learned.

Students of the socialization process use concepts of personality to show how this knowledge is acquired. Their further commitment is to show how a society induces its members willingly to accept these responsibilities. The question becomes one of the integration of society. As Schwartz and Merten (1968:1120) have phrased it: "How does a society make its members feel that the status they eventually must occupy is desirable as well as inevitable?" Relevant, then, are accurate descriptions of social structure, the interaction of individuals and groups, variations and cycles within groups, and the choices available to actors at various structural positions. The study of socialization process and personality, as thus described, has been over the years a major concern of psychological anthropology, and the literature to be reviewed here is immense.

Psychological anthropology emerged from a subfield of anthropology called "culture and personality." The main theoretical difference between the old label and the new, as well as between work done, say, prior to 1955 and work done more recently, is reflected in the difference between two concepts, coined by Wallace in 1961, "replication of uniformity" and "organization of diversity." Wallace argued that works which assumed that the process of socialization was the accomplishment of the replication of culture in the individual personality, with the corollary that each member of a culture was a uniform replication of every other, were elevating a tautology to the level of theory. Was personality really culture writ small? Was culture really personality writ large? Various theorists tried to obviate the necessity for replication of uniformity assumptions and the search was heightened as anthropologists worked in increasingly complex societies. Kardiner and Linton's "basic personality type" (Kardiner 1939) was an effort to provide theoretical understanding that certain basics were shared (read replicated) in every member of a culture, with individual differences emerging from fringes around the basics. DuBois's modal personality was an effort to provide a statistical description of a central tendency around which a culture's members could vary. However, by the 60s these adjustments had become stretched to the point where something better was needed. This is not to suggest that Kardiner and Linton's models did not continue to exert an effect, for example. Indeed the Whiting model of socialization discussed below is, in other respects, a direct descendant from the Kardiner model. However, by the 60s the field had become more conscious of, and more interested in, within-culture variations, and a recognition that "personality" and "cognitive map" were concepts which, while relatable to culture, were not synonymous with it.

This led to Wallace's conceptualization of culture as the organization of diversity of individual personalities. In this conceptualization behavioral expectations are shared, and the personality or cognitive map which produces individual behaviors is acknowledged as diverse (and, while not for Wallace, for us potentially unknowable—see above). This does not prevent the theorist from theorizing that people behave as they do because of a particular personality variable. It emphasizes that the test of the theory is how well that behavior is predicted, and that a successful prediction does not mean that all those behaving in a particular way are behaving in that way for the personality reason given. This conceptualization is responsive to our discussion of cognition above. This kind of theoretical conceptualization inevitably led to more statistical kinds of analyses, more careful data gathering, and the greater methodological rigor that has come to characterize the field of psychological anthropology throughout the sixties into the present.

Whiting's Model

The anthropological model of socialization most relevant to educational inquiry explicates the position that education is embedded in a sociocultural matrix and is therefore basic to the study of the integration of society. The mode of education, or child training practices in Whiting's model, is seen as arising in any particular culture setting, from the maintenance systems of the particular culture. To say this is to emphasize two points: 1) that any study of "education" which does not take into account its cultural context is incomplete, and 2) that since maintenance systems give rise to education more than vice-versa, educational systems are not a useful point to initiate change. This point becomes crucial in an examination of much of the recent literature on education. To criticize the schools for their failures, and to demand change, overlooks the functions and interrelationships of the school within the larger society. This is not to say that abuses in schools cannot be corrected or that reform is impossible. It is to say that for change to occur (as opposed to reform) a change in the society (maintenance systems) is prerequisite to change in educational structures. Wallace's widely known 1961 article makes a similar point to Whiting's model by emphasizing that the goal of schools will be different in what he calls conservative, reactionary, and revolutionary societies, in which the type of society determines the type of schooling and not vice-versa. The advantage of Whiting's formulation for educators is that it includes all education, not just schooling, in its scope. Thus, John Herzog (1962) was able to show that the type of instruction (whether deliberate or not, whether done by kin or not) varied by household type and type of society. This study provides empirical support for two points: 1) that type of education is determined by type of society and 2) that types (i.e., deliberate instruction) must be considered in the total context of child training practices of a society and not as synonymous with them. (See Figure 1.)

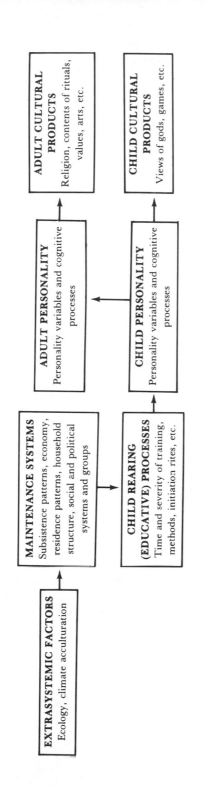

FIGURE 1. The Whiting Model. (Adapted from Harrington and Whiting 1972.)

Maintenance systems are described by Whiting and Child as the "economic, political, and social organizations of a society surrounding the nourishment, sheltering, and protection of its members." From structual anthropology (both the British and American versions) come working models and actual descriptions of maintenance systems. Examples of maintenance systems from the following sections include household composition, sexual division of labor, and residence patterns. Child training practices, in the broadest sense, are what is done to the child to bring about the behavior necessary for social life. In the term "child training" is implicit some intent on the part of the parent or surrogate, and some goal presumably defined by the culture. Schools, the fact that initial child training is done by women, and initiation rites, are examples of child training practices. Personality is the model of what the individual assimilates and of how he organizes what happens to him. In a sense, "personality" may be conceptualized as an individual's adaptation to his socialization. Here the study of socialization depends upon psychological anthropologists and, through them, upon the field of psychology itself, so that personality can be expressed in terms of measured variables. Such a personality variable is sex identity. Cultural products include religion, cultural values, art, games, or any other cultural features not immediately and practically involved in the satisfaction of basic biological needs. In the study of male initiation rites, the value of male solidarity would be an example, as well as the symbolic content of the initiation rites themselves.

While many psychological anthropologists would argue over fine points, most would agree that education can only be studied as part of an overall socialization process designed to meet goals specific to the culture examined. For a review of the literature supporting the Whiting model see Harrington and Whiting (1972).

In postulating that there is a causal sequence in illustrating the model in Figure 1, Whiting justifies his logic as follows:

The correlational method used in cross-cultural research cannot, of course, show the direction of causation. It must rest
upon other evidence suggesting the relative plausibility of one
or the other assumption as to causal direction...temperature
and climate cannot be reasonably assumed to be the effect of a
custom. Any association between a climatic variable and a
custom can plausibly be interpreted either as an effect of climate
upon the custom or as an effect of climate upon some other factor associated with such a custom. For example, in this paper it
is not plausible to assume that exclusive mother-infant sleeping
arrangements cause a warm winter, or that a long post-partum
sex taboo caused a rainy tropical climate. Thus, it is the
assumption of this paper that ecological variables determine the
customs associated with them (Whiting 1964:524).

The flow of causal arrows in this model is essentially from
left to right. It will be obvious to the reader that if everything is
working properly at any given point, there is feedback and support of what has gone before. That is, in the initiation rites'
literature, the symbols used in the ceremony are a cultural
product; yet they are part of the child training initiation rites
and their symbolic treatment of male and female reinforces the
social structure based upon sex differences, etc. Recent work
has focused upon various kinds of feedback. An example of
feedback was encountered by Roberts and Sutton-Smith in
their work with games. Following the model, in their 1966 article on games of chance, they suggest that such games may be
played in societies whose situations are not easily controlled by
skill or strategy, where uncertainty exists, "particularly in the
areas of environmental setting, food production, social and
political interaction, marriage, war and religion." These
uncertain conditions lead such societies to emphasize responsibility in child training and generate conflict in the area of sex,
aggression, and achievement, since the life situation is one
where "favorable and unfavorable outcomes may occur in an
uncertain way" (Roberts and Sutton-Smith 1966:143). Games
of chance can be viewed as a cultural product, an expression of

responses to the passivity of the player's normal life role incompatible with the role of diligent provider. Differential incidence of gambling in our own society emphasizes this point. Thus "antecedent conflicts produced by socialization...lead to involvement in models of all sorts, including games. These models represent activities in behavior spheres relevant to the antecedent conflicts" (Roberts, Hoffman, and Sutton-Smith 1965:17). Children learn through folklore and games what the culture requires them to know, but will not teach them directly. Referring to what they describe as a conflict-enculturation interpretation, Roberts and Sutton-Smith (1962) argue that

> 1) there is an overall process of cultural patterning whereby society induces conflict in children through its child raising processes;
>
> 2) that society seeks through appropriate arrays and varieties of ludic models to provide an assuagement of these conflicts by an adequate representation of their emotional and cognitive polarities in ludic structure; and
>
> 3) that through these models society tries to provide a form of buffered learning through which the child can make enculturative step-by-step progress toward adult behavior (Roberts and Sutton-Smith 1962:183-4).

Each type of game provides information to the child about chance, skill, and/or strategy in assuaging conflict and in learning to handle social life. As Roberts and Sutton-Smith say "between the ages of seven and twelve the child learns, in simple direct form, how to take a chance, how to show a skill, and how to deceive" (1962:183). In complex games he learns to combine these skills in circumstances more nearly approaching the conditions of real life. In subsequent studies these authors have demonstrated, for example, that skilled strategy players are more "strategic" in other areas of life (Sutton-Smith & Roberts 1967). Thus games can be viewed, not only as a projective technique or a cultural product, but also as a child training device. Hence a feedback arrow must be shown in the model, from the products of adults and children to child training.

In addition, Whiting et al. (1966) have argued that in a society which undergoes a change in maintenance systems due to extrasystemic pressure (see above), child training systems may overreact to the change. This might create cultural products of exaggerated values to bolster the new order (feedback of cultural product on maintenance system). Values like harmony, achievement, and virtue, however can be so overdrawn and idealized that living up to them is difficult. Thus, Whiting postulates a cultural defense mechanism to deal with failure to live up to the ideal. Projection of hostile feelings and bad thoughts onto witches or outside the group, and bragging about success even if none exists, are seen as culturally provided defense mechanisms against failure to meet the dominant values. This would be an example of feedback of cultural product upon personality systems. An interesting avenue of study is what happens in social change situations to these various parts when there is less than perfect fit. What if child training practices seek to inculcate behaviors appropriate to maintenance systems which no longer exist, thereby producing personality types which cannot function successfully within the new order? What if cultural products like values, religion, etc., do not reinforce these new behaviors? These and other questions await answers. Other extrasystemic factors recently investigated which are directly related to behavior described here include diet (Bolton 1973, Bolton and Vadheim 1973, Rohner 1970) and climate (Robbins, DeWalt and Pelto 1972).

Sex Role and Initiation

The intersection of two characteristics makes the cross-cultural study of sex role socialization and initiation rites a natural and basic part of any psychological anthropology of education. In the first instance, biological gender is something that varies in a constant way in all human societies, and societies are free to attend to the difference in allocating role responsibilities and constructing divisions of labor. Most attend to the difference (see Linton 1936:116), but the degree to which it matters varies a great deal (see D'Andrade 1966, Barry, Bacon, and Child 1957). Secondly, in effecting the transition from child (infant) to adult (or to male adult or female adult), societies often make use of ritualized initiation processes to mark the transition. These often include relatively formal instruction for the initiates as to their new obligations. This instruction, sometimes including "bush schools," is for many societies the only "formal" education setting that children will experience. Therefore much interest has been shown as to what these rites are about and how they accomplish what they set out to do. Some initiation rites seem concerned with making adults out of children (e.g., many North American Indian rites); others, in societies in which sex differences are important, are concerned with not just making adults, but particularly male as opposed to female (or vice versa) adults. The relationship of male initiation rites to the socialization of proper sex role behavior hasbeen extensively studied.

In their interpretation of male initiation rites, Whiting, Kluckhohn, and Anthony (1958) used the psychological concept of sex identity. Their cross-cultural study established the following:

1) A close relationship between mother and son during infancy as a consequence of either (a) their sleeping together for at least a year to the exclusion of the father, or (b) the mother being prohibited from sexual intercourse for at least a year after the birth of her child, or (c) both of these together, has measurable consequences which are manifested in cultural adjustments at adolescence.

2) These adjustments are either (a) a ceremony of initiation into manhood involving at least one and generally several of the following factors: painful hazing by the males of the society, tests of endurance and manliness, seclusion from women, and genital operations, or (b) a change of residence which involves separation of the boy from his mother and sisters and may also include some formal means for establishing male authority such

as receiving instructions from and being required to be respect-
ful to the mother's brother or the members of the men's house.

3) If both the factors specified in (1) are present, the consequences at adolescence tend to be more elaborate and severe
than if only one is present (1958:368-369).

The authors offered an interpretation of their findings based
upon the personality variable of sex identity. This interpretation was further refined and more completely stated by Burton
and Whiting (1961), who viewed the absence of the father as
leading to primary cross-sex (feminine) identity in boys. Initiation rites are designed to overcome primary cross-sex identity
and substitute male identity and behavior. If the identity conflict were not resolved, boys would retain behaviors inappropriate to the society's adult male role.

Burton and Whiting (1961) distinguish three kinds of identity: "attributed" (statuses assigned ego by others in his
society), "subjective" (statuses ego thinks he fills). and "optative" (statuses which ego wishes to occupy). The aim of
socialization is to produce adults whose three identities are congruent. Optative identity is not always a conscious wish, and in
fact can be assumed to be either an unconscious wish or a
cognitive style; subjective identity, on the other hand, is conscious.

Cross-sex identity, used in reference to males, means that
they identify with women, usually the mother. According to
Burton and Whiting, the individual forms "primary" or "optative sex identity" in infancy and "secondary" or "subjective
sex identity" in childhood, corresponding to the status arrangements encountered by him in those respective periods.
Primary cross-sex identity is linked to absence of the father as
measured by exclusive mother-child sleeping arrangements
and long post partum sex taboos. Secondary male identity, in
contrast, is linked to male influence as measured by patrilocality. The definition of father absence for primary cross-sex identity is different from that for secondary because the domain of
the child changes. When the child is an infant, his domain is

limited largely to where he sleeps; hence, the importance shifts from sleeping arrangements to whether the father is present in the household at all to the status males possess (for example, in a patrilocal or a matrilocal household).

The relationship of cross-sex identity to behavior depends upon the combination of primary and secondary identities. Primary cross-sex identity may be either reacted against or expressed, depending upon the secondary sex identity. Some societies institutionalize a means for resolving an underlying conflict in sex identities (primary, female; secondary, male) in favor of the secondary sex identity. Circumcision-type initiation rites are an example of this. The ceremonies occur in societies which differentiate boys from girls (Harrington, 1968) and presumably teach boys the appropriate male role. Thus they attempt to insure proper masculine role behavior by making it clear that the boys are now men and are different from the women who have raised them.

If there is a conflict between primary and secondary sex identities without a mechanism to resolve it, the individual reaction to primary feminine identity may be an exaggerated masculinity, through which the boy tries to resolve the conflict (see Munroe, Munroe, and Whiting 1965). Such hypermasculine traits have been linked to feminine identity by several researchers. B. Whiting (1965), for example, has explained aggression as "protest masculinity," and found it more often in those societies where the father has low salience in infancy but high status later in life. (See Whiting, 1965, for a summary of the literature on protest masculinity.) If glory in war is taken to be a reasonable index of hypermasculinity or the exaggerated need for men to defend themselves against feminity, then it should be found more commonly in societies with an exclusive relationship between a boy and his mother during his infancy, combined with a low salience of the father during this period. Such turns out to be true. Polygynous societies in which each child has a mother but at most half a father who often sleeps and eats elsewhere are more likely to value glory in war than do monogamous societies. Exclusive mother-son sleeping arrangements—a more explicit measure of a condition likely to produce cross sex identity—is also significantly associated with the glory in warfare score. Whiting, Kluckhohn, and Anthony consider juvenile delinquency in the United States to be another form of exaggerated masculinity:

> It has long been known that there is an association between certain types of juvenile delinquency and broken homes. We would predict that the probability of a boy becoming delinquent in such instances would be highest where the separation of the mother and father occurred during the early infancy of the boy and where she (later)...remarried (1958:370).

The macho complex among Mexican males would be another instance (Lewis 1951). A further case may be that described for the Cayman Islands (Howe 1966). Such reactions of exaggerated masculinity typically come about where there is an overlaying of male influence upon a child with primary cross-sex identity. Cultural mechanisms to resolve the conflict, such as circumcision-type initiation rites, are said to make such individual protests superfluous.

Cross-sex identity may be openly expressed if the primary and secondary identifications are both feminine. One institutionalized expression is couvade, a set of practices in which the man shares symptoms of pregnancy and childbirth with his wife (see Munroe, Munroe, and Whiting 1965). Burton and Whiting said couvade should be a good index of the wish "to act out the feminine role and thus symbolically to be in part a woman" (1961:91). Munroe, Munroe and Carson (1973) support this. Individual expressions of femininity are also possible. D'Andrade (1962) found that in the United States high feminine identification scores on the Franck Drawing Completion Test were strongly related to father absence during the first two years of life. Carlsmith (1963, 1973) as well as Sutton-Smith and Rosenberg (1968) found that father-absent male students had some feminine patterns on scholastic aptitude tests, or other expressions of cognitive cross-sex identity.

D'Andrade (1973) reports similar results with the Franck test, as a measure of cognitive cross-sex identity for boys, in a neighborhood composed of American blacks and third generation Barbadians outside Boston, for father absence in the first three years of life. Harrington (1970) was unable to produce such findings for a population of abnormally behaving adolescent boys, and argued, following recent findings in psychology, that father absence was too crude an approximation of a variable that had to describe the relationship of the father to the child: father salience. In addition, I argued that the role of the mother had to be taken into account, and following Sutton-Smith and Rosenberg (1968) I might also argue the importance of the sibship. Longabaugh (1973) explicitly investigates the effects of mother behavior on the effect of father absence. Although not dealing over a long period of time with the salience of the mother to the child, he investigates shorter term effects and, based upon brief observation, argues that mother behavior toward the son is a variable, moderating the relationship between father absence and femininity of the son's semantic style.

Munroe and Munroe (1973) investigate the individual expressions of femininity to be found, if genital mutilation initiation rites predicted by the theory outlined are not performed. They compare four East African societies, in which interviews were conducted with adult males during the wife's pregnancy. They report that men in a rites-absent society (Nilotic) report significantly more symptoms themselves during their wife's pregnancy than males in the societies in which such initiation rites are present, offering evidence of the efficacy of such rites in effecting cognitive changes in sex identity.

The connection between subjective cross-sex identity and overt behavior was specifically tested by Harrington (1970), for a group of hospitalized boys in the United States who had shown errors in sex role learning. Harrington found support for Whiting's explanation of male initiation rites in terms of primary and secondary sex identity. Boys with exaggeratedly masculine behavior more often had primary feminine identity and secondary masculine identity, as measured by personality tests, than boys who did not show errors in sex role learning. Boys whose behavior showed errors in the other extreme (behavior inappropriate to the male role) had both primary and secondary feminine identity. Thus the association of measures of primary and secondary sex role identity with the socialization of male role behaviors has been fairly well documented both cross-culturally and by within-culture replications.

Circumcision-type initiation rites are said to be necessary to overcome primary cross-sex identity and inculcate properly male identity and behavior. Recent work in symbolic anthropology, particularly in the work of Turner (1969) and the studies in Mayer (1970) suggest that by a careful analysis of what goes on within these rituals we may learn more about the dynamics by which they operate. What is particularly needed is a knowledge of what, if anything, these rituals actually accomplish in terms of socialization. John Herzog (1973) attempts to assess the effects of initiation rites. He administered questionnaires to groups of boys, one initiated in 1969, one postponing initiation till 1970, one till later. Each group was interviewed one month before the 1969 initiation and four to five months after by initiated males from the same community. The findings do not document an immediate impact of initiation itself; perhaps because of the short time between the pre- and post-states (see Harrington 1968 for an argument which would require effects to be measured over a longer period of time), and perhaps because of the interviews having been done by initiated youths, which might have tended to homogenize responses around a cultural norm. However, even in these circumstances, Herzog was able to show that a combination of initiation plus secondary education does have a recognizable impact on boys' self concepts. A recent study of Granzberg's (1973) begins to answer this question, not for circumcision-type initiation rites, but for rites like those of the Hopi, that emphasize the distinction between the child and adult roles (but see also Schlegel 1973).

Most of the cross-cultural studies of sex role learning reviewed here have been limited to males, reflecting a bias in the literature that may be accounted for to some extent by the fact that most of the authors are male. Judith Brown (1963) has redressed this imbalance in part with a fine study of female initiation rites. She draws three major conclusions. First, female initiation rites occur most often in societies where the girl, as an adult, will not have to leave her parents' domestic unit; second, those initiation rites that subject the initiated girl to extreme pain are found in societies in which infant and childhood sex identity are in conflict; this establishes a relation between painful female initiation rites and male genital mutilation rites. Third, female rites are found in those societies in which women are important in subsistence activities, thereby (according to Brown) giving her recognition for her contribution to the existence of the society. While much remains to be done on sex role learning by women, the work of Brown and Barry, Bacon and Child offers some useful beginnings.

Suicide is a trait which shows sex-linked findings. Threatening suicide is more often used by women than it is by men (see Farberow and Schneidman 1961) and more by boys with feminine rather than masculine identity (Harrington 1970). Cross-cultural studies of suicide have produced some findings which have relevance to students of education. Krauss offers data that frequency of suicide is linked to societal complexity, with low complexity societies having low suicide rates, medium complexity societies having high rates, with highly complex societies divided between low and high rates. Insofar as formal education is linked to societal complexity, there is a possibility of a direct, though possibly curvilinear, relationship between education and suicide. In addition, the cross-cultural evidence emphasizes the effectiveness of societies in binding members into patterned social relations (Krauss 1970); strong family ties and social structure (Gobar 1970) are preventive of suicide but not necessarily threats of suicide, (see Kreitman, Smith, and Tan 1970). As Hippler (1969) emphasizes, these represent inter-relationships of child-rearing variables, social structure, and cultural values, a set of problems of direct relevance to educators.

Recent research has also been conducted on sex-linked task assignments, sex preference and role performance. Ember (1973) hypothesized that boys observed to perform a great deal of "feminine" work (by Luo culture definitions) would tend to exhibit more "feminine" social behavior than other boys (measured on basis of egotistic behavior, altruistic, and pro-social behavior scales). A comparison of social behavior scores of boys doing little feminine work, boys doing a great deal of feminine work and girls, showed that boys who did a great deal of feminine work were intermediate in their social behavior between other boys and girls. Further analysis revealed that different types of work, all of which were considered feminine, were differently related to social behavior. Boys who did more feminine work inside the home were more feminine than other boys, but boys who did a great deal more feminine work outside the home were not more feminine than other boys. Perhaps this feminine task performance in the home implies task overlap with the mother and an identification component. Harrington (1970) shows that task overlap in the home with the mother, as opposed to the father, for boys is a useful predictor of cross-sex behavior. These findings emphasize the interplay of various socializing agents which needs to be considered by researchers in education.

Methods for Study

Over the past twenty years there have been increasing numbers of studies purporting to be about "socialization." Nearly all of these studies have contained deficiencies traceable, at least in part, to the existence of disciplinary boundaries. While many disciplines share a theoretical interest in socialization phenomena, their methodologies do not correspondingly overlap. Indeed, one can read about "anthropological methods," "psychological methods," and "sociological methods." Since methodology must follow from theory, not vice-versa, this is a paradox. What is needed is research which will develop in useable form an integrated set of methodologies for the study of socialization. These methodologies are presently associated with a number of different disciplines, but primarily with the fields of anthropology, psychology, and sociology

We need to bring the various methodologies into one integrated whole which can be used easily by all researchers in socialization. This is not to discourage interdisciplinary collaboration by researchers—quite the opposite would be my wish. However, reality dictates that opportunities for truly interdisciplinary research are often limited by discipline-organized academic structures, by the low probability of finding someone from just the right discipline at just the right time who is interested in, available to, and capable of collaboration. My experiences in even the most fortuitous of circumstances make me certain that all those interested in the study of socialization cannot find suitable collaborators. Even for the few who can, the process of collaboration, expecially in the early stages, is extremely time consuming, as each person explores—often for the first time—the other's academic world. While this is a fascinating process, assuming it goes well, it does effectively postpone the research for such a length of time that the nascent researcher faced with a choice between a "quick" within disciplinary effort and the uncertainties of an interdisciplinary encounter, may too often choose the former, to the detriment of the research.

We need to separate various research techniques from the disciplines to which tradition assigns them, while at the same time producing research into socialization which they would regard as legitimate. Such work will bring the strengths and fruits associated with interdisciplinary research without the actual necessity of members of a number of disciplines working together on the problem. The work must be as accessible to an anthropologist wanting to learn experimental procedures as it is to a psychologist wanting to learn participant observation techniques, and must be guided to some degree by the concept of "limits of naivete" proposed by the anthropologist Max Gluckman and economist Ely Devons (Devons and Gluckman 1964). You do not need to become an anthropologist to do participant observation, but you do need to know enough so that you do it in a way that will be acceptable by anthropologists. Similarly, you do not need to become a psychologist to do experimentation, but you need to know enough so that you do not produce research unacceptable to psychologists.

The study of socialization requires knowledge of *what* is to be learned as well as *how* it is to be learned. Accurate descriptions of the society, the culture, variations and cycles within groups, and the choices available to actors at various social positions and educational settings must be our first step. This is as true in dealing with our own society and its sub-cultures as it is when working cross-culturally. Only then can we investigate how appropriate behaviors are learned, using concepts of personality and theories of learning to show how the knowledge is acquired.

The delineation of what is to be learned and the investigation of how that learning occurs (in part by showing that it does) require in most cases different batteries of research techniques. But, the overall study requires a deliberate interweaving of the various research tools to provide a more complete and efficient investigation than would be possible with the techniques used in isolation. Each of the research techniques used is, I argue, best suited to particular information production purposes, and is relatively inefficient for others. But, a discipline's habits may force an experimental methodology for a research problem for which informant interviewing would be far better suited. Secondly, a combination of research techniques allows the use of some in settings in which they would otherwise be suspect.

For example, ethnographic data allow the consideration of cultural and sub-cultural differences in designing and conducting research on general psychological processes using experimental designs. Experimental design in isolation requires the experimenter to base many of his research decisions on his often implicit knowledge of the culture of the participants in his research. People really do not know about how their own cultures operate as well as they think they do, and know even less about how other (sub-) cultures operate. Such knowledge is prerequisite to experimental design. Working the other way for a moment, anthropologists are sometimes glib about how learning occurs. For example, Jules Henry as participant observer in a school classroom may tell us that "kids learn to be docile there" but such a conclusion (hypothesis) depends upon his intuition about how learning occurs, based upon his own feelings. What do the teenagers demonstrably learn in such a setting? Where is a test of the existence of the intuited outcome? (Henry 1955)

In the first instance use will be made of various informally cross checking methodologies subsumed under the rubric "participant observation" including informant interviewing, observation, recording of data, census taking, etc. In the assessment of learning outcomes systematic observation, experimental (both field and laboratory) techniques, and various cognitive and perception eliciting procedures are used. Other techniques could be used in either instance and include multidimensional scaling, survey techniques, various sociometric procedures, and networks analysis. The proposed methodology should be useful for many particular foci of socialization—political socialization, ethnic socialization, or any other.

There have been published recently reports about two studies into socialization which are by these definitions complete: the "six cultures project" and the research in Liberia by Cole and his associates discussed in the previous chapter. The six cultures project began twenty years ago and the final report on the systematic observation of children was not published until 1975, although the ethnographies were published in Whiting (1963) and a factor analysis of mother interviews in Minturn and Lambert (1964). The study included six fieldteams and scores of collaborators and assistants (see Whiting and Whiting 1975). Cole and his associates combined, albeit belatedly, ethnographic and experimental procedures in researching the Kpelle of Liberia over a period of several years (Cole *et al.*, 1971). Both the studies then were large scale team efforts, and took many years to complete. No one researcher can ever hope to do as much. However, both were exploratory efforts which charted new methodological and theoretical territory; both were wide ranging in behaviors under study.

Students of socialization need a set of research techniques more applicable to smaller scale problems. These socialization studies are essential to an understanding of educative processes in our own as well as other societies. The need for them is so pressing, and the quality of truncated researches into socialization can be so low, that a way more productive of results in a shorter time must be found and made generally available. Harrington, Gumpert, and Canavan-Gumpert (in preparation) attempts to do this.

III

Ethnicity and Culture Contact

We have said that psychological anthropology is that branch of anthropology concerned with the interface between individuals and their culture, that a natural concern for psychological anthropologists is how individuals are socialized, and particularly, as Henry Murray used to say, how one becomes in some ways like all persons, in some ways like some persons, and in some ways like no other person. Psychological anthropology is concerned mainly with the first two phenomena, leaving the last to psychology. Up to now we have been talking more about socialization in a whole culture. We are concerned here with the ways in which we categorize or divide people into groups, or how they divide themselves.

The purpose of this chapter is to review some significant research related to the very important social category or classification of ethnicity. I have chosen first to review the literature on some of the fundamental issues of ethnicity and schooling and then to discuss particular ethnic groups, not only to provide a body of information, but also to suggest a number of unresolved theoretical and practical problems in our understanding of cultural pluralism, which I feel are best illustrated in the research on particular ethnic groups. The resolution of these problems I feel is critical: how we understand and use the concepts of ethnicity and cultural pluralism will affect our ability to educate a multi-ethnic school population.

I first review the concept of ethnicity particularly as it relates to schooling, at the outset stressing the importance of our recognizing the possibility of different educational values among various ethnic groups, and how the ways in which a particular ethnic group evaluates competent performance may

be in conflict with another group's view. This is especially
significant if one is a minority ethnic group and the other is the
dominant sociocultural group. In the subsequent discussion of
Spanish speaking groups in New York City, I illustrate these
value conflicts and point to the kind of further research that is
needed to increase our understanding of ethnic children in the
schools. We next turn to Mexican Americans and review the
research on the factors affecting their school performance, particularly again the educational values and attitudes of students,
parents, and school people, but here pointing to the unfor-
tunate educational results of our failure to recognize properly
the cultural differences that exist between and among Mexican
Americans and Anglos and to respond adequately to them. A
discussion of blacks follows. Here, rather than reviewing the
research about cultural attitudes and values, about which
much is already known, we review some of the seminal works
conceptualizing black culture, which have had a profound effect on how we view black culture in its complex relationship to
the larger white culture. This discussion is important because
our perspective dictates our choices in educating not only this
group but also all minority ethnic groups with a distinct culture
that is variously affected by the majority culture. The next
discussion of Native Americans reviews some of the issues
already raised, showing their distinct character, particularly
the acculturation difficulties unique to these peoples. Here too
our conceptualization of this cultural group, possibly the most
removed from the mainstream culture, will affect any future
action for improving their educational opportunities. Finally,
we turn to the issue of cultural pluralism, the ways in which a
particular group can have a repertoire of behavior, and the
kinds of educational interventions that the society must provide
in order to educate a multi-ethnic school population.

Ethnicity in the Schools

I view ethnicity as a complex interaction of a variety of factors which may create important differences among groups of individuals. First, in order for a concept of ethnicity to be effective for use in the United States it must contain the factor of nationality. Extensive studies have been done by applied anthropologists from Columbia University in the past ten years concerning the various nationality groups found in New York City, studied not only in New York but also in their countries of origin before and during the process of migration. We have been able to identify critical sociological dimensions that affect the move to the United States, such as the demographic composition of the migrant group and the types of migration which occur, particularly the circulatory (or shuttle) migration practiced by Dominicans and increasingly by Puerto Ricans. It is clear that there are differences among these nationality groups and that these differences are not clearly understood by the staffs of many schools. Language is one variable that distinguishes among the nationality groups, although it can also link them. While there are more refined differences among them, Spanish speaking groups are often lumped together: many teachers—indeed many New Yorkers—assume that Spanish speaking students are all Puerto Rican. Such inference of nationality from language is not welcome by, for example, the Dominicans to whom it is applied. In addition to language differences, nationalities differ in the legal definition of their stay in the United States. Puerto Ricans are legally citizens of the United States. Dominicans are denizens. Those who are in the country legally may be waiting to meet eligibility requirements for citizenship. Even more confounding is the fact that an unknown proportion of Dominicans reside in this country illegally, that is they may have overstayed a visitor's visa (Hendricks 1971) and they must actively seek to hide their status from authorities. Thus Dominican parents are much less able to participate in school politics or to provide the school with accurate data about family size, birth place, and so forth.

In addition to the differences by nationality, language and legal status, there are also differences on an additional set of factors which contribute to a meaningful definition of ethnicity. Differences along these variables can be found to some degree within *all* the nationality groups. These factors are important in influencing relationships among adults, among children, and between the groups and school personnel. They include skin color; educational background and attainment by parents; migration from either rural or urban backgrounds; occupation and income; religion; and dialect differences that are found within language groups.

Research I carried out at Teachers College's Institute for Urban and Minority Education has strongly suggested that each of these variables can influence how a teacher responds to a child in class. Skin color is sometimes used by teachers as the sole criterion for judging a child's ethnicity and, through ethnicity, his ability; children of lighter skin receive more positive attention (see also Rubovits and Maehr 1973). Highly educated parents have been observed entreating and receiving special favors and treatment for their children. Teachers feel that children from rural areas face adjustment problems in New York City to a greater degree than urban children ("His parents are just peasant farmers—he has a long way to go"). Since teachers bear many norms of American culture as well as norms of the city culture, they also respond to occupation and money cues of parents. Dialect differences between spoken languages of the nationality groups are also used as cues to infer inferiority. Black English is "wrong"; Puerto Rican Spanish "does not sound good," and so forth (see also Campbell 1970). Observers have also described non-verbal communication habits being used as criteria for evaluation. For example, children attending a Spanish Heritage Day in a Spanish-dominant school assembly were upbraided (by a U.S. born, middle class black school administrator) for shouting approval and clapping, and haughtily told that " *here* we express approval only with our hands, *not* our mouths."

We perceive ethnicity not as a rigid category, but as a semi-fluid interaction of the variables outlined above. Indeed while these variables produce a very large number of combinations and hence an enormous potential number of ethnic categories, the actual diversity is not so great. For example, there are few Dominican immigrants from urban backgrounds; most have not been granted citizenship; and most are lower class *campesinos*. More important, in any given interaction an individual may choose to accent one variable and play down others, for example, as when a rural Puerto Rican with other Puerto Ricans emphasizes his "Puerto Ricanness" but when with Dominicans emphasizes his common Spanish language or rural origin.

Ethnicity and Performance

It is an anthropological commonplace that disparate cultural values will affect one group's evaluations of another's performance or one group's perceptions of another's competence. It would be unwise, however, to extend that commonplace and to assume we know specifically how disparate values are related to one group's evaluations or perceptions of another without testing them. This means first identifying the values held by the various ethnic groups which could affect their performance or competence as perceived by the school, and, second, demonstrating that these values in fact are reflected in the school's evaluations and perceptions.

Probably the best known account of how cultural values different from those of the school have affected performance evaluation, success, failure and perceptions of competence is work done among the Navajo and the schools run by the Bureau of Indian Affairs (see, for example, Leighton and Kluckhohn 1946). The Navajo value a democratic harmony. To be different from a norm is to be deviant and by definition to fail on this important standard. Teachers, however, judge achievement purely in terms of success on school tasks, and distribute rewards differentially on that basis. The literature describes an incident in which a student who achieved an "A" on a test in which "C" was the norm was praised in front of the class as an example to be emulated. The "successful" child, however, was filled with embarrassment and shame at being so exposed as different from his peers. He could be expected to take care not to "fail" in this way again.

The thrust of anthropological literature has been to demonstrate that different cultures allocate values differently and that these values have consequences for behavior. This literature has gone well beyond simplistic assertions that culture A is different from culture B. Anthropologists have been able to account for value differences by examining child raising practices, family, political, and economic organizations. Value systems, then, are deeply embedded within a cultural matrix and more difficult to change in an acculturation situation than knowledge or belief systems (see Whiting and Whiting 1960). Therefore the way the values of a particular cultural group lead them to evaluate tasks expected of their children in schools may lead to serious and pervasive conflict when schools are run by and attentive to the values of a different culture.

There is evidence from research to support a lack of responsiveness on the part of schools to the values of the children they serve. Wax (1967), examining high school dropouts from the Pine Ridge Sioux schools, documents the dissimilarity between the values of the Sioux culture and that of the middle class, white oriented schools. Fuchs and Havighurst (1972) point to the insubstantial Indian influence on curriculum design and content in schools for Indians and the predominance of non-Indian personnel in these schools. Judgments of success or excellence by school personnel may be at variance with judgments produced by a particular ethnic group. Indeed, what the school values as an objective may not be so perceived by a particular group being served, and what a particular group defines as a goal may seem inappropriate to the school. For example, many schools are setting up bilingual education programs in response to the obvious perceived needs of many Spanish speaking students. However U.S. born blacks object to the diversion of funds from their children, and "middle class" Puerto Rican parents object to their children being taught to read in Spanish because this will prevent them from getting "white" (English speaking) jobs.

Conversely, other Spanish speaking parents are actively concerned with maintaining their own ethnic identities with their linguistic heritage and want their children to read and write adequately in Spanish. At the same time, in more traditional schools there are no bilingual programs; even schools having 60% Spanish speaking children can have less than 1% staff who even speak Spanish. These schools clearly only value learning to read and write in English, and judgments of competence are often made solely on this criterion. In such a setting a student's *ability* to learn, no matter how well he can read or write Spanish, is evaluated solely by his scores on English reading tests.

These examples emphasize the contradictions that can exist between school goals and the goals of the ethnic groups which make up the school population. While the findings from psychology consistently suggest that competence on a particular task is rewarding, the anthropological literature would suggest that competence in a task valued by one's culture is more rewarding than competence in a task not valued by one's culture, and that failure at a task valued by one's culture is more costly than failure at a task not valued by one's own culture.

Spanish Speaking Groups in New York City

New York's Spanish speaking population is composed of several distinct ethnic groups, including Puerto Ricans, Dominicans, and Cubans. Puerto Ricans constitute the single largest group in New York's Hispanic population, and it is the case in fact that other large Spanish speaking groups are often confused with Puerto Ricans. The following discussion will focus on another of those large groups—the 400,000 Dominicans who live in New York—in part to correct this imbalanced view and in part because data on Dominicans usefully illustrate the disparity in values between ethnic group and school which we have described above.

Results from three major sources (Hendricks 1973, Walker 1973, and Foxworthy [n.d.]) argue that Dominican parents tend to view education as learning how to read and write. Tasks undertaken in school other than these are said to have no place. There is some evidence that Dominican children, at least when they first enter school, share their parents' views. Dominican parents perceive the purpose of schooling as the means by which their children can acquire a proficiency in English enabling them to get good jobs. Education is said to be seen by Dominican parents as a validation of the change of status brought about by their social mobility from the life of the *campesino* in the rural Dominican Republic to urban New York. While the prime reasons for migration are said to be economic, an educated child is evidence that the migration has been successful, for had it been necessary for the child to work in order to contribute to the support of his family, he could not have attended school.

Not only are Dominican parents' attitudes toward the content of education often at odds with those of the school, but discrepant values concerning the personal characteristics of teachers have been noted. Dominican parents expect the teachers of their children to be authoritarian and to maintain strict and effective discipline. Teachers who define their role in a more informal way (e.g. in an open classroom) are often interpreted by Dominicans as weak and incompetent. Further, if a child acts out Dominican parents expect the teacher to take care of the matter. A teacher who calls a parent to ask for a conference, to enlist the parents' cooperation or alert them to their child's conduct, is regarded as weak and unable to handle discipline. Teachers who attend to teaching reading and mathematics are valued; those who concern themselves more personally with the child are not.

It should be noted that not all ethnic groups in New York share the attitudes toward school described above. While some Puerto Ricans and U.S. born blacks, and nearly all Dominicans and Cubans, favor successful reading instruction and more formal aspects of education as the means by which their children can aspire to the middle class, others take a different view. More politically oriented sections of the Puerto Rican and black groups value verbal and social skills and denigrate school tasks as middle class "white" skills improperly imposed on a different culture. These groups appear to emphasize political and economic maneuvering in the gaining of resources. It is interesting that Cubans and Dominicans are disenfranchised while U.S. born blacks and Puerto Ricans are citizens and potentially politically potent. It seems to be the more politically secure groups which can support cultural pluralism (not surprising in view of our discussion of cultural pluralism below).

As much as we do know, further research is required if we are to achieve adequate understanding of these groups. We need to consider not only the ethnicity of family background but also the ethnicity of a comprehensive social milieu—that is, the composition of class, peer group, teachers, and the placement of ethnic groups in various neighborhood-defined hierarchies. We must ascertain what kinds of indigenous learning situations exist for the various populations outside of school, and what are the successes of these learning situations in achieving their goals, whether the goals are self-expressed or implicit. Identification of the impact of variables like socioeconomic status, language, cultural values, income, occupation, and religion must therefore be examined. We must analyze the kinds of rewards and sanctions used in those situations and the styles of instruction in each. Data must be col-

lected on a sufficient number of categories of educational set
tings to allow descriptions of the types of settings important for
each of the migrant groups and the characteristics of instruction in each setting type for each group.

We should also ascertain on the macro level the effect of
migration on educational processes in whatever setting they occur. Where possible, data relevant to pre-migrational instructional patterns must be collected, allowing gross comparisons
of a pre-post migrational kind. Some of these peoples have
moved to new sites to stay. Others have come here to work and
obtain resources so that they can return to their home country
with capital to establish businesses or otherwise improve their
status. Still others engage in what can only be described as circular migration, in which, for most individuals, two bases can
be said to exist. It makes considerable difference to schools
which pattern of migration is encountered. If children will
return to their native, non-English speaking homes, there is little need for special programs to teach them English; what is
needed is instruction in their native tongue. An important
question is how "individuals and small groups, because of
specific economic and political circumstances in their *former
position* and among the assimilating group, may change their
locality, their subsistence pattern, their political allegiance and
form, or their household membership" (Barth 1969:24).

Then, we ought to discover the implicit cultural values that
are relevant to schooling, specifically examining what is
perceived to be important to learn and what is not. We need to
determine which of two variables—language or cultural
values—is the most powerful predictor of school failure or success. If nationality were synonymous with ethnicity and
cultural values, knowing from school records which language is
spoken in the home and the birth place of the parents would
allow us easily to assess which variable is more potent. But nationality and ethnicity are not the same. Only by a thorough
knowledge of the family based upon ethnographic data can one
hope to identify truly cultural variables.

We need to understand the processes whereby children learn

about their own ethnicity and the ethnicity of others. The following observations from Foxworthy's New York City field notes illustrate the kinds of phenomena we need to understand more fully. In a sixth grade class:

> "A Cuban-Chinese boy is called 'Chino' by Dominican boys but not by Cuban boys." "Dominican boys never dance at class parties with U.S. born black girls, but dance with Dominican girls of the same skin color." "Friendship choices for girls tend to be across ethnic lines, while the choices of boys are always within ethnic lines."

In a fourth grade class:

> "The teacher starts a discussion about Dominican Independence Day and the Dominican leader Duarte. A Dominican boy asks the teacher if she is from the Dominican Republic. When she says no, Puerto Rico, he gives her a thumbs down sign and tells her that's bad...Santo Domingo is better." "There is a lot of talk between boys about whose hair is getting long enough to be an Afro, and whether Afros are good or bad. The children's discussions center on the trouble of combing it, however, while a similar discussion among adults, i.e. mothers, has racial considerations ('he'll look like an African') as the dominant feature."

The processes of development of such images in children, and their consequences, are important areas of study which have significance far beyond the particular setting under study.

Finally, we must shed light on the consequences of stereotyping in the process of the classroom. Rosenthal's (1968) study made an empirical argument that stereotypes, in this case of a pupil's ability, could become self-fulfilling stereotypes. Gumpert and Gumpert, while acknowledging defects in the statistical analysis of the Rosenthal book, find evidence to substantiate this point, (But see also Elashoff and Snow 1971.)

To summarize, in order to arrive at an understanding of ethnicity we need to know more about the interaction among variables which determine the life patterns and values of these groups, how they view themselves and how they are viewed by others. With this knowledge, directives for educational planning should become clearer.

Mexican Americans

Recent research on Mexican Americans has investigated specifically some of the factors influencing school performance which we discussed above with particular reference to the Spanish speaking groups in New York City. Several of these studies address the issue of values and attitudes—of students, parents, and school—from which we might draw conclusions about the nature of ethnicity which may have implications for educational practice.

Schwartz (1971) emphasizes that ethnicity must be defined by variables in addition to simple nationality labels. Her study compared Mexican American and Anglo secondary school age children. She found high expectations of school attendance for both groups but a higher generalized faith in mankind and more optimistic orientation toward the future among Anglos than among Mexican Americans. These variables were also related to achievement. More important, she showed that within the Mexican American group these values were not distributed evenly, and that Mexican American pupils of higher socioeconomic status were more similar to Anglos.

Evans and Anderson (1973), while not examining variations within the Mexican American group as did Schwartz, did find that stereotypes about this group held by educators and used to explain their relation to failure are seriously in error. Mexican American students, in comparison to Anglos, did have lower self concepts of ability, experienced less democratic parental independence training, had fatalistic present time orientations, had a high striving orientation, and lower educational aspirations; however, simple minded linkages to school attitudes do not work. The Mexican Americans were also found to come from homes where education was valued and stressed. Parental encouragement of schooling was linked to values and experiences which the authors attribute to a "culture of poverty."

Madsen and Kagan (1973) report a study of experimental situations in a small Mexican town and among Anglos in Los Angeles. Mothers of both groups rewarded their children for success, but Mexican mothers more often gave rewards for failure than did Anglo mothers. Anglo mothers chose higher and more difficult achievement goals for their children. Does this matter? Yes, but again not in the simple way one might expect—high achievement goals producing better performance. Madsen's 1971 study of cooperative-competitive behavior in the same populations as those in the preceding study shows a higher level of *cooperation* among Mexican than among Anglo American children. There are also increases in *non-adaptive* competition with age for the Anglo group.

The United States Commission on Civil Rights (1971) examined "the degree to which schools in the Southwest are succeeding in educating their students, particularly minority students." Using five measures of achievement—school holding power (the ability of the school to retain students until completion of course of study), reading achievement, grade repetition, overageness, and participation in extracurricular activities—the Commission concludes that there are great discrepancies in the outcomes of students of different ethnic groups. In all measures Mexican Americans achieve at a markedly lower rate than Anglo Americans. The United States Commission on Civil Rights (1972) deals with the issue of assimilation. It sketches the conflict between the emphasis on Anglo culture (and language) in the schools and a distinct Mexican American cultural pattern. This report addresses three aspects of cultural exclusion as practiced in schools: 1) exclusion of the Spanish language; 2) exclusion of the Mexican heritage; and 3) exclusion of the Mexican American community from full participation in school affairs.

Clearly then, we are not doing an adequate job of educating Mexican American children. It may be that positive identification with one's culture or ethnicity is a powerful motivation for tested achievement. Feeling of self worth seems adaptive in the face of neglect by the school for one's group, but how is it acquired in the face of everyday pressures?

Blacks

If we have much to learn about the cultural attributes which contribute to the ethnic characters of the migratory Spanish groups, a different challenge altogether is illustrated by the more settled, urban, English speaking ethnic group: blacks. In point of fact, those we commonly label blacks actually constitute at least two major groups. One is the migrants and their descendents from various British West Indian islands (predominantly Trinidad, Jamaica and Barbados). These groups represent a migrant population of long history and stability, and some of our most prominent blacks are in fact British West Indian descendants. The other is the black U.S. population located in this country since its inception, the group to whom we now turn our attention.

Recent psychological anthropological studies of U.S. urban blacks have brought to the fore the problem of perspective, or how to view a relatively stable, well known ethnic population. The most psychologically oriented of these recent studies is Hannerz' (1969). His book is also interesting because it marks (with Ogbu's 1974) attempts by non-American anthropologists to come to grips with black U.S. culture. Using the tools of the anthropologist, Hannerz describes life in the ghetto, but his particular interest is given to the development of male role behavior, a subject which also concerned Elliot Liebow in *Tally's Corner* (1969). In fact, in one way or another, much of the anthropological literature about the urban black ghetto has centered on male role behavior, either of teenagers (Walter Miller 1958, for example) or adults.

The literature about blacks can be classed according to the following three theoretical positions using male role as an example:

1) Behavior in a black ghetto is a deviant form of normal "mainstream" male role behavior. For example, black ghetto males are more aggressive because they are protesting their masculinity in terms defined as masculine by white, middle class people. That they overdo their behavior into a caricature of the white middle class male role is attributable to their coming from a subculture where matrifocal families predominate, depriving the child of male role models. Their inability to successfully carry out instrumental aspects of the male role results from their lack of training and exculsion from jobs.

2) Behavior in a black ghetto is evidence of a ghetto-specific or black culture-specific (see Young 1970) phenomenon; the ghetto is simply a different culture from white, middle class America. For example, it is a mistake to interpret male ghetto behavior as a reaction or in relation to white, middle class definitions. This is just the way ghetto males behave. Upholders of this position typically downgrade the "protest masculine" explanation as inappropriate, and also suggest it to be inaccurate since male influence in the ghetto is strong, particularly through extra-familial groups.

3) Behavior in a black ghetto is merely a local expression of a "culture of poverty" which is found worldwide. The critical dimension here is that the state of poverty, in a culture in which wealth is also present, creates certain behavioral patterns which hold, regardless of what mainstream culture is like. For example, matrifocal households and aggressive males are part of this "culture," and are therefore to be expected in our black ghetto.

So we have in anthropology a choice, and increasingly a dispute, among respectively the "subculture" (or subsociety), the "separate culture," and the "culture of poverty" schools in interpreting black ghetto behavior. Liebow upholds the first position and Valentine (1968) appears to lean toward it; Hannerz the second; and Oscar Lewis and his followers the third. Much of Hannerz' book *Soulside* is a justification of his own position. But all three schools and the dogmas which surround them may block our understanding of life in a ghetto, or anywhere. The concept of culture, instead of being an analytic tool, can *prevent* analysis by obscuring what it is we are talking about.

To pursue our argument further, Hannerz suggests that ghetto sex role behavior cannot be accounted for as protest against middle class values. Such an explanation would postulate that, for example, father absence leads to feminine identity and a subsequent exhibition of hypermasculine traits. Hannerz argues that since there *are* men in the ghetto who could serve as role models, the subculture position is fallacious; however his own argument is misdirected. Hannerz is right, if not original, in attacking a theory that fixates on father absence to explain sex role learning. Why not father salience, mother salience, sibling presence and salience, peer groups, etc., not to mention effects of street society, power positions, and so forth? But this has nothing to do with whether the black ghetto is a culture or a subculture.

There is a fair amount of psychological anthropological literature which talks about the effects of such variables regardless of a particular culture's definitions. But what we need for blacks are studies which link these influences to behavior. In our anthropological studies of the urban ghetto, we must see to what extent our *cross-cultural* findings of the last twenty years in the fields of perception, cognition and socialization can account for what we see in the ghetto. This, not polemic about what kind of culture or subculture ghetto life is (for example, Valentine 1968), is what is required. To say, as Hannerz does, that black male behavior is ghetto specific is *not* an explanation and is barely a description. But an extensive ethnographic study to account for behavior as a result of certain developmental and situational pressures which are themselves extensively treated and tested in anthropological literature is the kind of contibution I hope to see come out of psychological anthropology in the future.

Nevertheless, whether to conceptualize the black ghetto as a subculture, a culture, or a local manifestation of a culture of poverty *is* an important problem for educators. Each leads to different action and each position can find its defenders. All three are true to a certain extent; each perhaps helps us better understand one or another aspect of behavior. But I think none of them alone can help us very much. Further, the blacks are stratified so that for some groups one may matter more than for other groups.

Educators should therefore recognize the inadequacy of any one approach. Valentine (1972) comes close to this kind of approach in his discussion of "biculturation." He states:

> The collective behavior and community life of Afro-Americans can best be understood as bicultural in the sense that people regularly draw upon both an ethnically distinctive repertoire of beliefs and customs and, at the same time, make use of behavior patterns from the European American cultural mainstream (p.33).

It would be useful to educators to understand contemporary human behavior, to specify the importance of what goes on outside of school to the learning of social behavior, and to study the techniques of instruction that exist there, and the processes of learning that are involved. In some ways we know more about Samoa than about what happens six blocks east of my office.

Native Americans

Studies of Native Americans present a special case to the psychological anthropologist concerned with determining the factors which contribute to a definition of ethnicity of these peoples, and resultant implications for education. A great deal of anthropological research was carried out more than twenty years ago because North American cultures provided an easily accessible "laboratory" for the study of acculturation (for summaries see Honigmann 1972, Barnouw 1973, Haring 1956). Some recent studies have focused on the phenomena occuring as these peoples, perhaps the most removed from mainstream culture, are brought up against urban life. However, recent studies sometimes lose sight of the differences among the groups that fall under the label "American Indians." These differences, in addition to obvious "tribal" distinctions, involve all the variables listed in our earlier discussion of ethnicity, and the reader should not lose sight of them. Some of the problems that have been noted in our discussions of other ethnic groups—values and value conflict, ethnic identity and community, the perspective from which to view a cultural group—are demonstrated in studies of American Indians, as well as acculturation difficulties unique to these peoples.

Graves (1970) has written with eloquence about the Native Americans for whom urban migration is chosen as a result of inadequate economic opportunities on the reservation, and who then find the economic role of the migrant in the city to be only marginal (Sanday, 1973, has gone so far as to call them culturally marginal). To this economic insecurity he attributes, in large part, their extremely high rate of arrest in Denver for drinking and drinking related offenses. His ten year study of 259 Navajo male migrants reveals the economic, social and psychological pressures and constraints (see also Graves 1973). Trible (1969) has compared the psycho-social characteristics of employed and unemployed western Oklahoma male Indians representing nineteen tribes. Several salient differences were found which reinforce Graves's thesis: while level of training and education were unrelated to employment status, self concept variables were clearly linked.

Robbins (1973) describes an increase in interpersonal conflict as a concomitant of economic change. He describes the drinking behaviors of the Naskapi of Quebec and claims an increase in frequencies of identity struggles and the development of ritualized or formalized social interactions which serve as identity resolving forums. He concludes (Robbins 1971) that drinking behaviors provide an arena in which individuals can make status claims. Those who are successful wage earners (a status formerly achieved through hunting) make such claims by gift giving. Those who are failures make status claims through aggressive behavior. Robbins argues then that aggressive drinking behavior provides the Naskapi with a means for taking an identity he has not been able to achieve through the new economic channels. This research is a cut above the usual studies of the linkages between stress and alcoholism because of its analysis of the behaviors associated with drinking rather than drinking per se.

Savard (1968) concludes that the Navajo alcoholic seems to use alcohol not as an escape but as a means of entree into social relationships. Group fellowship among drinkers is seen as countering an inability to function in as large a variety of social groups as nonalcoholics function in. Explanations of culturally sanctioned responses for dealing with stresses of acculturation are congruent with the description in Whiting et al. (1966) of culturally sanctioned defense mechanisms for handling a failure to live up to cultural norms. A considerable promise for future research in this area can be assured.

Of course not all cultures succeed in establishing such cultural defenses, and individual expressions of stress-induced anger are possible. For example, Ackerman (1971) relates juvenile delinquency among Nez Perce to marital instability, loss of communal discipline, loss of patrilocality, and sex role definition changes. Levy and Kunitz (1971), studying the Navajo, argue that feelings of anomie are not responses to acculturation but should be seen rather as persisting elements of Navajo culture. And Boag (1970) feels that the social problems faced by Arctic groups resemble those of underprivileged minorities elsewhere. While traditional patterns of psychopathology are obscured by social change, they are replaced by familiar identity and family disorganization pathologies. It is worth noting that we have heard this debate before. To make the linkage clear, for some theorists stress reactions are Indian culture-specific, for others they represent reactions to new role demands made by the larger Anglo society, and for others they represent yet another manifestation of a culture shared by poor minorities elsewhere. Again, more data are needed to adequately sort out for which areas of life these processes operate.

More directly relating cultural attributes of Native Americans to education, Fuchs and Havighurst (1972) examined data on residents of Chicago. In the last twenty years Chicago has experienced a surge of migration by Native Americans. The authors claim that although approximately seven thousand reside in Chicago only 237 children were found in attendance at the schools located in the area of highest concentration. They assert that urban life has not suppressed indigenous values of these Native people and attribute the educational isolation to feelings on the part of youth that schools are punitively directed against them, to their unfamiliarity with educational prerequisites to careers and socioeconomic success, to their isolation from the mainstream, and to influence of peers. (For linguistic variables, see Philips 1970.) The authors conclude:

> Indian education is an essential part of the complete process by which the Indian peoples make progress toward their own goals as individuals and as social groups. For this, they must secure a higher material standard of living, and more *real* options for themselves as individuals, families, and tribes (author's emphasis, p. 314).

However, how are they to achieve these options *and* change their pattern of underdevelopment? The authors suggest that the "dominant society [will] act in good faith, mainly through the Federal Government." This is hardly likely in the light of history and their own ethnographic evidence.

Cultural Pluralism

In this section we have been building to an argument for a greater orientation in schools to the cultural pluralism of the peoples they serve. Cultural pluralism is a cultural diversity. It refers to differences brought about by group norms, resulting in different behavioral styles among various ethnic and linguistic groups. Group identity is nourished; attempts to minimize group differences and achieve melting pot models are eschewed. We distinguish cultural pluralism from social stratification. It is an important differentiation. Social stratification is the differential incorporation of various population categories into the opportunity structure of the society. It prevents some groups from achieving the social and economic status which others are able to achieve; racism is an example. One can talk about maintaining cultural differences and, at the same time, providing the learning experiences required successfully to compete for resources. Presumably this prevents cultural pluralism from becoming structural. But is this in fact true or possible in a society so used to differentially incorporating race and sex and nationality populations in its opportunity structure?

Ethnic differentiation is clearly the most basic form of cultural pluralism (see van den Berghe 1973). When ethnicity corresponds to racial divisions, however, the more structural forms of pluralism emerge. Examples are not difficult to come by to suggest that in many societies, including our own, racial identification has been important and necessary to support an exploitative, subordinating relationship (e.g., slavery and colonialism). Exploitation and subordination *need not* be aspects of *cultural* pluralism, but because of its context in our own de facto economically stratified society, is a completely benign cultural pluralism really possible?

Educators must be aware that schools form only a part of a child's life. The education of American minority group children takes place within the context of the way in which our soci ety is actually stratified. For example, Ogbu (1974) argues that black and Mexican American students reduce their efforts in school tasks to the level of rewards they expect as future adults. We must ask what differences in children we can reasonably expect through our educational innovations, given the everyday reality of growing up in an economically discriminated segment of the population. This is especially important in evaluating what we do. For example, we must not judge the effects of school integration too quickly when there is so much that remains segregated in our lives.

Yet schools must do a better job, must not turn or help cultural pluralism maintain or increase social stratification. Our directives point in the following ways. We need to increase the diversity of educational environments to increase the likelihood of children finding one within which they can function. We need to increase the number and diversity of educational outcomes sought for assessment and the procedures for measuring them. We need to nurture the legitimacy of multiple educational outcomes that foster cultural pluralism without reinforcing socio-economic differences. We must insist on curriculum definitions that allow the examination of what goes on in school as part of a larger context—the rest of the child's life.

Let me end with a warning. We have been reviewing a wide range of literature on a number of ethnic variables as they relate to processes of schooling. It would indicate a serious misunderstanding if the information we have given about the various groups were used to construct yet more stereotypes, however refined, about these groups. The reader should remember that we have been dealing with the second aspect of Murray's aphorism. The other two still operate and, however much a child may be like other children because of ethnicity, there are still ways in which he is like all other children regardless of ethnicity. That is, he is still human, able to learn, able to think and able to feel. The ethnic differences we have been describing are small compared to these.

In other ways a particular child is like no other and knowing something about the culture from which he comes or the ethnic group to which he belongs does not excuse an educator from his obligation to know the child as an individual unique from other individuals and respond to his own special needs with a personally designed plan of instruction. The information about ethnicity growing out of research described in this chapter is, I think, important and valuable for educators to have, but it is not the only information that they need in planning their actions.

IV

Conclusions

I have suggested that much of psychological anthropology is relevant to education. Chapter I presented the development of the trends I see emerging in the study of perception and cognition, which those interested in education should find valuable. I emphasized the crucial role that culture plays in learning and thinking, and that the content of perception is culturally determined and culturally learned. The data argued against assuming that biological differences can account for group differences in perception and suggested that certain perceptual styles, emphases, and skills are also culturally influenced, and not biologically determined. An understanding of these factors is important to any foundation of educational inquiry. Chapter II reviews research in the socialization process, emphasizing that education is embedded in a sociocultural matrix. Providing a bridge between psychological and social anthropology, I argued that educational practices, in any given culture, arise from the requirements of the maintenance systems of that culture (e.g., school "failure" cannot be discussed without examining the functions and interrelationships of the school in the larger society). Chapter III noted the importance of historical context (migration and change) and situational factors (minority status). We also examined specific research with various ethnic groups in whom the educational literature has interest.

My purpose in this chapter is not simply to summarize points made above. They are more limited. I hope to: (1) Recommend how psychological anthropologists might more effectively influence educational research; (2) delineate likely priority problems for such research; and (3) as an overview, take up a fundamental criticism which might appear to argue that psychological anthropology, despite what has been said, should not enter and would not further the study of education. I will discuss each of these in turn.

How Psychological Anthropology Can Influence Education

The methods and theories of psychological anthropology have produced a large and growing body of research of sufficiently high quality so as to convince me of their importance to educational inquiry and of their potential to move us in a direction where we will be better able to address educational problems. But this promise can be achieved only if two conditions are met: There must be more involvement of the psychological anthropologists in applied research and more overt linkages to it.

Several years ago, Paul Bohannan argued that anthropologists had contented themselves with a smug certainty of the value of their research to understanding their own culture, thinking the relevance of their investigations for sociologists and psychologists in the United States to be self-evident. Anthropologists soon recognized that while their work was not totally ignored, it was nevertheless true that if they wanted anthropologically informed research done in America they were going to have to do it themselves. Similarly, psychological anthropologists have been content to do their research confident that their work's significance to others would be so obvious that educators and others would apply anthropological findings in the formulation and construction of their own research.

There is little to justify their contentment. Anthropologists have had an affect on a small group of cross-cultural psychologists but they have not, in turn, been influential in education. The time has come for researchers to accept the fact that it is up to them to demonstrate the relevance of their work to educational researchers and educational policy makers. If they do not, no one else will. And by *demonstrate* I do not mean simply pleading for its importance or pointing to its significance. Demonstration puts additional burdens on the anthropologist, but to want to influence education, but not take an active role, is self-delusion.

Much of the literature I have reviewed is directly and urgently needed by and relevant to educators, yet I have no confidence that simply asserting and explaining will have any effect. Too many will find it "very interesting" and then go on exactly as before, doing the things they were trained to do, not what needs to be done. In various educational settings over the years, I have become more convinced of the need for direct involvement. The problems out there facing educators are real and immediate. Other disciplines have promised results which while "quick" are often "dirty." Anthropology is a time-consuming discipline. It questions basic principles in its cross-cultural stance that other disciplines and policy people simply take for granted. Unless we become directly involved, it is easy for others to ignore our ideas as untested and view us as aliens.

Neglect exists not just in the camp of the nonanthropologist. Will the psychological anthropologist, comfortable in his academic department, leave its safety for a tour of duty at "the education school?" I know of one such anthropologist fundamentally interested in doing applied educational research who restrains herself, lest she jeopardize her chances for tenure at a large prestigious institution. All academics seem willing to be applied researchers in the "relevance" sections for their grant proposals, but few follow up and test the real importance of their research.

The educational institutions of a society can only be understood within the total sociocultural context where they occur. It is fair to ask why our academic society continues to perpetuate the myth of poor quality research in education to the point of stigma (ample evidence existing for both sides of the question). Is it important to a conservative educational establishment to keep the innovative, creative, "quality" people out? Why did a leading sociologist tell me recently that he was free to indulge his interests in education only after establishing his reputation as pure sociological researcher? It is not an unusual pattern. Why does the academic community exact such a penalty from the scholar who is concerned with the implications of his results that he dares risk it only when "established?" Is it because the academic community wants to protect young scholars from the dangers of being seduced into evaluative and contract research and away from theoretically important problems, or is it because of its own need for a system to placate the academics' consciences when they are troubled by the problems that face us? There was after all really "nothing we could do." Or, are we unwilling to tackle large problems lest we find answers which will engender a loss of confidence in the relevance of our mission to solve problems? While one may want to distinguish between research and the application of its results (although the former without the possibility of the latter is hard to contemplate), there is no such thing as totally "pure" research. Yet the myth persists, and the more pure is the more holy.

The final irony in the research mythology is that applied research is accused of selling out to the "system." In an era of Project Camelot, the CIA, Watergate, and "Big Government," applied researchers are suspected of oiling the creaking gears of the big oppressive machine. Rather than seeing that the degree to which this has been true in the past results from the self-selection processes described above, it is used to provide additionally negative loadings for the applied researcher. This necessitates an Orwellian doublethink in the ranks. Getting a grant from NIMH is not selling out or researching for the system, but working directly for NIMH and such organizations is. Until we break free of the self-fulfillingly prophetic myths, few psychological anthropologists may be willing to undergo the penalties of applied research. This also applies to other disciplines new to education. Until there is a willingness to take risks, no one is likely to have much impact.

Research Priorities

Psychological anthropology ought to improve our ability to recognize, discover, and measure human diversity in varied populations. Such work is badly needed when compared with the unidimensional and culture-bound attitudes of current educational practice. One has but to watch a Spanish-speaking child in New York City being assigned to a grade or track on the basis of his performance on an English reading test to know how much room there is for improvement. Psychological anthropology can provide us with the ability to do research on diverse cognitive and behavior styles which does not confuse differences with deficit; research which is sensitive to the meaning and consequences of ethnicity, and how ethnic cues are learned; and research which investigates a diversity of learning styles and strategies and their relationship to various kinds of "academic" performance—not one arbitrary standard.

We need further research in the nature and diversity of educational environments, in school and out, and how these factors interact with the diversity of the populations served. In particular it is important to ask "What are the goals of education for individuals and populations?"

Ethnic differentiation is the most basic form of cultural pluralism. When ethnicity corresponds to racial cleavage, the more extreme forms of pluralism materialize. The societies which provide the best (and only) examples of racial cleavage have been those where racial identification has been important (or necessary) to exploitative subordinating relationships like slavery and colonialism. Thus, while exploitation and subordination need *not* be an aspect of cultural pluralism, because of its context in our society pluralism has come to mean a de facto asymmetrical economic relationship, not a completely benign cultural pluralism. If we, however reluctantly, accept this view then an important research question is "What are the consequences for children who recognize that the groups to which they belong do not participate fully in the opportunity structure?" We return to this in the next section.

In all cultures it is necessary to examine the effects on education of historical and sociocultural factors external to the group
studied—specifically, the history of migration, and the general
placement of a cultural group in acculturation positions. Such
research emphasizes the importance of examining the effects of
migration, ethnic, and cultural contact phenomena on individuals and groups and through them on education. What
are the prerequisites for functioning in these situations? Are
they acquired equally for all groups? How are they acquired?
What are the motivational consequences of imbalances in the
distribution of education and other resources? These all com-
prise priorities for research.

For blacks and Mexican-Americans in California, Ogbu
finds an adaptation of school failure *specific* to these groups.
Since "they have been given inferior education and those
among them who managed to receive good educations have
been excluded from the social and economic rewards awarded
to whites...blacks responded, more or less unconsciously, by
reducing their efforts in school tasks to the level of rewards they
expected as future adults. This mode of adaptation results in a
high proportion of school failure." (Ogbu 1974.) For blacks
this adaptation reduces the pain of working as hard or harder
than do whites for fewer rewards. For whites, this adaptation
provides an excuse for the uneven allocation of resources by
showing that blacks just cannot make it, giving rise to the
perseverance and popularity of Jensenist theories about inferior ability.

We turn to Ogbu's analysis now as it raises another question: Is there room for "psychologizing" in an anthropology of
education?

Are We Just "Yet More Psychologists"?

For Ogbu, "Burgherside" children fail, in part, because of
the attitudes held by the school staff toward them; and fun-

damentally because the school system treats the school failure adaptation, which he describes for the group, in "psychological and clinical terms," rather than as a pattern embedded in the structure of the larger society. Ogbu dismisses these psychological and clinical explanations (e.g., cultural deprivation, school inferiority, or genetic inferiority). For him the real source of school failure is the unequal rewards distributed for education by the larger society. With that view, psychological research is reductionist and ignores the predominant social reality: the pervasiveness of the subordination of minority groups in the larger society. However, like so many who eschew psychological accounts Ogbu's replacement is itself a psychological theory, and a largely untested one at that. He is asserting that there is an impact of prejudice and unequal allocation of resources on *motivation* to learn, and motivation is surely a most psychological concept. Ogbu's explanations, rather than throwing out psychological accounts, call for better psychologizing to enable the examination of the phenomena he describes.

In other words, psychological anthropology must attend to situational and historical factors and not be vigorously childhood-deterministic. We need to learn more about competence motivation, and how children respond to diverse competence feedbacks. We need to investigate how people handle conflicts between the ideal and the real, frustration of goal and self-concept formation. These are social psychological phenomena, and perhaps it is long overdue that psychological anthropologists now interact with social psychologists as much as they have in the past with cognitive and developmental psychologists.

Ogbu is undeniably right when he calls for greater attention to the historical context. We have tried to do something of the same thing by suggesting ways by which psychological anthropologists have or could examine such phenomena. Psychologizing about blacks without taking such factors into consideration is reminiscent of several past debates in anthropology

about the relative importance of childhood vs. situational or
historical accounts. It is useful to review two of them here to
emphasize that psychological anthropology has been attentive
to this issue, and as a field is not concerned with constructing a
single minded "diaperology"—the cross cultural study of toilet
training—but rather with a more eclectic view of man.

In 1958 G. Morris Carstairs described Hindu males as
hostile, paranoid, and suspicious—quite the opposite of the
Gandhi image most Americans had come to accept. He related
his findings to a single-minded application of classic Freudian
theory, the while oblivious of the fact that he, a white physician
and a colonial to boot, was doing his research in immediately
post-independence India! Did one need to seek out early infancy explanations of suspicion and distrust, or would a more parsimonious account deal with how people relate to him at that
time and place? There are many other instances in Carstairs's
book in which obvious historical accounts are ignored and
Freudian accounts produced with single-minded devotion. For
example, the Hindu refusal to eat meat is explained as a repres-
sion of his desire to eat his father's penis! Such howlers as this
were thoroughly explored in M. Opler's review of Carstairs's
book (Opler 1959, 1960).

Douglas Haring (1953) was disturbed by accounts of
Japanese national character which emphasized Freudian or
developmental theory to the exclusion of situational and
historical factors. He argued that the Japanese national
character, to be understood, had to be viewed as an adaptation
to life in a totalitarian police state. Much as Ogbu was to argue
20 years later for blacks, Haring—a psychological anthropologist—was arguing that much psychological anthropology research was ignoring the predominant social reality for pre-1945 Japan: the pervasiveness of the police state
techniques for maintaining order.

Now while it is fair to say that the field of psychological anthropology as a whole has emphasized some factors to the detriment of others, it is not fair to assert that psychological an-

thropology has no relevance for education because of this imbalance. There are tools, and there is an existing literature
which does focus on the relevant and the important variable, as
we have strived to show throughout this report. The literature
also makes clear that it makes little sense to revert to an opposite stance by ignoring childhood developmental factors in
the many situations where they have been demonstrated to
have an effect. Part of the research question to be answered for
particular problems is which kinds of variable are having the
most potent effects for the phenomena under investigation.
Regrettably, however, this openness is sometimes obscured by
polemic. For example, shortly after Haring's position was
reported, Geoffrey Gorer, an English "diaperologist,"
published a paper linking English national character to the
London bobby. Haring (in a personal communication) felt bit-
terly that this was a caustic attempt to satirize and misrepresent
his viewpoint (Gorer 1955).

Suffice it to say here then that psychological anthropology
has been willing to acknowledge the legitimacy of historical or
situational accounts. Since these factors seem very much for
our own society's minorities a significant part of the input into
how learning and thinking are structured, the attention of
psychological anthropologists to such phenomena, perhaps in
collaboration with different kinds of psychologists (e.g., social)
than we have been used to, is a priority of future research.

We need to ask "What are the goals of any educational
research?" Assuming that our theory is sophisticated enough
that we can find out what is important to measure, and how to
measure it for whatever group of interest, why are we doing
this research? Are we discovering talent, or providing the
larger society with another excuse for discriminating against
those said to lack it? Are we helping developing countries best
utilize their scarce educational resources by putting their
money where it is most likely to win, or are we helping them to
rationalize their inability to serve 90 percent of their population? Are we searching for information and data to foster and

improve the likelihood of cultural pluralism and diversity? Or are we engaged in more label making and stereotyping, to which others can apply negative loadings? We cannot ignore these dangers. Indeed, we must constantly be alert to them.

Overview

Most generally, the research I have reviewed from psychological anthropology calls for the following programmatic priorities to which we should turn our efforts in the years ahead:

1. Increasing the diversity of educational environments to increase the likelihood of children finding one within which they can function.
2. Increasing the diversity of research methods by securing funding for research which would combine more standard anthropological techniques with longitudinal, experimental, and quasi-experimental designs;
3. Increasing the diversity of research personnel so as to increase the number of disciplines represented, and to involve the people being studied in the decisions that will ultimately concern them;
4. Increasing the number and diversity of educational outcomes sought for assessment, and the procedures for measuring them;
5. Nurturing the legitimacy of multiple educational outcomes that foster cultural diversity without reinforcing social stratification;
6. Insisting on curriculum definitions that allow the examination of what goes on in school as part of a larger context —the rest of the child's life—and the rest of American Society, or whatever society the program is in;
7. Encouraging the involvement of "mainstream" psychological anthropology in educational programs and breaking through the self-fulfilling prophecy syndrome of the quality of educational research.

My purpose in this book has been to delineate a field of inquiry—psychological anthropology and education—with the goal of effecting future research. The reader will have to assess the potentiality of the payoff for education from psychological anthropology. One way is to assess the academic rigor and power of the theories and methods examined. A second way is to examine the programmatic priorities just enunciated. They emerge from the literature reviewed, but they also involve human values and ethical choices. To a certain degree the success of a field of inquiry is determined not just by its academic fruitfulness but by its values. Is there some congruence between the ethical stance implicit in the field and ethics of the potential scholar or educational consumer? I invite the reader to apply both tests in assessing the value of psychological anthropology for education.

References Cited

Ackerman, Lillian A.
1971. Marital Instability and Juvenile Delinquency Among the Nez Perces. *American Anthropologist* 73:595.

Adams, Frances M. and Charles E. Osgood
1973. A Cross-Cultural Study of the Affective Meanings of Color. *Journal of Cross-Cultural Psychology* 4:135.

Adler, Norman M. and Charles Harrington
1970. *The Learning of Political Behavior.* Chicago: Scott, Foresman.

Al-Issa. I. and W. Dennis
1970. *Cross-Cultural Studies of Behavior.* New York: Holt, Rinehart, & Winston.

Allen, Martin J.
1967. Childhood Experience and Adult Personality—A Cross-Cultural Study Using the Concept of Ego Strength. *Journal of Social Psychology* 71:53-68.

Almy, M.
1970. The Usefulness of Piagetian Methods for Studying Primary School Children in Uganda. In *Studying School Children in Uganda.* M. Almy, J.L. Davitz, and M.A. White. New York: Teachers College Press.

Ardener, Edwin, Ed.
1971. *Social Anthropology and Language.* A.S.A. Monographs, No. 10. London: Tavistock.

Asch, S.E.
1956. Studies of Independence and Conformity: A Minority of One Against a Unanimous Majority. *Psychological Monographs* 70:414.

Ayres, Barbara C.
1954. "Personality Determinants of Food and Sex Taboos During Pregnancy." Doctoral dissertation. Cambridge, Radcliffe College.
1968. Effects of Infantile Stimulation on Musical Behavior. In *Folk Song Style and Culture.* Alan Lomax, et al., Eds. American Association for the Advancement of Science, pp. 211-221.
1973. Effects of Infant Carrying Practices on Rhythm and Music. *Ethos* 4:387.

Bacon, M.K., Irvin Child and Herbert Barry,
1963. A Cross-Cultural Study of Correlates of Crime. *Journal of Abnormal and Social Psychology* 66:291-300.

Barclay, A. and D. R. Cusumano
1967. Father Absence, Cross-Sex Identity and Field Independent Behavior in Male Adolescents. *Child Development* 38:243-50.

Barnes, J.A.
1954. Class and Committees in a Norwegian Island Parish. *Human Relations 7:39-58.*

Barnouw, Victor
1973. *Culture and Personality.* Homewood, Illinois: The Dorsey Press.

Barry, Herbert A.
1957. Relationships Between Child Training and the Pictorial Arts. *Journal of Abnormal and Social Psychology* 54:380-383.
1968. Sociocultural Aspects of Alcohol Addiction. In *The Addictive States.* Association for Research in Nervous or Mental Disease, Vol. XLVI. Baltimore: Williams and Wilkins Co.

Barry, Herbert A., M.K. Bacon and Irvin Child,
1957. A Cross-Cultural Survey of Some Sex Differences in Socialization. *Journal of Abnormal and Social Psychology* 55:327-332.
1959. Relation of Child Training to Subsistence Economy. *American Anthropologist* 61:51-63.

Barry, Herbert A. and L.M. Paxon
1971. Infancy and Early Childhood: Cross-Cultural Codes. 2. *Ethnology* 10:466.

Barry, Herbert A. and J. Roberts
1972. Infant Socialization and Games of Chance. *Ethnology* 11:296.

Barth, Frederick
1969. *Ethnic Groups and Boundaries: The Social Organization of Cultural Difference.* Boston: Little, Brown & Co.

Battilla, Bonfil
1966. Conservative Thought in Applied Anthropology: A Critique. *Human Organization* 25:89.

Benedict, Ruth
1934. *Patterns of Culture.* Boston: Houghton Mifflin.

Berlin, B. and A.K. Romney
1964. Descriptive Semantics of Tzeltal Numeral Classifiers. In *Transcultural Studies in Cognition.* A.K. Romney, and R.G. D'Andrade, Eds. *American Anthropologist* 66:79-98.

Berry, John W.
1966. Temne and Eskimo Perceptual Skills. *International Journal of Psychology* 1:207-229.
1970. Marginality, Stress and Ethnic Identification in an Acculturated Aboriginal Community. *Journal of Cross-Cultural Psychology* 1:239.

Berry, John W. and P. R. Dasen
1974. *Culture and Cognition.* London: Methuen Press.

Berry, John W. and H. Witkin
1975. Psychological Differential in Cross-Cultural Perspective. *Journal of Cross-Cultural Psychology* 6(1).

Biener, Lois B.
1972. "The Effect of Message Repetition on Attitude Change: A Model of Informational Social Influence." Ph.D. dissertation, Columbia University.

Boag, Thomas J.
1970. Mental Health of Native Peoples of the Arctic. *Canadian Psychiatric Association Journal* 15:115.

Boas, Franz
1911. *The Mind of Primitive Man.* New York: MacMillan.

Bock, Philip K.
1967. Love Magic, Menstrual Taboos and the Facts of Geography. *American Anthropologist* 69:213-217.

Bolton, Ralph
1973. Aggression and Hypoglycemia Among the Qola: A Study in Psychobiological Anthropology. *Ethnology* 12:227.

Bolton, Ralph and Constance Vadhein
1973. The Ecology of East African Homicide. *Behavior Science Notes* 8:319.

Bovet, Magali C.
1968. Comparative Investigation of Intellectual Development and Learning Process. *Schweizerische fur Psychologie und ihre Anwendungen* 27:189-199.

Brown, Judith K.
1963. A Cross-Cultural Study of Female Initiation Rites. *American Anthropologist* 65:837-853.

Bruner, J.S. and R.R. Oliver
1963. *Development of Equivalence Transformations in Children.* Monograph. Society for Research in Child Development 28:125-143.

Burling, Robbins
1964. Cognition and Componential Analysis: God's Truth or Hocus-Pocus? *American Anthropologist* 66:20-28.

Burnett, Jacquetta H.
1974. *Anthropology and Education: An Annotated Bibliographic Guide.* New Haven: HRAF Press for the Council on Anthropology and Education.

Burton, Roger and John W.M. Whiting
1961. The Absent Father and Cross-Sex Identity, *Merrill-Palmer Quarterly* 7:85-95.

Campbell, D.T.
1964. Distinguishing Differences in Perception from Failures of Communication in cross-Cultural Studies. In *Cross-Cultural Understanding: Epistemology in Anthropolgy.* F.S.C. Northrop, Ed. New York: Harper & Row, pp. 308-366.
Campbell, D.T., and J.C. Stanley
1966. *Experimental and Quasi-Experimental Designs for Research.* Chicago: Rand McNally.
Campbell, Russell N.
1970. English Curricula for Non-English Speakers. In *Bilingualism and Language Contact.* James E. Alatis, ed. Proceedings of the Georgetown University Round Table on Language and Linguistics 1970, Washington D.C.: Georgetown University Press.
Carlsmith, Karolyn Kuckenberg
1963. "Effect of Father Absence on Scholastic Aptitude." Ph.D. dissertation, Harvard University.
1973. Some Personality Characteristics of Boys Separated from their Fathers During World War II. *Ethos* 1(4):466-477.
Carpenter, Edmund, Frederick Varley and Robert Flaherty
1959. *Eskimo.* Toronto: University of Toronto Press.
Carstairs, G.M.
1958. *The Twice Born.* Bloomington: Indiana University Press.
1960. Rejoinder. *American Anthropologist* 62:504.
Cattell, Raymond B.
1968. The Theory of Fluid and Crystallized Intelligence: Its Relationship to Culture Free Tests and Its Verification in 9-12 Year Old Children. *Bolletino de Psicologia Applicata* 88-90:3-22.
Caudill, William
1973. The Influence of Social Structure and Culture on Human Behavior in Modern Japan. *Ethos* 3:343.
Chance, Norman A.
1973. Minority Education and Transformation of Consciousness. In *Learning and Culture.* Proceedings of the 1972 Annual Spring Meeting of the American Ethnological Society. Solon T. Kimball and Jacquetta H. Burnett, Eds. Seattle: University of Washington Press.
Cheng, Tsu-Hsin and Mei-Ke Lei
1960. An Investigation into the Scope of the Conception of Numbers among 6-7 Year Old Children. *Acta Psychological Sinica* 1:28-35.
Child, Irvin L.
1968. The Experts and the Bridge of Judgement that Crosses Every Cultural Gap. *Psychology Today* 2:24-29.

Clement, David E., Frank Sistrunk and Zenita C. Guenther
1970. Pattern Perception Among Brazilians as a Function of Pattern Uncertainty and Age. *Journal of Cross-Cultural Psychology* 1:305.

Cohen, Yehudi
1964. *The Transition from Childhood to Adolescence.* Chicago: Aldine.

Cole, M., J. Gay and J. Glick
1968. Reversal and Nonreversal Shifts among a West African Tribal People. *Journal of Experimental Psychology* 76:323-324.

Cole, Michael, John Gay, Joseph A. Glick and Donald W. Sharp
1971. *The Cultural Context of Learning and Thinking.* New York: Basic Books.

Cole, Michael and Sylvia Scribner
1974. *Culture and Thought.* New York: John Wiley and Sons.

Conklin, H.C.
1955. Hanunóo Color Categories. *Southwestern Journal of Anthropology* 11:339-344.

Cremin, Lawrence A.
1970. *American Education: The Colonial Experience 1607-1783.* New York: Harper & Row.

Cuceloglu, Dogan M.
1967. "A Cross-Cultural Study of Communication Via Facial Expressions." Ph.D. dissertation, University of Illinois.

D'Andrade, Roy G.
1962. "Paternal Absence and Cross-Sex Identification." Ph.D. dissertation, Harvard University.
1966. Sex Differences and Cultural Institutions. In *The Development of Sex Differences.* E. Maccoby, Ed. Stanford: Stanford University Press.
1973. Father Absence, Identification, and Identity. *Ethos* 1:440.

Dalton, William, Nancy Foxworthy and Frances Schwartz
1972. *The Dynamics of an Open Classroom in a New York City School.* Mimeo. Center for Urban Studies and Programs. Teachers College, Columbia University.

Dasen, Pierre R.
1972. Cross-Cultural Piagetian Research: A Summary. *Journal of Cross Cultural Psychology* 3:23.

Dawson, John L.M.
1963, "Psychological Effects of Social Change in a West African Community." Ph.D. dissertation, University of Oxford.
1966. Kwashiorkor, Gynaecomastia and Feminization Processes. *Journal of Tropical Medicine and Hygiene* 69:175-179.
1967. Cultural and Physiological Influences upon Spatial-Perceptual Processes in West Africa. Parts I and II. *International Journal of Psychology* 2:115-128 and 171-185.

1967. Cultural and Physiological Influences Upon Spatial-Perceptual Processes in West Africa Part I. *International Journal of Psychology* 2:115-125.

Dawson, John L.M., Brian M. Young and Peter P.G. Choi
1973. Developmental Influences on Geometric Illusion Susceptability Among Hong Kong Chinese Children. *Journal of Cross-Cultural Psychology* 4:49.

DeLacey, P.R.
1971a. Classificatory Ability and Verbal Intelligence among High-Contact Aboriginal and Low-Socioeconomic White Australian Children. *Journal of Cross-Cultural Psychology* 2:393-396.

DeLemos, M.M.
1969a. Conceptual Development in Aboriginal Children: Implications for Aboriginal Education. In *Aborigines and Education.* S.S. Dunn, and C.M. Tatz, Eds. Melbourne: Sun Brooks, pp. 244-263.
1969b. The Development of Conservation in Aboriginal Children. *International Journal of Psychology* 4:255-269.
1973. The Development of Spatial Concepts in Zulu Children. In *Culture and Cognition: Readings in Cross-Cultural Psychology.* J.W. Berry, and P.R. Dasen, Eds. London: Methuen & Co. Ltd.

Dempsey, A.D.
1971. Time Conservation Across Cultures. *International Journal of Psychology* 6:115-120.

Dennis. W. and R.W. Russell
1940. Piaget's Questions Applied to Zuni Children. *Child Development* 11:181-187.

Deregowski, Jan B.
1968. Difficulties in Pictorial Perception in Africa. *British Journal of Psychology* 59:195-204.
1969. Perception of the Two-Pronged Trident by Two and Three Dimensional Perceivers. *Journal of Experimental Psychology* 82:9-13.

Deregowski, Jan B. and William Byth
1970. Hudson's Pictures in Pandora's Box. *Journal of Cross-Cultural Psychology* 1:315-323.

Deutsch, M. and H.B. Gerard
1955. A Study of Normative and Informational Social Influences Upon Individual Judgment. *Journal of Abnormal and Social Psychology* 51:629-636.

Devons, Ely and Max Gluckman
1964. Introduction, in *Closed Systems and Open Minds.* Chicago: Aldine.

Dollard, John
1935. *Criteria for a Life History, With Analyses of Six Notable Documents.* New Haven: Yale University Press.

Douglas, Mary
1970. *Natural Symbols, Explorations in Cosmology.* London: Barrie and Rockliff.

Dubois, Cora
1944. *The People of Alor.* Minneapolis: University of Minnesota Press.

Dubreuil, G. and C. Bosclair
1960. Le Réalisme Enfantin à la Martinique et au Canada Francais. Etude Genetique et Esperimentale. In *Thought from the Learned Societies of Canada.* Toronto: Gage, pp. 83-95.
1966. Quelques aspects de la Pensée Enfantine à La Martinique. In *Les Sociétés Antillaises: Etudes Anthropologiques.* J. Benoist, Ed. Department of Anthropology, University of Montreal, pp. 79-99.

Durkheim, Emile and Marcel Mauss
1903. De Quelques Formes Primitives de Classification. *Année Sociologique.*

Easton, David and Jack Dennis
1970. The Child's Acquisition of Regime Norms: Political Efficacy. *American Political Science Review* 61:25-38.

Edgerton, Robert B.
1971. A Traditional African Psychiatrist. *Southwestern Journal of Anthropology* 27:3.

Eells, K.W., A. Davis, R.J. Havighurst, R.W. Tyler and V.E. Herrick
1959. *Intelligence and Cultural Differences.* Chicago: University of Chicago Press.

Ekman, Paul and Wallace V. Friesen
1971. Constants Across Cultures in the Face and Emotion. *Journal of Personality and Social Psychology* 17:124-219.

Ekman, Paul, Richard E. Sorenson and Wallace V. Friesen
1969. Pan Cultural Elements in Facial Displays of Emotion. *Science* 164:86-88.

El-Abd, Hamed A.
1970. The Intellect of East African Students. *Multivariate Behavioral Research.* 5:423-433.

Elashoff, Janet and Richard E. Snow
1971. *Pygmalion Reconsidered.* Worthington, Ohio: Charles A. Jones.

Ember, Carol R.
1973. Feminine Task Assignment and the Social Behavior of Boys. *Ethos* 1:424-439.

Endleman. Robert
1967. *Personality and Social Life.* New York: Random House.

Epstein, A.L.
1961. The Network and Urban Social Organization. *Rhodes-Livingston Journal* 29:29-61.

Etuk, E.
1967. "The Development of Number Concepts: An Examination of Piaget's Theory with Yoruba-Speaking Nigerian Children." Ed.D. dissertation, Teachers College, Columbia University.

Evans, Francis B. and James G. Anderson
1973. The Psychocultural Origins of Achievement and Achievement Motivation: The Mexican-American Family. *Sociology of Education* 46:396.

Farberow, Norman L. and Edwin S. Shneidman, Eds.
1961. *The Cry for Help.* New York: McGraw-Hill.

Fischer, John L.
1959. Art Styles and Cultural Cognitive Maps. Paper presented at American Anthropological Association Annual Meetings, Mexico City, December.

Foxworthy, Nancy
n.d. Unpublished Field Notes: Applied Anthropology Program, Teachers College, Columbia University.

Freed, Stanley A. and Ruth Freed
1971. A Technique for Studying Role Behavior. *Ethnology* 10:107.

French, D.
1963. The Relationship of Anthropology to Studies in Perception and Cognition. In *Psychology: A Study of a Science;* Vol. 6. S. Koch, Ed. New York: McGraw Hill. pp. 388-428.

Friendly, Joan P.
1956. "A Cross-Cultural Study of Ascetic Mourning Behavior." Senior honors thesis, Radcliffe College.

Frijda, N. and G. Jahoda
1966. On the Scope and Methods of Cross-Cultural Research. *International Journal of Psychology* 1:110-127.

Fuchs, Estelle and Robert J. Havighurst
1972. *To Live on the Earth: American Indian Education.* Garden City: Doubleday.

Garbett, G.K. and B. Kapferer
1970. Theoretical Orientations in the Study of Labour Migration. *New Atlantis* 2.

Gay, J., and M. Cole
1967. *The New Mathematics and an Old Culture.* New York: Holt, Rinehart, & Winston.

Gearing, Fred O., Murray L. Wax and Stanley Diamond
1971. *Anthropological Perspectives on Education.* New York: Basic Books.

Gladwin, T.

1970. *East is a Big Bird.* Cambridge, Massachusetts: Harvard University Press.

Gladwin, T., and W.C. Sturtevant

1972. *Anthropology and Human Behavior.* Washington, D.C.: Anthropological Society of Washington.

Gluckman, M.

1944. The Logic of African Science and Witchcraft. *Rhodes-Livingstone Journal* 1:61.

Gobar, A,H,

1970. Suicide in Afghanistan. *British Journal of Psychiatry* 116:493-496.

Goldschmidt, Walter

1973. Guilt and Pollution in Sebei Mortuary Rituals. *Ethos* 1:75.

Goodnow, J.J.

1969a. Cultural Variations in Cognitive Skills. In *Cross-Cultural Studies.* D.R. Price-Williams, Ed. Baltimore: Penguin Books.

1969b. Problems in Research on Culture and Thought. In *Studies in Cognitive Development: Essays in Honor of Jean Piaget.* D. Elkind, and J.H. Flavell, Eds. New York: Oxford University Press, pp. 439-462.

Gorer, Geoffrey

1955. Modification of National Character: The Role of the Police in England. *The Journal of Social Issues* 2(2):24-32.

Granzberg, Gary

1973. Twin Infanticide: A Cross-Cultural Test of a Materialistic Explanation. *Ethos* 1:405.

Graves, Theodore D.

1970. The Personal Adjustment of Navajo Indian Migrants to Denver, Colorado. *American Anthropologist* 72:35.

1973. The Navajo Urban Migrant and his Psychological Situation. *Ethos* 3:321.

Green, Helen B.

1971. Socialization Values in West African, Negro and East Indian Cultures: A Cross-Cultural Comparison. *Journal of Cross-Cultural Psychology* 2:309.

Greenfield, P. Marks

1966. On Culture and Conservation. In *Studies in Cognitive Growth.* J. S. Bruner, R. R. Oliver and P. M. Greenfield, Eds. New York: Wiley, pp. 225-256.

Greenfield, P. M., and J. S. Bruner

1966. Culture and Cognitive Growth. *International Journal of Psychology* 1:89-107.

Gumpert, Peter and Carol Gumpert
1968. The Teacher as Pygmalion: Comments on the Psychology of Expectation. *The Urban Review* 3(1):21-25.

Gumpert, Peter and Charles Harrington
1972. Intellect and Cultural Deprivation. *Teachers College Record* 74(2):261-273.

Gunders, S. M. and John W. M. Whiting
1964. The Effects of Periodic Separation from the Mother During Infancy upon Growth and Development. Paper presented at the International Congress of Anthropological Sciences, Moscow.

Hallowell, A. I.
1951. Cultural Factors in the Structuralization of Perception. In *Social Psychology at the Crossroads*. J. H. Rohrer, and M. Sherif, Eds. New York: Harper & Row.

Halsey, A. H., Jean Floud and C. Arnold Anderson
1961. *Education, Economy and Society*. New York: The Free Press.

Hamer, John H.
1969. Guardian Spirits, Alcohol, and Cultural Defense Mechanisms. *Anthropologia* 11:215-241.

Hannerz, Ulf
1969. *Soulside*. New York: Columbia University Press.

Hargreaves, David
1967. *Social Relations in a Secondary School*. London: Routledge and Kegan Paul.

Haring, Douglas G.
1953. Japanese National Character: Cultural Anthropology, Psycho-Analysis and History. *The Yale Review* 42:373-392.

Haring, Douglas G., Ed.
1956. *Personal Character and Cultural Milieu*. Syracuse: Syracuse University Press.

Harrington, Charles
1968. Sexual Differentiation in Socialization and Some Male Genital Mutilations. *American Anthopologist* 70:952-956.

1970. *Errors in Sex-Role Behavior in Teen Age Boys*. New York: Teachers College Press.

1973. Pupils, Peers and Politics. In *Learning and Culture, Proceedings of the 1972 Annual Spring Meeting of the American Ethnological Society*. Solon T. Kimball and Jacquetta H. Burnett, Eds. Seattle: University of Washington Press.

1974. *Schooling and Socialization of Migrant Groups in a Bi-lingual and Culturally Diverse Metropolitan Area*. Mimeo. Applied Anthropology Program, Teachers College, Columbia University.

1975a. *Psychological Anthropology and Education*. Mimeo. Washington, D.C. National Academy of Education, Committee on Anthropology and Education.

1975b.A Psychological Anthropologist's View of Ethnicity and Schooling. *IRCD Bulletin* 10(4).

1976. Psychological Anthropology and Educational Practice. *Teachers College Record* 78(1):69-76.

Harrington, Charles, Peter Gumpert and Donnah Canavan Gumpert

n.d. *Methods of Inquiry*. Cambridge: Winthrop.

Harrington, Charles and John W. Whiting

1972. Socialization Process and Personality. In *Psychological Anthropology*. Francis L. K. Hsu, Ed. Cambridge: Schenkman.

Hart, J. A.

1965. "A Study of the Cognitive Capacity of a Group of Australian Aboriginal Children." M. A. qualifying examination thesis, University of Queensland.

Hartley, Eugene L. and Ruth E. Hartley

1952. *Fundamentals of Social Psychology*. New York: Knopf.

Hellon, C. P.

1970. Mental Illness and Acculturation in the Canadian Aboriginal. *Canadian Psychiatric Association Journal* 15:136-139.

Hendricks, Glenn

1971."The Dominican Diaspora: The Case of Immigrants from the Dominican Republic in New York City." Ed.D. dissertation.Teachers College, Columbia University.

1973. La Raza en Nueva York: Social Pluralism and Schools. *Teachers College Record* 74(3):379-394.

Henry, Jules

1955. Docility, or Giving Teacher What She Wants. *Journal of Social Issues.* 11:33

Heron, A.

1968. Studies of Perception and Reasoning in Zambian Children. *International Journal of Psychology* 3:23-29.

Heron, Alastair and Wendy Dowel

1973. Weight Conservation and Matrix-Solving in Papuan Children. *Journal of Cross-Cultural Psychology* 4:207.

Herskovits, Melville

1948. *Man and His Works: The Science of Cultural Anthropology*. New York: Knopf.

Herzog, John D.

1962. Deliberate Instruction and Household Structure: A Cross-Cultural Study. *Harvard Educational Review* 32:301-342.

1973. Initiation and High School in the Development of Kikuyu Youth's Self-Concept. *Ethos* 1:478.

Hess, Robert D. and Judith V. Torney
1967. *The Development of Political Attitudes in Children.* Chicago: Aldine.

Hippler, Arthur E.
1969. Fusion and Frustration: Dimensions in the Cross-Cultural Ethnopsychology of Suicide. *American Anthropologist* 71:1074.

Honigmann, John J.
1967. *Personality in Culture.* New York: Harper & Row.

1972. North America. In *Psychological Anthropology.* Francis L. K. Hsu, Ed. Cambridge: Schenkman.

Howe, James
1966, "Caymanian Drinking Behavior." Honors thesis, Department of Anthropology, Harvard University.

Hsu, Francis L. K., Ed.
1972. *Psychological Anthropology.* Cambridge: Schenkman.

Hudson, W.
1960. Pictorial Depth Perception in Sub-Cultural Groups in Africa. *Journal of Social Psychology* 52:183-208.

1962. Pictorial Perception and Educational Adaptation in Africa. *Psychologia Africana* 9:226-239.

1967. The Study of the Problem of Pictorial Perception Among Unacculturated Groups. *International Journal of Psychology* 2:90-107.

Ianni, Francis A. J. and Edward Storey
1973. *Cultural Relevance and Educational Issues.* Boston: Little, Brown and Company.

Irvine, S. H.
1967. How Fair is Culture? Factorial Studies of Raven's Progressive Matrices in Africa. *International Workshop on Educational Testing.* Berlin: Pedagogisches Zentrum.

1970. Affect and Construct: A Cross-Cultural Check on Theories of Intelligence. *Journal of Social Psychology* 80:23-30.

Irving, Douglas Dorset
1970. "The Field-Dependence Hypothesis in Cross-Cultural Perspective." Ph.D. dissertation, Rice University.

Jahoda, G.
1966. Geometric Illusions and Environment: A Study in Ghana. *British Journal of Psychology* 57:183-189.

1970. A Cross-Cultural Perspective in Psychology. *The Advancement of Science* 27:1-14.

Jahoda, Gustav and Barrie Stacey
1970. Susceptibility to Geometrical Illusions According to Culture and Professional Training. *Perception and Psychophysics* 7:179-184.

Jensen, Arthur
1969. How Much Can We Boost IQ and Scholastic Achievement? *Harvard Educational Review* 39:1-123.

Kagan, Jerome and Howard A. Moss
1961. *Birth to Maturity.* New York: Wiley.

Kardiner, Abram
1939. *The Individual and His Society, The Psychodynamics of Primitive Social Organization.* New York: Columbia University Press.

Keddie, Nell
1971. Classroom Knowledge. In *Knowledge and Control.* Michael F. D. Young, Ed. London: Collier & McMillan Publishers.

Kellagham, T. P.
1965. "The Study of Cognition in a Non-Western Society with Special Reference to the Yoruba of South Nigeria." Doctoral thesis, University of Belfast.

Kellaghan, Thomas
1968. Abstraction and Categorization in African Children. *International Journal of Psychology* 3:115-120.

Kelly, M. R.
1971. Some Aspects of Conservation of Quantity and Length in Papua and New Guinea in Relation to Language, Sex and Years at School. *Territory of Papua and New Guinea Journal of Education* 7:55-60.

Kibuuka, P. M. T.
1966 "Traditional Education of the Baganda Tribe." Unpublished MS, National Institute of Education, Makerere University

Kidd, A. H. and J. L. Rivoire
1965. The Culture-Fair Aspects of the Development of Spatial Perception. *Journal of Genetic Psychology* 106:101-111.

Kilbride, Philip L.
1971 "Individual Modernization and Pictorial Perception Among the Baganda of Uganda." Ph.D. dissertation, University of Missouri, Columbia.

Kilbride, Philip L. and Michael C. Robbins
1969. Pictorial Depth Perception and Acculturation Among the Baganda. *American Anthropologist* 71:293.

Kimball, Solon T. and Jacquetta H. Burnett, Eds.
1973. *Learning and Culture, Proceedings of the 1972 Annual Spring Meeting of the American Ethnological Society.* Seattle: University of Washington Press.

Kluckhohn, Clyde
1939. Theoretical Bases of an Empirical Method of Studying the Acquisition of Culture by Individuals. *Man* 39:98–105.
Krauss, Herbert H.
1970. Social Development and Suicide. *Journal of Cross-Cultural Psychology* 1:159-167.
Kreitman, Norman, Peter Smith and Eng Seong Tan
1970. Attempted Suicide as Language: An Empirical Study. *British Journal of Psychiatry* 116:465-473.
Kuske, Irwin I.
1970. "Psycholinguistic Abilities of Sioux Indian Children." Ed.D. dissertation, University of South Dakota.
Lacey, Colin
1970. *Hightown Grammar.* Manchester: Manchester University Press.
Lambert, W. W., Leigh Triandis and Margery Wolf
1959. Some Correlates of Beliefs in the Malevolence and Benevolence of Supernatural Beings: A Cross-Cultural Study. *Journal of Abnormal and Social Psychology* 58:2.
Landauer, Thomas K.
1973. Infantile Vaccination and the Secular Trend in Stature. *Ethos* 1:499.
Landauer, Thomas K. and John W. M. Whiting
1964. Infantile Stimulation and Adult Stature of Human Males. *American Anthropologist* 66:1007-1028.
Langness, L. L.
1965. *The Life History in Anthropological Science.* New York: Holt, Rinehart, and Winston.
Lee, Dorothy
1950. Lineal and Nonlineal Codifications of Reality. *Psychosomatic Medicine* 12:89-97.
Leighton, D. and C. Kluckhohn
1946. *Children of the People.* Cambridge: Havard University Press.
Lesser, Alexander
1961. Education and the Future of Tribalism in the United States: The Case of the American Indian. Occasional paper No. 3 of the Phelps-Stokes Fund. Reprinted in the *Social Science Review* 35:1-9.
Lesser, G. D., G. Fifer and D. H. Clark
1965. *Mental Abilities of Children from Different Social Class and Cultural Groups.* Child Development Monograph 30.
LeVine, Robert A.
1960a. Witchcraft and Marital Relations in East Africa: A Controlled Comparison. Paper presented at the American Anthropological Association Meeting, Minneapolis, Minnesota.

1960b. The Internalization of Political Values in Stateless Societies. *Human Organization* 19:51-58.

1970. Cross-Cultural Study in Child Psychology. In *Carmichael's Manual of Child Psychology*, Volume II, 3rd edition, P. H. Mussen, Ed. New York: John Wiley & Sons.

1973. *Culture and Personality*. Chicago: Aldine.

LeVine, Robert A. and Douglas Price-Williams
1974. Children's Kinship Concepts: Cognitive Development and Early Experience Among the Hausa. *Ethnology* 3:25.

Levi-Strauss, Claude
1966. *The Savage Mind*. Chicago: University of Chicago Press.

Levy, Jerrold E. and Stephen Kunitz
1971. Indian Reservations, Anomie and Social Pathologies. *Southwestern Journal of Anthropology* 27:97.

Levy-Bruhl, L
1923. *Primitive Mentality*. London: Allen & Unwin.

Lewis, Oscar
1951. *Life in a Mexican Village: Tepoztlan Restudied*. Urbana, Illinois: University of Illinois Press.

1961. *The Children of Sanchez*. New York: Vintage Books.

1965. *La Vida*. New York: Random House.

1969. *A Death in the Sanchez Family*. New York: Random House.

Liebow, Elliot
1969. *Tally's Corner*. Boston: Little, Brown and Company.

Linton, Ralph
1936. The Study of Man. New York: Appleton-Century-Crofts.

Lloyd, Barbara B.
1971. The Intellectual Development of Yoruba Children: A Re-Examination. *Journal of Cross-Cultural Psychology*. 2:29.

Lombardi, Thomas P.
1969, "Psycholinguistic Abilities of Papago Indian Children." Ed.D. dissertation, University of Arizona.

Longabaugh, Richard
1973. Mother Behavior as a Variable Moderating the Effects of Father Absence. *Ethos* 1:456.

Lopate, Carol
n.d. Structure, Hierarchy and Political Learning. Mimeographed. New York: Applied Anthropology Program, Teachers College, Columbia University.

Lugo, James O.
1970. "A Comparison of Degrees of Bilingualism and Measure of School Achievement Among Mexican-American Pupils. Ph.D. dissertation, University of Southern California.

MacArthur, R. S.
1967. Sex Differences in Field Dependency for the Eskimo. *International Journal of Psychology* 2:139-140.
Madsen, Millard C. and Spencer Kagan
1973. Mother-Directed Achievement of Children in Two Cultures. *Journal of Cross-Cultural Psychology* 4:221.
Malinowski, Bronislaw
1948. *Magic, Science and Religion.* New York: Doubleday.
Masland, R. L., S. B. Sarason and T. Gladwin
1958. *Mental Subnormality: Biological, Psychological and Cultural Factors.* New York: Basic Books.
Mayer, Philip
1963. *Townsmen or Tribesmen.* Cape Town: Oxford University Press.
1970. *Socialization: The Approach from Social Anthropology.* London: Tavistock Publication.
McManus, Marianne
1970. Behavior on Nonoutcome Problems of United States and Caribbean Island Preschool Children. *Proceedings of the Annual Convention of the American Psychological Association* 5:69-70.
Menyunk, Paula
1969. *Sentences Children Use.* Research Monograph 52, Cambridge: MIT Press.
Miller, George A.
1971. Foreword. In *The Cultural Context of Learning and Thinking.* Michael Cole, John Gay, Joseph A. Glick, and Donald W. Sharp. New York: Basic Books, Inc.
Miller, Walter
1958. Lower Class Culture as a Generating Milieu of Gang Delinquency. In *The Sociology of Crime and Delinquency.* M. E. Wolfgang, L. Savitz and N. Johnson, Eds. New York: Wiley.
Minturn, Leigh and William W. Lambert
1964. *Mothers of Six Cultures: Antecedents of Child Rearing.* New York: J. Wiley.
Mitchell, J. C.
1969. *Social Networks in Urban Situations.* Manchester: Manchester University Press.
Monberg, Torben
1970. Determinants of Choice in Adoption and Fosterage on Bellon Island. *Ethnology* 2:99.
Moon, Shiela
1970. *A Magic Dwells: A Poetic and Psychological Study of the Navaho Emergence Myth.* Middletown, Conn: Wesleyan University Press.

Morgan, M.
1959. A Study in Perceptual Differences Among Cultural Groups in South Africa Using Tests of Geometric Illusions. *Journal of the National Institute of Personnel Research* 9:39-43.

Moscovici, S., E. Lage and M. Naffrechoux
1969. Influence of a Consistent Minority on the Responses of a Majority in a Color Perception Task. *Sociometry* 32:365-380.

Muensterberger, Warren, Ed.
1969. *Man and His Culture: Psychoanalytic Anthropology after "Totem and Taboo."* New York: Taplinger.

Mundy-Castle, A. C.
1966. Pictorial Depth Perception in Ghanaian Children. *International Journal of Psychology* 1:290-300.

Mundy-Castle, A. C. and G. K. Nelson
1962. A Neuropsychological Study of the Knysna Forest Workers, *Psychologia Africana* 9:240-272.

Munroe, Ruth H. and Robert L. Munroe
n.d. Household Density and Infant Care in an East African Society. *Journal of Social Psychology.*
1973. Psychological Interpretation of Male Initiation Rites: The Case of Male Pregnancy Symptoms. *Ethos* 1:490.

Munroe, Robert L., Ruth H. Munroe and Margaret T. Carson
1973. The Couvade: A Psychological Analysis. *Ethos* 1:30.

Munroe, Robert L., Ruth H. Munroe and Robert E. Daniels
1969. Effects of Status and Values on Estimation of Coin Size in Two East African Societies. *Journal of Social Psychology* 77.

Munroe, Robert L., Ruth Munroe and John W.M. Whiting
1965. Structure and Sentiment: Evidence from Recent Studies of the Couvade. Paper read at the American Anthropological Association Meeting, Denver, Colorado.

Munroe, Robert L., John W.M. Whiting and David J. Hally
1969. Institutionalized Male Transvestism and Sex Distinctions. *American Anthropologist* 71:87-91.

Murdock, George P.
1951. Cultural Determination of Paternal Attitudes: The Relationship Between the Social Structure, Particularly Family Structure, and Parental Behavior. In *Problems of Infancy and Childhood.* Milton J.E. Sean, Ed. New York: Josiah Macy, Jr. Foundation.
1957. World Ethnographic Sample. *American Anthropologist* 59:664-687.

Nadel, S.F.
1951. *Foundations of Social Anthropology.* Glencoe: Free Press.

Nedler, Shari and Peggy Seber
1971. Intervention Strategies for Spanish Speaking Preschool Children. *Child Development* 42:259-267.

Nurcombe, B.
1970a. Deprivation: An Essay in Deprivation with Special Reference to Australian Aborigines. *Medical Journal of Australia.* 2:87-92.
1970b. Precausal and Paracausal Thinking. Concepts of Causality in Aboriginal Children. *Australia and New Zealand Journal of Psychiatry* 4:70-81.

Ogbu, John
1974. *The Next Generation.* New York: Academic Press.

Opler, M.
1959. Review of Carstairs' Twice Born. *American Anthropologist* 61:140-142.
1960. The Hijara (Hermaphrodites) of India and Indian National Character: A Rejoinder. *American Anthropologist* 2(3):505-511.

Otaala, B.
1971. "The Development of Operational Thinking in Primary School Children: An Examination of Some Aspects of Piaget's Theory among the Iteso Children of Uganda." Ph.D. thesis, Teachers College, Columbia University.

Padelford, William B.
1969. "The Influence of Socioeconomic Level, Sex, and Ethnic Background upon the Relationship between Reading Achievement and Self-Concept." Ed.D. dissertation, University of California, Los Angeles.

Peluffo, N.
1967. Culture and Cognitive Problems. *International Journal of Psychology* 2:187-198.

Philips, Susan U.
1970. Acquisition of Rules for Appropriate Speech Usage. In *Bilingualism and Language Contact.* James E. Alatis, Ed. Proceedings of the Georgetown University Round Table on Language and Linguistics 1970. Washington, D.C.: Georgetown University Press.

Piaget, Jean and A. Morf
1956. Recherches sur le Developpement des Perceptions XXX, Les Comparaisons Verticales a Faible Intervalle. *Archives de Psychologie* 35:289-319.

Piker, Steven
1973. Comments on the Integration of Thai Religion. *Ethos* 3:298.

Poirer, Frank
1973. Socialization and Learning Among Nonhuman Primates. In

Learning and Culture. Proceedings of the 1972 Annual Spring Meeting of the American Ethnological Society. Solon T. Kimball and Jacquetta H. Burnett, Eds. Seattle: University of Washington Press.

Poole, H.E.
1968. The Effect of Urbanization upon Scientific Concept Attainment among Hausa children of Northern Nigeria. *British Journal of Educational Psychology* 38:57-63.

Price-William, D.R.
1961. A Study Concerning Concepts of Conservation of Quantities Among Primitive Children. *Acta Psychologica* 18:297-305.

Prince, J.R.
1969. *Science Concepts in a Pacific Culture.* Sydney: Angus & Robertson.

Protho, E. Terry
1960. Patterns of Permissiveness among Preliterate People. *Abnormal and Social Psychology* 61:151-154.

Provins, K. A., C. R. Bell, S. Biesheuvel and W. T. Adiseshiah
1968. The Crosscultural measurement of Perceptual and Motor Skills in Relation to Human Adaptation. *Human Biology* 40:483-493.

Ramirez, Manuel and Alfredo Castaneda
1974. *Cultural Democracy, Bicognitive Development, and Education.* New York; Academic Press.

Rautman, A. L. and Edna Brower
1951. War Themes in Children's Stories: Six Years Later. *Journal of Psychology* 31:263-270.

Read, M.
1949. *Children of Their Fathers.* London: Methuen.

Resnick, H. L. and Larry H. Dizmang
1971. Observations on Suicidal Behavior Among American Indians. *American Journal of Psychiatry* 126:882-887.

Reuning, H.
1959. Psychologische Versuche mit Buschleuten der Kalhari. *Die Umshau in Wissenschaft und Technik* 17:520-523.

Rivers, W. H. R.
1901. Introduction and Vision. In *Physiology and Psychology, Part I. Report of the Cambridge Anthropological Expedition to the Torres Straits.* Cambridge: Cambridge University Press.
1905. Observations on the Senses of the Todas. *British Journal of Psychology* 1:321-396.

Robbins, Michael C., Billie R. DeWalt and Perti J. Pelto
1972. Climate and Behavior: A Biocultural Study. *Journal of Cross-Cultural Psychology* 3:331.

Robbins, Michael C. and Philip L. Kilbride
1971. Sex Differences in Dreams in Uganda. *Journal of Cross-Cultural Psychology* 2:406.
Robbins, Richard H.
1970. "Drinking Behavior and Identity Struggle:" Ph. D. dissertation, University of North Carolina at Chapel Hill.
1973. Alcohol and the Identity Struggle: Some Effects of Economic Change on Interpersonal Relations. *American Anthropologist* 75:99.
Roberts, John M. and Brian Sutton-Smith
1962. Child Training and Game Involvement. *Ethnology* 1:166-185.
1966. Cross-Cultural Correlates of Games of Chance. *Behavior Science Notes* 3:131-144.
Roberts, John M., H. Hoffman and Brian Sutton-Smith
1965. Pattern and Competence: A Consideration of Tick Tack Toe. *El Palacio* 62:17-30.
Rohner, Robert P.
1970. Parental Rejection, Food Deprivation and Personality Development: Tests of Alternative Hypotheses. *Ethnology* 9:414.
Rosenblatt, Paul
1966. A Cross-Cultural Study of Child Rearing and Romantic Love. *Journal of Personality and Social Psychology* 4:338-343.
Rosenthal, Robert and L. Jacobson
1968. *Pygmalion in the Classroom.* New York: Holt, Rinehart & Winston.
Rubovits, P. C. and M. L. Maehr
1973. Pygmalion, Black and White. *Journal of Personality and Social Psychology* 25:210-218.
Salzman, Znedek
1970. *Contribution to the Study of Value Orientations among the Czecks and Slovaks.* Massachusetts, Department of Anthropology Research Reports, 4, University of Massachusetts at Amherst.
Savard, Robert J.
1968. "Cultural Stress and Alcoholism: A Study of their Relationship among Navaho Alcoholic Men." Ph.D. dissertation, University of Minnesota.
Savishinsky, Joel S.
1971. Mobility as an Aspect of Stress in an Arctic Community. *American Anthropologist* 73:604.
Schlegel, Alice
1963. The Adolescent Socialization of the Hopi Girl. *Ethnology* 12:449.
Schneider, David
1965. Some Muddles in the Models. In *The Relevance of Models for Social Anthropology.* A.S.A. Monographs I. London: Tavistock Publications.

Schwartz, Audrey J.
1971. A Comparative Study of Values and Achievement: Mexican-American and Anglo Youth. *Sociology of Education* 44(4):438-462.

Schwartz, Gary and Don Merten
1968. Social Identity and Expressive Symbols: The Meaning of an Initiation Ritual. *American Anthropologist* 70:1117-1131.

Schwartz, Theodore
1973. Cult and Context: The Paranoid Ethos in Melanesia. *Ethos* 2:153.

Sears, R. R.
1961. Transcultural Variables and Conceptual Equivalence. In *Studying Personality Cross-Culturally*. B. Kaplan, Ed. Evanston, Illinois and New York: Row, Peterson, pp. 445-455.

Segall, Marshall H., Donald T. Campbell and Melville J. Herskovits
1966. *The Influence of Culture on Visual Perception*. Indianapolis: Bobbs-Merrill.

Sharp, Lauriston
1969. *The Dream Life of a Primitive People: The Dreams of the Yir Yoront of Australia*. Anthropological Studies 1. Washington: American Anthropological Association.

Shirley, R. W. and A. K. Romney
1962. Love Magic and Socialization Anxiety. *American Anthropologist* 64:1028-1031.

Sigel, Roberta
1970. *Learning about Politics*. New York: Random House.

Sipes, Richard G.
1973. War, Sports and Aggression: An Empirical Test of Two Rival Theories. *American Anthropologist* 75:64.

Spiro, Melford and Roy G. D'Andrade
1958. A Cross-Cultural Study of Some Supernatural Beliefs. *American Anthropologist* 60:456-466.

Spradley, James
1969. *Guests Never Leave Hungry*. New Haven: Yale University Press.

St. George, Ross
1970. The Psycholinguistic Abilities of Children from Different Ethnic Backgrounds. *Australian Journal of Psychology* 22:85-89.

Stephens, William N.
1961. A Cross-Cultural Study of Menstrual Taboos. *Genetic Psychology Monographs* 64:385-416.

Strodtbeck, F.
1964. Considerations of Meta method in Cross-Cultural Studies. *American Anthropologist* 66:223-229.

Sutton-Smith, Brian and J. M. Roberts
1963. Game Involvement in Adults. *Journal of Social Psychology* 60:15-30.
1964. Rubrics of Competitive Behavior. *Journal of Genetic Psychology* 105:13-37.
1967. Studies in an Elementary Game Strategy. *Genetic Psychology Monographs* 75:3-42.
Sutton-Smith, Brian and B. A. Rosenberg
1968. Father-Absence Effects on Families of Different Sibling Composition. *Child Development* 39:1213-1222.
Sweet, Louise E.
1969. Child's Play for the Ethnographer. *Behavior Science Notes* 4:237.
Trible, Joseph E.
1969. "Psychosocial Characteristics of Employed and unemployed Western Oklahoma Male American Indians." Ph.D. dissertation, University of Oklahoma.
Turner, Victor
1969. *The Ritual Process*. Chicago: Aldine.
United States Commissions on Civil Rights
1971. Report II: *The Unfinished Education*.
1972. Report III: *The Excluded Student*.
Valentine, Charles
1968. *Culture and Poverty: Critique and Counter proposals*. Chicago: University of Chicago Press.
1972. Black Studies and Anthropology: Scholarly and Political Interests in Afro-American Culture. *McCaleb Module 55*, pp. 1-53.
van den Berghe, Pierre L.
1973. Pluralism. *In Handbook of Social and Cultural Anthropology*. John Honigmann, Ed. Chicago: Rand McNally, pp. 959-977.
Van Velsen, J.
1967. The Extended-Case Method and Situational Analysis: In *The Craft of Anthropology*. A.L. Epstein, Ed. London: Tavistock Publications.
Vernon, P.E.
1965. Environmental Handicaps and Intellectual Developments: Parts I and II. *British Journal of Educational Psychology* 35:9-20, 117-126.
1967. Abilities and Educational Attainments in an East African Environment. *Journal of Special Education* 1:335-345.
1969. *Intelligence and Cultural Environment*. London: Methuen.
Vincent, Joan
1974. The Structure of Ethnicity. *Human Organization* 33:375-379.

Walker, Malcolm T.
1973. *Politics and the Power Structure: A Rural Community in the Dominican Republic.* New York:Teachers College Press.
Wallace, Anthony F.C.
1961a. *Culture and Personality.* New York: Random House.
1961b. Schools in Revolutionary and Conservative Societies. In *Anthropology and Education.* F. Gruber, Ed. Philadelphia: University of Pennsylvania Press.
Walters, Sister Annette
1942. A Genetic Study of Geometrical-Optical Illusions. *Genetic Psychology Monographs* 25:101-155.
Washburn, S.
1963. The Study of Race. *American Anthropologist* 65:521-531.
Watson, Graham
1970. *Passing for White.* London: Travistock Publications.
Watson, Lawrence C.
1973. Marriage and Sexual Adjustment in Guajiro Society. *Ethnology* 12:153.
Wax, Murray
1963. American Indian Education as a Cultural Transaction. *Teachers College Record* 64:693-704.
1973. Cultural Pluralism, Political Power, and Ethnic Studies. In *Learning and Culture, Proceedings of the 1972 Annual Spring Meeting of the American Ethnological Society.* Solon T. Kimball, and Jacquetta H. Burnett, Eds. Seattle: University of Washington Press.
Wax, Rosalie H.
1967. The Warrior Dropouts. *Transaction* 4(6):40-46.
Wechsler, D.
1944. *Measurement of Adult Intelligence.* Baltimore: Williams and Wilkins.
Weisner, Thomas A.
1973. The Primary Sampling Unit: A Nongeographically Based Rural-Urban Example. *Ethos* 1:546.
Werner, Emmy E.
1972. Infants Around the World: Cross-Cultural Studies of Psychomotor Development from Birth to Two Years. *Journal of Cross-Cultural Psychology* 3:111.
Werner, Heinz and S. Wapner
1955. The Innsbruck Studies on Distorted Visual Fields in Relations to an Organismic Theory of Perception. *Psychology Review* 62:130-138.
Whiting, Beatrice
1950. *Paiute Sorcery.* New York: Viking Fund Publication in Anthropology No.15.

1965. Sex Identity Conflict and Physical Violence: A Comparative Study. *American Anthropologist* 67:123-140.

Whiting, Beatrice, Ed.
1963. *Six Cultures: Studies of Child Rearing.* New York: Wiley.

Whiting, Beatrice and John Whiting
1975. *Children of Six Cultures.* Cambridge, Harvard University Press.

Whiting, John W.M.
1941. *Becoming a Kwoma.* New Haven: Yale University Press.
1959a. Sorcery, Sin and the Superego: A Cross-Cultural Study of Some Mechanisms of Social Control. In *Symposium on Motivation.* Lincoln: University of Nebraska Press, pp. 174-195.
1959b. Cultural and Sociological Influences on Development. In *Maryland Child Growth and Development Institute June 1-5,* pp. 5-9
1960. Resource Mediation and Learning by Identification. In *Personality Development in Children.* I. Iscoe and M. Stevenson, Eds. Austin: University of Texas Press.
1961. Socialization Process and Personality. In *Psychological Anthropology.* F.L.K. Hsu, Ed. Homewood, Illinois: The Dorsey Press.
1962. Comment. *American Journal of Sociology.* 67: 391-393.
1964. Effects of Climate on Certain Cultural Practices. In *Explorations in Cultural Anthropology.* Ward H. Goodenough, Ed. New York: McGraw Hill, pp. 511-544.

Whiting, John W.M., et al.
1966. The Learning of Values. In *People of Rimrock: A Study of Values in Five Cultures.* E.Z. Vogt and E.M. Albert, Eds. Cambridge: Harvard University Press.

Whiting, John W.M. and Irvin Child
1953. *Child Training and Personality.* New Haven: Yale University Press.

Whiting, John W.M., Richard Kluckhohn and Albert Anthony
1958. The Function of Male Initiation Ceremonies at Puberty. In *Readings in Social Psychology,* 3rd ed. Eleanor E. Maccoby, Theodore H. Newcomb and Eugene L. Hartley, Eds. New York: Holt, Rinehart & Winston, pp. 359-370

Whiting, John W.M. and T.K. Landauer
1968. Infantile Immunization and Adult Stature. *Child Development* 39:59-67.

Whiting, John W.M. and Beatrice B. Whiting
1960. Contributions of Anthropology to the Methods of Studying Child Rearing. In *Handbook of Research Methods in Child Development.* Paul H. Mussen, Ed. New York: John Wiley.

Witkin, H.A., R.B. Dyk, H.F. Faterson, D.R. Goodenough and S.A. Karp
1962. *Psychological Differentiation*. London: Wiley.
Wober, M.
1967. Adapting Witkin's Field Independence Theory to Accomodate New Information from Africa. *British Journal of Psychology* 58:29-38.
Wolcott, Harry F.
1969. *A Kwakiutl Village and School*. New York: Holt, Rinehart and Winston.
Wright, G.O.
1956. Projection and Displacement: A Cross-Cultural Study of Folk-Tale Aggression. *Journal of Abnormal and Social Psychology* 49:523-528.
Yinger, J. Milton
1960. Contraculture and Subculture. *American Sociological Review* 25:625-635.
Young, Francis A., et al.
1970. Refractive Errors. Reading Performance, and School Achievement among Eskimo Children. *American Journal of Optometry and Archives of American Academy of Optometry* 47:384-390.
Young, Frank
1962. The Function of Male Initiation Ceremonies: A Cross-Cultural Test of an Alternative Hypothesis. *American Journal of Sociology* 67:379-391.
1965. *Initiation Ceremonies: A Cross-Cultural Study of Dramatization*. New York: Bobbs-Merrill.
Young, Frank and A.A. Bacdayan
1965. Menstrual Taboos and Social Rigidity. *Ethnology* 4:225-240.
Young, Virginia H.
1970. Family and Childhood in a Southern Negro Community. *American Anthropologist* 72:269-288.

Annotations of Selected Additional Sources

PERCEPTION AND COGNITION

Al-Issa, Ihsan and Wayne Dennis, 1970, *Cross-Cultural Studies of Behavior.* New York: Holt, Rinehart & Winston.

Twenty-nine of the articles are reprinted from psychology or psychiatry journals, two from anthropology sources, and eight from other disciplines. The articles are divided into six chapters: "Cross-Cultural Studies of Perception," "Cross-Cultural Studies of Intellectual Functioning," "Cross-Cultural Studies of Personality," "Cultural Differences in Child Rearing and Child Behavior," "Psycholinguistics," and "Cross-Cultural Studies of Mental Health." The book "proposes to introduce the reader (whether he is a student of integrated social science, psychology, sociology, or of any related field in any country) to what can be achieved in human understanding when one steps outside of his own culture"(p. v.).

There are no chapter introductions, no bridges. While each reading has an introduction, it is usually particular to the article, and provides scant context for what we are to read.

The perception chapter is a mixed bag of the old and nearly new; the intellectual functioning chapter only takes a minimal view at its topic given the literature available; the personality chapter selections (Benedict, Klineberg, Sears, Triandis, and Pettigrew) seem even more limited; the child rearing chapter is itself half personality; the psycholinguistics chapter is very heavy on Osgood; and the mental health chapter moves diffidently from psychoses, depressions, and schizophrenia to crime and alcohol.

[Author or journal abstracts have been used verbatim where they are available and intelligible. They are marked AA and JA respectively. Annotations prepared by Elizabeth Sklar.]

Berry, John W., 1971, Muller-Lyer Susceptibility: Culture, Ecology or Race? *International Journal of Psychology*, 6(3):193-197.

The author briefly discusses the three lines of research which attribute the cause of the Muller-Lyer illusion respectively to a perceptual differentiation factor, an ecological factor ("carpentered world" or not), and to a retinal pigmentation factor. He examines each of these variables in 10 experiments of subjects which vary according to their ecological environment and their culture. The hypothesis of retinal pigmentation seems to be the most highly supported; the least highly supported is the ecological hypothesis, and the role of differential perception receives no support or confirmation from culture to culture. (JA, translated from French)

Bornstein, Marc H., 1973, Color Vision and Color Naming: A Psychophysiological Hypothesis of Cultural Difference. *Psychological Bulletin*, 80(4):257-285.

Proposes an hypothesis which relates physiological differences in visual processing to semantic categorization. A comparison of primary color-naming systems across cultures reveals a regular geographic patterning of color-naming confusions. These semantic data indicative of a short wavelength (blue) insensitive, so-called tritan, color vision have been corroborated by psychophysically measured depressions in spectral sensitivity and confusions in color matching. Yellow intraocular pigmentation which is biometeorologically adaptive and which attenuates effective short wavelength radiation is assessed to contribute in varying degrees toward mimicry of the tritan color-vision complex. Furthermore, the density of yellow intraocular pigmentation is found to parallel the worldwide distribution of collapsed color-naming systems. (JA)

Brockman, Lois M. and Henry N. Ricciuti, 1971, Severe Protein-Calories Malnutrition and Cognitive Development in Infancy and Early Childhood. *Developmental Psychology* 4(3):312-319.

Observed the effects of severe protein-calorie malnutrition during infancy on cognitive development. Twenty protein-calorie deficient 11.8-43.5 month old children and nineteen controls without a history of malnutrition were tested with ten different sorting tasks. Following twelve weeks of further nutritional treatment, the experimental *S*s were retested. Analysis of the total test scores indicate that malnourished *S*s performed significantly lower than controls, and the younger *S*s (less than 24 months) lower than the older (qreater than 24 months) *S*s. On retest, the malnourished *S*s showed no significant increase in test scores. Test scores of experimental *S*s were correlated negatively with all body measure percentages at admission, and positively with changes in body length and head circumference percentages between admission and first testing, length of time in nutritional treatment, and medical ratings of nutritional recovery. (JA)

Chandra, Subhas, 1972, An Assessment of Perceptual Acuity in Fiji: A Cross-Cultural Study with Indians and Fijians. *Journal of Cross-Cultural Psychology* 3:401.

110 Indian and 83 Fijian of ages 15 through 20 were administered Gough and McGurk's 30-item visual *Perceptual Acuity Test* (PAT). In accord with prior findings in French, Italian, Swiss, and American applications, scores correlated significantly with age (r = .26); in addition, mean weighted scores increased for each older subsample by age. Insignificant differences in performances were observed between Fijian and Indian Ss, and between two small subsamples of delinquents and nondelinquents matched for age. Sex was related to performance, with men attaining higher scores. PAT performance was essentially unrelated to school achievement, and to ability as measured by Raven's Matrices. It may be concluded that the PAT is a promising device for cross-cultural study of age gradients in the development of perceptual acuity. (JA)

Chapra, Sukhendra Lal, 1968, Measured Intelligence and Academic Achievement as Related to Urban-Rural Residence. *Rural Sociology,* 33(2):214-217.

The purpose of this study was to compare intelligence test scores and academic achievement of students from urban and rural areas when matched on socioeconomic home background.

Differences in the mean intelligence test scores and the mean high school marks for urban and rural students, when matched for home background, did not reach even the .05 level of significance. The conclusion is that the apparent superiority of urban students in other studies is probably due to economic disparities and differences in the home background rather than simple residence in urban areas. With the gradual improvements in the rural areas (e.g., in India) the urban-rural differences may gradually decline.

Cole, Michael and Sylvia Scribner, 1974, *Culture and Thought: A Psychological Introduction.* New York: John Wiley.

This textbook reviews the major fields of research relating culture and cognition, discussing the history of speculation concerning culture-thought relations in perception, language, memory, classification, and problem solving. The book is appealingly presented and up to date but emphasizes the psychological literature more than the anthropological.

Cole, Michael, John Gay and Joseph Glick, 1968, A Cross-Cultural Investigation of Information Processing. *International Journal of Psychology* 3:93-102.

One hundred and twenty American *S*s (Yale students, seven to nine and ten to twelve year olds) were compared with 120 illiterate adults, school children, and illiterate children of the Kpelle tribe of Liberia on number recognition of random and patterned dots. Although American subjects were significantly more accurate than Kpelle *S*s, the results can be variously interpreted, e.g., in terms of differences of informational requirements of the two cultures. Study of relationships of performance with a culture may aid in eventual treatment of differences between cultures. However trivial, alternatives are not likely to account for these patterns of results. (AA)

Dasen, Pierre R., 1972, The Development of Conservation in Aboriginal Children: A Replication Study. *International Journal of Psychology* 7(2):75-85.

Ninety full-blooded and part aboriginal *S*s of similar background, 10 of each age from 6-12 years and 5 each from 13-16 years, performed conservation tasks. Results on qualitative aspects of operative development confirm that European and aboriginal children do not differ in qualitative aspects although developmental rhythm tends to be slower for aboriginal *S*s. Replication results show no quantity-weight reversals or genetic differences in acquiring concrete operations (revealed through chi-square values) for full and part aboriginal *S*s.

David, Kenneth H., 1967, Effect of Verbal Reinforcement on Porteus Maze Scores among Australian Aborigine Children. *Perceptual and Motor Skills* 24:986.

Purpose: To determine whether verbal reinforcement would increase Maze Test scores among a group of Australian aborigines. *Method:* Maze test scores administered to 46 Australian aborigine grade school children (seventeen males, twenty-nine females) aged eight to fifteen years. One half of *S*s were given immediate positive reinforcement by E each time they correctly traced a maze. The others received no reinforcement. A 2 x 2 analysis of variance (males versus females and reinforced versus non-reinforced) for unequal cell frequencies was performed on the test quotients. *Results:* There were no significant differences for the A, B, or A x B effects (p less than .05), indicating that reinforcement did not affect test performance. The mean Test Quotient for all *S*s was 109.13. These results suggest that *S*s were performing at an optimal level under both reinforced and non-reinforced treatments.

DeLacey, P. R., 1970, A Cross-Cultural Study of Classificatory Ability in Australia. *Journal of Cross-Cultural Psychology* 1:293-304.

Classificatory tests based on those of Piaget and Inhelder were administered to four groups of 6-10 year old *S*s: aborigines with and without extensive contact with European children living in Australia. Only a small subsample of high-contact aborigines performed on a par with the European children, leading to the interpretation that environmental differences were the major influence in the performance differences found. (JA)

Deregowski, Jan B., 1968, On Perception of Depicted Orientation. *International Journal of Psychology* 3(3):149-156.

The two experiences described here indicate that, as far as pictorial perception is concerned, individuals in certain cultures, aside from those whose depth perception is relatively assessed, encounter difficulties in correct orientation perception. The extent of errors correlated with the interpretation of orientation in designs and drawings seems to depend upon the perspective in which the combination of the stimuli is represented, the position of the objects in relation to the appearance and meaning implicit in the total representation. (JA, translated from French)

Deregowski, Jan B., 1969, A Pictorial Perception Paradox. *Acta Psychologica* 31(4):365-374.

Hypothesized that *S*s who prefer chain type drawings to conventional drawings will find the latter form of drawings easier to interpret correctly when trying to identify depicted objects. As *S*s, 107 men and 97 women from rural areas of Zambia served in simple choice situations using geometric and meaningful stimuli. The data obtained with the former support the hypothesis, while those obtained with the meaningful stimuli fail to do so. (JA)

Edwards, Carolyn P., 1975, Societal Complexity and Moral Development: A Kenyan Study. *Ethos* 3(4).

Purpose: To suggest that one of the reasons that "higher stages of moral judgment are not culturally universal" has to do with the level of complexity of the society in question, the greater the complexity, the "higher" the capacity for moral judgment. To propose that "peoples' differing frames of reference are related to differing moral concepts." *Method:* Interview data (moral judgment scores) on sub-

jects from both modernized and more traditional "contexts" in
Kenya: students at University of Nairobi and students from seven
communities located in different parts of Kenya (central and western
provinces) all of whom were considered to be "moral leaders" of their
communities. (Kohlberg's moral judgment stages). *Results:* (1)
Neither sex nor ethnic group are signiicant variables in level of moral
judgment. (2) Nor is age. (3) Nor is lack of "moral concern." The
critical variables in *S*s' responses proved to be that University students
were oriented more toward "professional jobs" in modern sectors of
Kenyan economy than were community leaders. (4) Education and
occupation related positively to moral judgment scores. *Conclusion:*
Different modes of moral decision-making are appropriate for tribal
versus national frames of reference. New mechanisms of social control
are developed in transition from tribal to civilized society; hence new
modes of moral judging may evolve as a result of the same social
forces. Modes of moral judgment are adaptive structures developed by
people to accomplish important cognitive tasks at hand.

Evans, Judith L. and Marshall H. Segall, 1969, Learning to
Classify by Color and by Function: A Study of Concept-Discovery by
Ganda Children. *Journal of Social Psychology* 77(1):35-53.

Three concept-discovery experiments were performed in Uganda
with Ganda children, both schooled and unschooled, and with adults.
All *S*s had to learn to sort pictures on the basis of the color and function
of the objects pictured. Color sorting was learned more easily by all *S*s
except children in their fifth year of primary school. Age, school, and
grade differences were interpreted as demonstrating the importance of
formal schooling for the development of habits of superordinate concept formation.

Fitzgerald, L., 1969, The Use of Psychological Testing in Rehabilitation Planning for Alaskan Native People. *Australian Psychologist*
4:146-152.

Of Native Alaskans, 70 were individually administered either the
WAIS (N = 42) or the Revised Beta Test (N = 28) to determine
rehabilitation guidance possibilities. Results indicate that while scores
on subtests of the Revised Beta test did not differ significantly, poorest
scores were in the area of visualization of similarities and dissimi-
larities and in the ability to envision a whole from the parts on a two-
dimensional plane. The WAIS Performance IQ scores were
significantly higher than Verbal IQ scores, with highest scores in the
Object Assembly subtest and lowest scores in the Arithmetic subtest.
Results support the "impression that the Alaska Native has a greater
facility in the handling of concrete problems." It is concluded that
while an IQ test alone cannot measure the abilities of native Alaskans,

a good test can be useful in evaluating rehabilitation potential by providing a distribution of abilities and an indication of the degree to which such abilities differ from a normative population. (JA)

Foster, George M., 1973, Dreams, Character, and Cognitive Orientation in Tzintzuntzan. *Ethos* 1:106.

The thesis advanced in this paper is that dreams in Tzintzuntzan, Michoacan, Mexico, when analyzed for manifest content, reflect remarkably accurately large areas of basic character and collective cognitive orientations of the villagers.

Gorsuch, Richard L. and M. Louise Barnes, 1973, Stages of Ethical Reasoning and Moral Norms of Carib Youths. *Journal of Cross-Cultural Psychology* 4:283.

Ethical development was investigated in a cross-cultural context by examining both the cognitive structure of ethical reasoning and the content of perceived moral norms in Carib boys. No evidence was found for the position that the stages might be a function of cultural norms. Other results were also as expected by stages theory: villagers were at a lower stage than the older youths. However, only the first two cognitive stages were found and the cultural invariance of the perceived moral norms was as great as that of the stages. (AA)

Harkness, Sara, 1973, Universal Aspects of Learning Color Codes: A Study in Two Cultures. *Ethos* 2:175.

The research described in this article addresses itself to questions such as: if color lexicons do evolve in a stable order, then might there be some cognitive logic behind it? For instance, do children learn colors in "evolutionary order?" Are there differences in adults' knowledge of color terms in their own language? How do various colors function cognitively for both children and adults? And, finally, why do some cultures have more basic color terms than others?

Heider, Eleanor, 1972, Universals in Color Naming and Memory. *Journal of Experimental Psychology,* 93(1):10-20.

Investigated the hypothesis that there are salient areas of color space ("focal colors") which are universally the most linguistically "codable" and the most easily remembered. Exp. I used twenty English-speaking female undergraduates and ten foreign students to complete previous location of these focal colors on the dimensions of hue, value, and saturation. In Exp. II, twenty-three speakers of different languages named a sample of focal and nonfocal colors. In Exp. III, twenty English speakers and twenty-one New Guinea Dani, speakers of a language which lacks hue names, remembered and recognized focal and nonfocal colors. In Exp. IV, Dani learned names for focal and nonfocal colors in a paired-associates task. Results show that focal colors (a) were given the shortest names and named most rapidly across languages, (b) were the most accurately recognized by both English and Dani speakers, and (c) could be paired with names with fewest errors. On the basis of these findings, linguistically caused interpretations of earlier language-cognition studies using color are challenged.

Heron, Alastair, 1971, Concrete Operations, "g," and Achievement in Zambian Children, *Journal of Cross-Cultural Psychology* 2:325.

A comparison is made between Zambian elementary school children in the range of "stated ages" 7–17 years who provided evidence of weight conservation behavior and those who did not do so. The principal dependent variable is performance on locally-developed psychometric measures of reasoning ability, and further data were available in the form of scores on an objectively-marked national Secondary School Selection examination. Very little connection is found between the conservation-status of the subjects and their performance on these variables, and the implications for a possible rapprochement between psychometric and Piagetian approaches to human intelligence are discussed in the light of cultural factors. An experimental approach to the problem is recommended. (AA)

Irvine, Sydney H., 1969, Figural Tests of Reasoning in Africa: Studies in the Use of Raven's Progressive Matrices Across Cultures. *International Journal of Psychology* 4:217-228.

Experiments involving *S*s from various educational groups in Africa and Great Britian, using Raven's Progressive Matrices, compared item difficulty and describe strategies employed. Factorial analysis shows that environmental variables, whether verbally loaded or not, are not associated for central African *S*s. Cross-cultural analysis reveals that item difficulties change from culture to culture, and that test scores approach Western patterns as the groups adopt Western value systems. Appearance of differing individual strategies in problem solving renders it unwise to assume that the same total score provides evidence of identical samples of psychological behavior. Research with African *S*s shows "that sources of variance exist that call for some revision of. . . assumptions about the reduction of cultural bias in figural test items." (JA)

Irwin, Marc, Patricia L. Engle, Robert E. Klein and Charles Yarborough, 1976, Traditionalism and Field Dependence: A Failure to Replicate. *Journal of Cross-Cultural Psychology* 7(4):463-472.

The relationship between preschool children's field dependence-independence and mother's traditionalism and intellectual stimulation provided in the home was investigated in rural Guatemala. Contrary to several previous studies—which have not measured traditionalism at the level of the family, but rather compared children from more and less traditional communities—EFT scores were found to be unrelated to traditionalism. EFT scores were related to both material sources of stimulation as well as to the presence of better educated older siblings in the home. It was argued that in previous studies traditionalism has been confounded with other variables such as the availability of intellectual stimulation. (JA)

Kilbride, Janet E., Michael C. Robbins and Philip L. Kilbride, 1970, The Comparative Motor Development of Baganda, American White, and American Black Infants. *American Anthropologist* 72:1422-1428.

Examined the developmental motor quotients (DMQs) of 71 male and 92 female 1-24 month old rural Baganda infants. *S*s were found to be significantly more advanced in motor development in the 1st year of life when compared to samples of white and black American children. As age increased, DMQ decreased, but at the age of 24 months, *S*s still obtained an average DMQ higher than either American sample.

Kilbride, Philip and Michael Robbins, 1968, Linear Perspective, Pictorial Depth Perception and Education among the Baganda. *Perceptual and Motor Skills* 27:601-602.

A positive and significant relationship between the amount of formal education and the use of linear perspective due to pictorial depth perception was found among 523 subjects living in Uganda. (JA)

Kuczynska-Stoffels, M. J., 1970, Figurative Responses of Congolese to the Lowenfeld Mosaic Test. *Revue de Psychologie Appliqué* 20:41-57.

Reports results of administering the Lowenfeld Mosaic Test to 662 Congolese 7-30 year old *S*s (313 were between the ages of 9-10 inclusive). The proportion of figurative responses was low. Specific figures of 10-year old Congolese are found among 5-year-old Europeans. The theme most common both in Europe and in the Congo is that of a "home." Distinctive themes preferred by Europeans—trees, plants, flowers, animals and human beings—do not seem to inspire Congolese. (JA)

Kundu, Chuni L., 1970, Comparison of Intelligence Test Scores of Bhil and High Caste Hindu Delinquents and Nondelinquents. *Journal of Social Psychology* 81:265-266.

A cross-cultural study was conducted to determine whether there are significant differences in intelligence test scores between delinquents and nondelinquents belonging to two strikingly different cultural groups—one from the high caste Hindu communities, and the other from jungle-dwelling illiterate Bhil tribesmen. Significant differences were found at .01 levels on Batia's Battery of Performance Tests of Intelligence. (AA)

Kugelmass, Sol, Amia Lieblich and Chedvah Ehrlich, 1972, Perceptual Exploration in Israeli Jewish and Bedouin Children. *Journal of Cross-Cultural Psychology* 3:345.

A sample of 104 Israeli Bedouin children were tested in an attempt to clarify further the factors influencing developmental trends in visual perception exploration. In addition to a further demonstration of the influence of the specific characteristics of the language of school instruction, the findings suggest the importance of extra-school reading opportunities. A discrepancy between two indices of perceptual exploration was related to different aspects of reading development. While the Bedouin children's perceptual exploration might be considered less mature in some ways related to reading, this was not the case with other aspects of perceptual exploration. (JA)

Lave, Jean, 1977, Cognitive Consequences of Traditional Apprenticeship Training in West Africa. *Anthropology and Education Quarterly.* VIII, 3:177.

By combining intensive ethnographic work with formal experiments it is possible to demonstrate that a traditional form of education—apprenticeship training—does teach general problem-solving skills. An arithmetic test, anchored with problems drawn directly from tribal tailors, apprenticeship training, was administered to a sample of Vai and Gola tailors in Liberia. The tailors differ on tailoring experience and formal schooling characteristics. Both tailoring experience and schooling contribute strongly to arithmetic problem-solving success on unfamiliar problems. (AA)

LeVine, R. A., 1970, Cross-Cultural Study in Child Psychology. In *Carmichael's Manual of Child Psychology,* Vol. 2. 3rd. edition P. H. Mussen, Ed. New York: Wiley. pp. 559-612.

An important critical survey of methods used in cross cultural studies in psychology.

Lloyd, Barbara B. and Rian Easton, 1977, The Intellectual Development of Yoruba Children: Additional Evidence and a Serendipitous Finding. *Journal of Cross-Cultural Psychology* 8(1):3-16.

In re-examining Yoruba children from educated (ELITE) and traditional (DJE) families after five years, we find that those growing up in a privileged environment showed increasingly superior mental age scores. A partial replication of the original study from Yoruba children of three and one-half to seven years confirmed the original findings of highly significant age and background effects. Analysis of the nine age groups in the second stage also yielded a significant age and family background interaction. The predictive power of the 1968 scores, transformed as intelligence quotients, was examined in a regression analysis. An unexpected result was the failure of the 1968 scores for boys to predict performance in 1973. The regression coefficients for both ELITE and DJE girls were significantly greater than zero. Although these findings might suggest biological determinants, these are difficult to specify—as are any aspects of socialization which would be similar in both ELITE and DJE families but which would differentiate the treatment of boys and girls. (JA)

McGurk, Harry and Gustav Jahoda, 1975, Pictorial Depth Perception by Children in Scotland and Ghana. *Journal of Cross-Cultural Psychology* 6(3):279-296.

An experimental study of the development of pictorial depth perception, conducted in Scotland and Ghana, is reported. Subjects constructed three-dimensional models representing the size and spatial relationships between figures in pictorial scenes in which three depth cues—elevation texture, gradient, and linear perspective—were manipulated. For both samples size accuracy increased with the amount of depth information available; it also increased with age in the Scottish but not in the Ghanaian sample. Spatial accuracy increased with age in both samples, but was influenced by type of depth cue only in the Scottish sample. Scottish children were more accurate throughout than Ghanaian children. However, the evidence reported does not support the view that African children are grossly deficient in perceiving pictorial depth. (JA)

MacArthur, Russell S., 1969, Some Cognitive Abilities of Eskimo, White and Indian-Metis Pupils Aged Nine to Twelve years. *Canadian Journal of Behavior Science* 1:50-59.

Factor analysis of ability tests for Eskimo, White and Indian-Metis pupils 9-12 years of age, indicated for each sample two highly correlated oblique factors. When native *S*s were scored on white T-score norms, least ethnic differences and least decline with age relative to white *S*s occured in reasoning from non-verbal stimuli. Written memory was an outstanding exception. There were almost no sex differences in the sample.

Mallory, Sadie A., 1970, Effect of Stimulus Presentation on Free Recall of Reflective and Impulsive Mexican-American Children. *Journal of Psychology* 76:193-198.

Identified 19 reflective and 19 impulsive second grade Mexican-Americans by the Matching Familiar Figures Test. One-half of each group was presented auditorily or audiotactually a twelve-word noun list. Free recall was significantly better for clustering and total words for audiotactual reception. Reflectivity and impulsivity did not influence free recall responses. (AA)

Martin, William A., 1969, Word Fluency: A Comparative Study. *Journal of Genetic Psychology* 114:253-262.

A slightly adapted version of Thurston's word fluency test was administered to several groups of Maori and European high school children (n = 143). It was found that the Maori had a significantly higher word fluency than their European counterparts; that the female pupils had, on the average, higher word fluency scores than males, and that the racial differences revealed that this held true within sex, as well as urban and rural categories. This Maori superiority could not be explained in terms of intelligence, sample selection bias, or verbal ability, nor could it be attributed to their greater age alone. Some evidence was found which suggested that this word fluency superiority derived from a definite intellectual ability.

Meade, Robert D. and James O. Whitaker, 1967. A Cross-cultural Study of Authoritarianism. *Journal of Social Psychology, 72:3-7.*

Purpose: To investigate the personality dimension of authoritarianism in six culturally disparate groups of college students; Americans, Arabs, Rhodesian Africans (Mashona), Chinese, Indians, and Brazilians. *Method:* Administration of the California F Scale printed in the language used for instruction in *S*s colleges. *Results:* None of the mean scores for male and female respondents in the 6 groups differed significantly. All five cultures, when compared with American students, show a significantly higher degree of authoritarianism. (In order; U.S., Brazil, Arabia, Hong Kong, Rhodesia, India—highest authoritarianism last). Degree of difference from one to the next is not significant.

Myambo, Kathleen, 1972, Shape Constancy as Influenced by Culture, Western Education, and Age. *Journal of Cross-Cultural Psychology* 3:221.

Shape constancy responses, obtained by asking *S*s to match the shape of an inclined circular test object with one of a series of comparison ellipses, were obtained for adult groups of educated Senas, uneducated Senas, and educated Europeans, as well as for uneducated Mang 'nja children between the ages of 5 and 15 years and Mang 'nja adults. The uneducated African *S*s tended to respond to the true shape of the objects regardless of age while the European *S*s tended to respond to the retinal image shape; the educated Africans gave responses which were intermediate between those of the uneducated Africans and the educated Europeans. The differences between African *S*s and European *S*s on shape matching responses were believed to be due to cultural influences, but it could not be determined by the present shape matching method whether the response differences were due to differential responding to the instruction by the cultural groups or to differences in perception. (JA)

Noesjirwan, Jennifer, 1970, Attitudes to Learning of the Asian Student Studying in the West. *Journal of Cross-Cultural Psychology.* 1:393

An hypothesis that the Asian student has an attitude to learning that is markedly different from his Western counterpart is presented. He is more dependent on authority, less able to think independently, and more dependent on memorization. Such an attitude is an impediment to successful academic performance in a Western university. A questionnaire measuring various aspects of this attitude was administered to a group of Asian students and to a similar group of Australian students. The items were subject to a components analysis and three factors were extracted. The first two factors described the attitudes as hypothesized, and both significantly discriminated Asian from Australian groups. The First Factor was found to predict academic performance for the Asian group to a significant extent.

Omari, Issa M. and Walter H. Mac Ginitie, 1974, Some Pictorial Artifacts in Studies of African Children's Pictorial Depth Perception *Child Development,* 45:535-539.

Pictorial depth perception of Tanzanian children in grades one, three, five, and seven was investigated using two versions of Hudson's pictures—the original version, widely used in prior studies of pictorial depth perception in developing countries, and a revised version, using the same depth cues but with familiar characters in neutral poses. Revised-version scores were higher and increased with grade; original-version scores were very low in all grades. Urban children scored higher than children from a remote area. Earlier studies showing severe and continuing deficits must be reinterpreted. (JA)

Pande, C.G., 1970, Sex Differences in Field Dependence: Confirmation with Indian Sample. *Perceptual & Motor Skills* 31:70.

Administered H.A. Witkin's colored Embedded-Figures Test (EFT) to 70 male and 70 female undergraduates to find whether sex difference in field-dependence, observed earlier, also exists for an Indian sample. Women were found to be significantly more field-dependent than men as found in earlier investigations with American and Western European samples. Some differences from Witkin's original results are demonstrated. *Ss'* consistency throughout the trials of EFT and its reliability as a measure of field-dependence are noted. (AA)

Pomerantz, Norman E., 1971, An Investigation of the Relationship Between Intelligence and Reading Achievement for Various Samples of Bilingual Spanish-Speaking Children. Ed.D. dissertation, New Mexico State University.

Problem: The purpose of this study was to investigate the relationship between intelligence scores (performance on the California Test of Mental Maturity (CTMM)) and reading achievement scores for various samples of bilingual Spanish-speaking children. This study evaluated the ability of the CTMM to predict reading achievement scores for different categories of bilingual third graders. The predictive validity of the CTMM was investigated in an effort to (a) discover the combination of score yielding the maximum correlation with three reading achievement scores, and (b) determine if the CTMM could discriminate between achieving and nonachieving readers.

Price-Williams, Douglass, William Gordon and Manuel Ramirez III, 1969, Skill and Conservation: A Study of Pottery-Making Children. *Developmental Psychology* 1(6):769.

Hypothesis: Experience in pottery making should promote early conservation at least in the concept of substance (in which clay is the experimental medium). *Method:* Piagetian conservation tests administered to twenty-four children in Tlaquepaque, Jalisco, Mexico, and to thirty-two children in San Marcos, Jalisco, Mexico, all from six to nine years of age. In the Tlaquepaque sample, Fisher's exact probability test was used for each of the five conservation tests. *Results:* Nonsignificant on tasks of number, liquid, weight, and volume, but significant for substance in Tlaquepaque (differences between potters' sons and control group of non-potters' sons).

Conclusions: The role of skills in cognitive growth may be important; manipulation may be a prior and necessary prerequisite in the attainment of conservation, but a skill embodies a set of operations with a recognizable end.

Sankoff, Gillian, 1971, Quantitative Analysis of Sharing and Variability in a Cognitive Model. *Ethnology* 10:389

In this article the issues raised are: to what extent are cognitive maps shared, which aspects of them are not shared, how do these latter aspects vary from individual to individual, and, in effect, how is intracultural diversity organized? The specific data discussed are of the Buang, a mountain people of northeastern New Guinea. This system is characterized by a high degree of variability both in informants' verbal reports of the affiliation of individuals and in their assignment of agricultural plots to kin groups. Verbal statements assigning both individuals and plots to Kin groups vary both among different informants and between reports made by the same informant on different occasions.

Serpell, Robert, 1971, Preference for Specific Orientation of Abstract Shapes among Zambian Children. *Journal of Cross-Cultural Psychology* 2:225.

Experiment I replicates and extends among Grade 3 and Grade 5 urban Zambian schoolchildren findings obtained by Ghent (1961) among U.S.A. pre-school children. The *S*s showed consistent preferences for specific orientations of abstract, geometrical shapes, including some of the designs used in the Bender-Gestalt and Koh's Block tests. Three hypothetical determinants of these preferences are discussed: (1) "location of focal part," (2) "stability," and (3) "familiarity." Experiment II attempts to assess directly the relative importance of (1) and (3) as well as to examine age-trends among rural and urban Zambian schoolchildren and urban "Western-educated" expatriate children. In both experiments, only limited support was found for the "familiarity" hypothesis. It is concluded that intrinsic perceptual features of abstract shapes give rise, independently of cultural background, to consistent preferences for certain specific spatial orientations of those shapes. A tentative theoretical integration of this phenomenon is made with other results showing cross-cultural differences in the difficulty of copying orientation.

Siann, Gerda, 1972, Measuring Field Dependence in Zambia: A Cross-Cultural Study. *International Journal of Psychology* 7(2):87-96.

Zambian infants and non-Zambians underwent the rod-and-frame test (RFT), the embedded-figures test (EFT), and a verbal test. The author studied the intercultural differences for the two sexes in relation to the concept of field dependency. Following the presentation of obtained results, a second method is proposed for the calculation of results on the RFT. The results were not supportive of the concept of field dependency to interpret the spatial aptitude of Zambian subjects (JA, translated from French)

Tyler, S., 1969, *Cognitive Anthropology*. New York. Holt, Rhinehart and Winston.

A collection of articles form the 50's and 60's emphasizing issues of ethnoscience and dealing with the fallacy of assigning psychological reality to analytic models. The book is designed for use as a text, and is intended to be representative of the field labelled cognitive anthropology as it existed then.

Welsh, George S., 1969, Preferences for Basic Geometric Shapes by American and Egyptian Subjects. *International Journal of Symbology* 1:58-66.

The Welsh Figure Preference Test was used to determine whether there is consistent order of preference for five basic geometric shapes: circle, triangle, square, pentagon, and Greek cross. Results were obtained for fourteen groups of American Ss and sixteen groups of Egyptian students. It was found "that the Egyptian and the American orders of preference differ only for the cross and the circle which are either first or second for both cultural samples." The remaining shapes fall in the order triangle, pentagon, square and in this sense is an order of preference common to American and Egyptians. Some minor inconsistencies appear when individual group orders are examined. Cultural explanations of the results are held to be inadequate and it is suggested "that the symbology of geometric shapes may be approached through the psychology of individual personality." (JA)

Witkin, Herman A. and John W. Berry, 1975, Psychological Differentiation in Cross-cultural Perspective. *Journal of Cross-Cultural Psychology* 6(1):4-87.

"Discusses the major propositions of psychological differentiation theory, cross-cultural studies of the theory's validity and generality, and problems in the existing research evidence and lines of further study that are suggested by the theory. Operative variables in the cross-cultural situation, including socialization, social tightness, ecological adaptation, and biological effects, are identified and discussed as antecedents to the developments of psychological differentiation. It is suggested that characteristic levels of differentiation are adaptive to the ecological and cultural settings which societies occupy, and that levels of psychological differentiation do make a difference in the process of acculturation. The need for extending research findings on acculturation and differentiation back to the social and cultural settings that nurtured differentiation theory itself and the tools for its measurement are noted." (L. Gorsey in *Psych. Abs.*)

SOCIALIZATION

Ainsworth, Mary D. Salter, 1967, *Infancy in Uganda*. Baltimore: Johns Hopkins Press.

Ainsworth describes methods of infant care used by the Ganda during the first fifteen months of a child's life and considers the effects of these methods on the child's psychosocial development. In particular, she seeks to ascertain the effect of variations in infant-care practices upon the growth of attachment.

Method: An interview schedule concerned with factors of socialization and infant development was administered to mothers of twenty-eight babies, fifteen boys, and thirteen girls, aged two days to eighty weeks, in twenty-three households. Observations were also made through informants. Mothers of infants were the most useful informants. Such factors as weaning age, vocalization, cleanliness, sleeping, discipline, and health practices were observed.

Conclusions: The child is born with a behavioral repertoire which includes responses already biased toward mediating social interaction. Thus the potential for attachment is part of the equipment of the newborn, although only gradually acquired in developmental course. The Ganda investigation gives some evidence that attachment does not rest on need gratification. Babies become attached very early to people who have little or no responsibility for gratifying their basic needs—fathers and selected siblings. Stranger anxiety, although related to the growth of attachment, is not its sole criterion, nor is separation anxiety. Attachment is said to grow through feedback in response to active behavior.

Ayres, Barbara, 1967, Pregnancy Magic: A Study of Food Taboos and Sex Avoidances. In C.S. Ford, ed. *Cross Cultural Approaches*, pp. 111-125. New Haven: HRAF Press.

This study seeks to explain why the number, importance, and duration of food and sex taboos vary, and why violation of the taboos is felt to be more hazardous in some societies than in others. Through positive and negative fixation mechanisms, response tendencies are said to be established which exert an influence on adult behavior (behavior which has been highly rewarded during childhood tends, in adult life, to be regarded as a potential source of gratification; behavior which has been severely punished is regarded as a potential source of harm or danger). In terms of dependency, this suggests that women whose dependency needs were rewarded during childhood would be most likely to respond to pregnancy by an increase in dependent behavior in those societies where child-training practices include high reward of dependent behavior. If food taboos represent necessary societal restraints on such behavior, the largest number of food taboos should be observed in societies where there is a high reward of dependency during childhood. Sex taboos are hypothesized to be avoidances motivated by anxiety concerning sexual behavior, suggesting a positive correlation between severity of punishment for sexual behavior and the duration of the sex taboo during pregnancy.

Conclusions: Food and sex taboos are found to be two different types of phenomena. Food taboos are most numerous in societies where child-training practices develop a strong tendency to respond to frustration and anxiety with dependent behavior. Sex taboos are associated with "punishment for heterosexuality." Food and sex taboos do have in common the fact of a psychological or motivational component, and neither the form, intensity, nor function of these customs can be fully understood apart from their psychic value to the individuals involved as well as their cohesive value to society. However, they cannot be fully accounted for on the basis of sociological functions alone.

Bach, G. R., 1946, Father-Fantasies and Father-Typing in Father-Separated Children. *Child Development* 17:63-80.

The fantasies of twenty father-separated six to ten year-old children, and those of twenty control, father-home children are compared through doll-play techniques. The father-separated children produce more idealistic and feminine fantasy pictures of the father compared with the control children. Clinical and theoretical implications of these results are discussed.

Barron, Frank and Harben Boutourline Young, 1970, Personal Values and Political Affiliation Within Italy. *Journal of Cross-Cultural Psychology* 1:355.

The philosophy of life of 82 young Italian males was analyzed in relation to their preferences in politics. The political spectrum from Right to Left was identified by the following continuum of party affiliation: Facist, Monarchist, Liberal Christian Democratic, Socialist, Communist, Popular Front Socialist. Statements in a questionnaire organized around personal and social philosophy were then correlated with positions of the young men on this continuum. The results showed clearly that the influence of the Catholic Church in matters of custom and morality is an important source of divisiveness in Italian political life. The Left splits sharply from Center and Right on matters having to do with divorce and sexual freedom, the Center is less exclusively determined by dogma but still is clearly orthodox and conservative, while the Right is dominated by its hatred of Communism and its emphasis on formalism and central authority. (JA)

Bartlett, Edward W. and Charles P. Smith, 1966, Childrearing Practices, Birth Order and the Development of Achievement-Related Motives. *Psychological Reports* 19:1207-1216.

The influence of parental demands and sanctions on the achievement-related motives of thirty-one boys (ages eight to ten) is examined. The findings of an earlier study by Winterbottom were not replicated. However, boys with high as compared with low need for achievement were more often first-born; their mothers more often expressed disappointment with unsatisfactory behavior, less often told them how much they loved them as a reward; and reported making fewer demands for achievement and independence. Age of demands was unrelated to need for achievement. Boys with high as compared with low test anxiety had lower IQs, lower grades, later birth order, and higher teacher-ratings of dependence. Their mothers tended to make later demands for independence and to praise their sons' behavior less often. (AA)

Batt, Carl E., 1969, Mexican Character: An Adlerian Interpretation. *Journal of Individual Psychology* 25:183-201.

An "ideal type" is offered including a discussion of the sociocultural situation, cult of manliness, woman's role, and childhood situation. (JA)

Berrien, F. Kenneth, 1969, Familiarity, Mirror Imaging and Social Desirability in Stereotypes: Japanese vs. Americans. *International Journal of Psychology* 4:207-215.

Japanese and Hawaiian samples of 240 males and 240 females were compared with 225 males and 118 females from the United States on judgments of national groups based upon items from the EPPS. Even with social desirability partialed out, Japanese see Americans as more contrasting with themselves than appears for American *S*s who compare themselves with Japanese. The Hawaiian sample falls in between the other samples. Data suggest that the strain-toward-consistency theories, derived largely from Western cultures, may not be applicable to Oriental respondents. "Further analyses of cognitive mechanisms in various cultures may lead to important revision in these theories and may also have a bearing on international bargaining styles." (JA)

Bhalla, Salma and Castellano Turner, 1971, A Cross-Cultural Comparison of Interpersonal Schemas. *Proceedings of the Annual Convention of the American Psychological Association* 6:355-356.

Investigated differences in interpersonal schemas (cognitive interpersonal plan) among individuals coming from 2 very different cultures (those of India and the United States). The focus was on 2 particular interpersonal schemas, the superior-subordinate relationship and the heterosexual relationship. After pointing out the major differences between the 2 cultures with regard to these relationships, it was hypothesized that Indians would show more distant interpersonal schemas than Americans on superior-subordinate and heterosexual placements. These hypotheses were supported, and the results were interpreted in terms of cultural variations leading to schemas. (AA)

Biller, Henry, 1969, Father Absence, Maternal Encouragement and Sex-Role Development in Kindergarten-Age Boys. *Child Development* 40 (2):539-546.

Compared to seventeen father-absent *S*s father-present *S*s were found to be much more masculine in projective sex-role orientation and slightly more masculine in game preference but were not significantly different in terms of rating scale measure of overt masculinity. For father-absent, but not for father-present *S*s, degree of maternal encouragement of masculine behavior was related to masculinity of game prefenence and the rating scale measure of overt masculinity. (JA)

Blane, Howard T. and Kazuo Yamammoto, 1970, Sexual Role Identity Among Japanese and Japanese-American High School Students. *Journal of Cross-Cultural Psychology* 1:345.

Sexual role identity was investigated by administering short forms of the Gough (CPI) femininity scale and the Franck Drawing Completion Test to 369 Japanese-American and Causacian-American high school students in Hawaii and to 93 students in Japan. Across sex, Japanese were more feminine on both measures than either American group; within the American group, Japanese-Americans were more feminine than Caucasian-Americans on the Gough measure, but did not differ from them on the Franck. Sex-by-ethnicity results showed that males followed the ethnic pattern on both measures, whereas Japanese females were less feminine on the Gough than Japanese-American females and were equal to Causacian-American females. Higher feminity of Japanese males may be understood as reflecting an Oriental factor of greater femininity related to definitional models of masculinity common to the East, in contrast to Western proof-of-masculinity models. Lower femininity of

Japanese women may result from shifting conceptions of femininity in Japan and the East generally, while higher femininity among Japanese-American females may be a subcultural expression related to the history and origins of Japanese in Hawaii. (JA)

Blount, Ben G., 1971, Socialization and Pre-linguistic Development Among the Luo of Kenya. *Southwestern Journal of Anthropology* 27:41.

The pre-linquistic period of child development, the period during which the child's vocalization is devoid of linguistic meaning, is customarily divided into a cooing and babbling stage. Furthermore, the vocalizations are considered to be conditioned by biological and physiological, but not by social factors. A study of interaction between Luo adults and infants shows, however, that the interactional framework changes as the children progress in their phonative skills and that the alteration facilitates the linguistic and social dvelopment of the children. Luo adults key on the children's ability to interact vocally, reducing the complexity of linguistic input initially and then increasing it gradually as the children gain competence.

Bowden, Edgar, 1973, Further Implications of Cultural Surgency and Sex-Dominance. *American Anthropologist* 75:176.

In the process of standardizing an Index of Sociocultural Development, it was found that male-dominant and equidominant societies differ significantly in their order of acquistion of developmental traits, their cultural elaboration and cultural surgency, the population of their largest settlements and possibly also their population density. These relationships are discussed in terms of the theoretical meaning of sex-dominance and cultural surgency and their dynamic significance for social change. (AA)

Bradburn, Norman, 1963, N Achievement and Father Dominance in Turkey. *Journal of Abnormal and Social Psychology* 67(5):464-468.

This study presents cross-cultural data to support the hypothesis that father dominance is associated with low need achievement (n Ach) in men. Evidence for the hypothesis was obtained (a) by testing groups of American and Turkish junior executives and (b) by comparing n Ach scores of Turks who differ in the degree to which they were dominated by their fathers. The American junior executives, as compared with the Turks, were found to have significantly higher n Ach scores. In three independent samples, Turks who were less dominated by their fathers, as measured by Ss' age when their fathers died or when they first lived apart from their fathers, had significantly higher n Ach scores than did men who were more dominated by their fathers. Such a relationship was not found, however, when dominance was measured by Ss' reports of who had had the greatest influence in their lives. (JA)

Brown, Jennifer, 1971, The Cure and Feeding of Windigos: A Critique. *American Anthropologist* 73:20.

This paper suggests that, contrary to a view recently expressed, the usual treatment of windigo psychosis is not nutritional in nature. When ingestion is involved (which is rare) its sequel (vomiting to expel the windigo heart of ice) is given more curative importance, challenging the view that the northern Algonquins somehow "grasped" the idea of a nutritive cure for windigos. Nor is evidence at this point clear on nutritional cause of windigo. (AA)

Brown, Judith K., 1970, A Note on the Division of Labor by Sex. *American Anthropologist* 72:1073-1078.

Although sexual division of labor is a universal, the contribution that women make to subsistence varies markedly from society to society. It is suggested in this article that the degree to which women participate in subsistence activities depends upon the compatibility of the latter with simultaneous child-care responsibilities. Women are most likely to make a substantial contribution when subsistence activities have the following characteristics: the participant is not obliged to be far from home; the tasks are relatively monotonous and do not require rapt concentration; the work is not dangerous, can be performed in spite of interruptions, and is easily resumed, once interrupted. (AA)

Brown, Judith K. 1973, The Subsistence Activities of Women and the Socialization of Children. *Ethos* 1:413.

Presents a cross-cultural view of the relationship between the role of women in the subsistence activities of non-industrialized societies and socialization practices as it appears to apply to the research concerning maternal employment in our society.

Findings: 1) The employment of mothers of young children is as much a vehicle for social change as it is the product of such change. Employed mothers appear to rear children who are less egoistic and who do not fit the self-assertive, achieving mold. The question is no longer whether maternal employment is good or bad for children, but how the society can absorb the less egoistic progeny of employed mothers. Alternative 2) Women's vocational choices could be broadened to the less "helpful" professions, their work could be seen as important to their self-realization and not merely as a way of helping the family. Were these changes to occur and were they communicated to children, employed mothers would present an egoistic model.

Burton, Roger V., 1973, Folk Theory and the Incest Taboo. *Ethos* 4:504.

Hypothesis: Incest taboo arose from a direct awareness by primordial humans of the deleterious effects of familial inbreeding. Data: The detrimental effects of consanguineous marriages support the possibility of this more parsimonious theory. Consideration was also given to the possibility that the same complex social custom could arise under different conditions and that it might be necessary to consider more than a single hypothesis to account for the total occurrence of such a custom. These alternative hypotheses seemed insufficient to account for the establishment of a taboo, but were seen as contributing to the conditions necessary for the dramatically visible deleterious effects of intrafamilial breeding to be expressed.

Burton, Roger V., 1972, Cross Sex Identity in Barbados. *Developmental Psychology* 6(3):365-374.

Hypotheses derived from Whiting's theory of identification—the status envy hypothesis—received support in this study. Degree of father presence measured by household structure was positively related for boys to sex of first drawing, size of male drawings, and differential size of drawings. Alternative explanations based on availability of male role models were not supported consistently. Controlling on age, ordinal position, achievement in school, and sex, age, and number of siblings did not affect these findings. Evidence suggests that both conflict of cross-sex identity and consistency of feminine identification occur in father-absence males in Caribbean culture. Comparisons of discrete and continuous measures of father absence supported a critical period hypothesis for absence during the first two years of infancy. (JA)

Caldwell, Bettye, Leonard Hersher, Earle L. Lipton, Julius Richmond and George Stern, 1963, Mother-Infant Interaction in Monomatric and Polymatric Families. *American Journal of Orthopsychiatry* 33:653-664.

Patterns of mother-infant interaction in families where mothering is provided by only one person (monomatric) or by more than one person (polymatric) are compared. A closer emotional attachment was found in the monomatric families. There was evidence that this may have been influenced by prenatal personality factors as well as by the exclusiveness of the postnatal mother-infant dyad. (JA)

Carlsmith, Lyn, 1973, Some Personality Characteristics of Boys Separated from Their Fathers During World War II. *Ethos* 1:466.

Purpose: A comparison between aptitudes, interests, and other personality characteristics of boys whose fathers were absent during World War II with boys whose fathers were not absent. *Sample:* 40 (20 of each group) students in the Harvard class of 1964. *Method:* Individual session lasting two hours, conducted by a single female, interview, Strong vocational interest test. The directions for all tests were simple and straightfoward; a brief descrition of each test is presented, along with the results in the following sections. *Results:* (1) Feminine cognitive styles in those whose fathers were absent. (2) More of the traits and interests typically associated with the female role in our culture than in boys who were not separated from their fathers. (3) Boys raised in stable middle class American families which apparently value intellectual and academic pursuits are able to find satisfying and socially approved modes of behavior that do not require an overtly masculine sex-role identity. The father-absent boys in this sample appear to be generally content with their present role identity and manifest no symptoms of conflict or anxiety concerning it. It should be recalled that the father-absent students have a weaker evaluation of adult men, project their own ideal self closer to women, and are more reticent to enter the adult professional world than are the father-present students.

Chartier, George M. and Norman D. Sundberg, 1969, Commonality of Word Listing, Predictability, and Chunking: An Anaysis of American and Indian Ninth Graders. *International Journal of Psychology* 4:195-205.

Indian *S*s of varied socioeconomic status from three communities in northern Indian manifested significantly greater variability in word-naming commonality than appeared among American *S*s. This finding runs counter to the conception of American individuality as opposed to Indian group orientation. American *S*s mentioned significantly more children than adults in a word-naming task, while the reverse held true for Indian *S*s. This finding supports the interpretation of greater peer orientation among Americans than among Indians. Girls in American but not Indian groups gave more identical words than did boys. No relationships appeared between commonality, predicatability, and originality. Further study could cast light upon which aspects of language or environment or both produce the marked similarities between cultural groups. (JA)

Choungourian, A., 1970, Lebanese and American Aspects of Personality: A Cross-Cultural Comparison. *Journal of Social Psychology* 81:117-118.

Examined differences between the behavior tendencies of Lebanese and American student samples with respect to 6 aspects of personality: orality, anality, sexuality, aggresion, independence, and achievement. The mean scale scores for self-descriptive statements on an always-never continuum indicated that on the whole the Americans show greater total orality and sexuality than the Lebanese, while the Lebanese exhibit more total aggresion than Americans. Cross-and same-sex differences within and across the 2 cultures were also found. (AA)

Cravioto, J., H. G. Bird, E. De Licardie, et al., 1969, The Ecology of Growth and Development in a Mexican Pre-industrial Community. *Monographs of the Society for Research in Child Development.* 34(5).

This report examines all children born during one year in a rural pre-industrial community situated in the hot semi-humid zone of Mexico. The condition of the children at birth and their physical and behavioral progress during the first month of postnatal life are assessed. This report—the first of a series deriving from the longitudinal study of the children—includes the design of the study and the methods used for the collection of data on the community, the children, and the familes.

Dennis, Wayne and Pergrouhi Najarian, 1957, Infant Development Under Environmental Handicap. *Psychological Monographs* 71(4):436.

Purpose: To report upon the developmental status of two age groups of severely institutionalized children in Beirut, Lebanon; describe environmental conditions; and discuss the relationship of the study to previous studies, and to theories of child development. *Method:* For subjects under one year of age, the Cattell infant scale was employed. At four and a half to six year level, the tests used were the Goodenough draw-a-man test, the Knox cube test, and the Porteous maze test. The infant tests were given to forty nine institutionalized infants and forty one control infants. The Goodenough tests were given to thirty subjects, and the Knox cube test and the Porteous maze test were each given to twenty five subjects. *Results:* The infant comparisons were not significantly different from each other or from "American norms." However, at all ages beyond 3.0 months the institutionalized infants score definitely lower than either the comparison or the normative groups, whose records are indistinguishable. There is a very significant difference (P less than .001) between three to twelve month-old infants who were institutionalized and those who were not. There is evidence that the institutional environment produces only a slight retardation among four and five-year-olds on the Goodenough and Knox cube and Porteous maze tests. *Conclusions:* It is uncertain whether the normality of behavior at two months shows that maturation plays a major role in early development, or whether experience, limited as it was, provided the essential requirements for learning the responses which were tested. The retardation prevailing between three and twelve months of age seems to be due to lack of learning opportunities in situations comparable to the test situations. It is possible that an observational approach in the day-by-day situation might reveal that some behaviors developed normally. The infants did not undergo loss of emotional attachment. There is nothing to suggest that emotional shock, or lack of mothering, or other emotionally arousing conditions were responsible for behavioral retardation. Retardation in the last nine months of the first year to the extent of a mean developmental quotient of sixty five does not result in a generally poor performance at four and a half to six years, even when the child remains in a relatively restricted environment. The study therefore does not support the doctrine of the permanency of early environmental effects. It is believed that the objective data of other studies, as well as this one, can be interpeted in terms of the effects of specific kinds of restrictions upon infant learning.

Dennis, Wayne, 1957, A Cross Cultural Study of the Reinforcement of Child Behavior. *Child Development* 28(4):431-438.

Purpose: To report some data obtained with a method which should enable a researcher to investigate in nearly any society those reinforcements which play a major part in the socialization of the child. *Method:* Critical incident technique, developed by Fanagan et al. involving asking the subject to describe instances of behavior, in this case, behavior on his part for which he has been praised. Data gathered through interviews of school children in Beirut, Lebanon: American, Arab, Jewish and Armenian children. Incidents and rewarding persons were categorized and counted. *Results:* In the American group, praise for academic performance constituted only five percent of total while in other groups from twenty-eight percent to forty-one percent of total, a decline with age in rate of academic achievement-importance among Lebanese subjects. Jewish group highest among Lebanese in emphasis on academic achievement. Armenian not different significantly from Arab. In all groups, child is praised for helping mother more often than for helping other individuals. *Conclusions:* (1) Near Eastern groups receive relatively more praise than Americans for academic achievement, for assisting unfortunates, and for being quiet, polite, and obedient. (2) This is an indication of value system. (3) Critical incident technique is valuable tool for cross-cultural behavioral studies.

Dennis, Wayne, 1960 Causes of Retardation among Institutional Children: Iran. *Journal of Genetic Psychology* 96:47-59.

Purpose: To examine child care in three institutions in Tehran and to gain insight into the "nature of environmental factors which influence motor development." *Method:* Quantitative observations on behavioral status of groups of children in each of the three institutions were made with regard only to motor coordination. Each child was classified according to his ability to (1) sit alone, (2) creep, (3) stand by holding, (4) walk by holding, (5) walk alone. *Results:* The institutions with better "environment" had children with more motor capabilities. *Conclusions:* (1) Retardation was probably due to *paucity of handling,* including failure of attendants to place children in sitting and prone positions, depriving them of the motor experiences listed in *method* above. (2) Retardation was also due to "restriction of specific kinds of learning opportunities." (3) "The *explanation of retardation* as due *primarily* to *emotional factors is believed to be untenable.*"

Diaz-Guerrero, Rogelio, 1971, The Teaching of Research in Psychology in Latin America: A Paradigm. *Revista Latinoamericana de Psicologia* 3:5-36.

The teaching of research in psychology in Latin America is not a simple technical problem. The lack of tradition of research, the absence of economic backing, the flooding of ready-made conceptions and operationally defined tools from the industrialized countries pose unique questions. A paradigm is described which has thus far proved successful in teaching research attitudes and practices in Mexican students. The model is a large cross-cultural research program in which students become aware of both techniques and the cultural differences that their local populations have vis-a-vis samples of another culture. Cross-cultural research is described as an excellent model, for it forces the realization of the large number of variables that intervene in human behavior. (JA)

Eckhardt, Kenneth W., 1971, Exchange Theory and Sexual Permissiveness. *Behavior Science Notes* 6:1.

An exchange theory of social behavior is advanced to explain intersocietal differences in sex codes. An examination of 153 societies drawn from Murdock's World Ethnographic Sample (1957) and from the HRAF-Micro-files indicates modest support for the thesis that the location of power and resources as they influence social interaction and exchange are contributory forces in accounting for the level of sexual permissiveness found in society.

Elsarrag, M. F., 1968, Psychiatry in the Northern Sudan: A Study in Comparative Psychiatry. *British Journal of Psychiatry* 111:945-948.

Compared Northern Sudanese psychiatry to British psychiatry. Differences are emphasized, attributing these to differences in cultural patterns. The hypotheses given to account for the differences cited are in need of further research and verification. (JA)

Erchak, Gerald M., 1976, The Nonsocial Behavior of Young Kpelle Children and the Acquisition of Sex Roles. *Journal of Cross-Cultural Psychology* 7(2):223–234.

Further evidence of the close relationship between aspects of child training and behavior and later adult economic role suggested by previous researchers is presented. An analysis of the nonsocial behavior of twenty Liberian Kpelle one to six year olds and the responses of adults to that behavior as these relate to the acquisition of sex roles are included. Nonsocial behavior is behavior that is individual, self-initiated, and egocentric. The methods of systematic behavior observation and coding developed by the Whitings are described and were employed. Because of the greater importance of women than men in Kpelle subsistence activities, girls become more self-reliant and responsible than boys at an earlier age. The nonsocial behavior of boys reflected their greater free time and lack of responsibilities. The responses of adults were inconclusive, but consistent with the findings on children's behavior. (JA)

Faris, James C., 1969, Sibling Terminology and Cross-Sex Behavior: Data from the Southeastern Nuba Mountains. *American Anthropologist* 71:482.

Contrary to certain of the assumptions of Nerlove and Romney (1967) on sibling terminology and cross-sex behavior, the sibling terminology of the Southeastern Nuba manifests a primary sex-of-speaker component and is shown to be conjunctive. Other data appear to weigh against their functional hypothesis for the cross-parallel distinction in sibling terminology but support a general conclusion that there may be different levels of explanation in kinship usage and that attention should be paid to cultural conceptions of cross-sex relations. (AA)

Garibay Patron, Miguel, 1969 Psychology of the Mexicans. *Revista Mexicana de Psicologia* 3:350–354.

Psychologists doing research in Mexico should be aware of the two specific cultural aspects of Mexico which reflect personality differences peculiar to Mexico as compared with the typical cultural values in the United States. The first characteristic considered and discussed is "Machismo," defined as a type of inferiority complex. This shows up in bravado, alcoholism, and women-chasing behavior as characteristic of typical Mexican male. The second cultural characteristic is that of the self-denying Mexican women. A Mexican woman is expected to be completely submissive to a man or the men in her life.

Gordon, C. Paul and Ronald Gallimore, 1972, Teacher Ratings of Behavior Problems of Hawaiian-American Adolescents. *Journal of Cross-Cultural Psychology* 3:209.

Teachers in rural Hawaii completed the Behavior Problem Checklist for 196 Hawaiian and part-Hawaiian students. Two factors were extracted, reflecting disruptiveness and passive withdrawal. Similar studies in the United States have typically reported three factors; the two obtained in the Hawaii study, and an immaturity-inadequacy factor. Failure to find the latter factor was attributed to the cross-cultural nature of the situation. The results were interpreted to indicate that behavior problems reported by teachers vary little from situation to situation and culture to culture, due to the stimulus conditions inherent in the typical school situation.

Gorzhowska, Krystyna, 1969, Changes in Children's Attitudes to Other Nationalities as Elected by Participation in the Malta Camp. *Prleglad Psychologiczny* 17:29-46.

Investigated by questionnaire and projective techniques changes in attitude of 435 12-17 year old Polish children to children of other nationalities during an International scouting encampment. Both positive and negative changes were found in 50% of the *S*s, with the number of negative changes being slightly higher. Results showed that a) prolonged, organized contact appeared to reduce prejudices, while short sporadic contact strengthened them: b) negative attitudes may be more easily changed when not accompanied by negative evaluations of the characteristics of a given nationality; c) direct contact exerted a greater influence on opinions than on emotional attitudes.

Granzberg, Gary, 1972, Hopi Initiation Rites—A Case Study of the Validity of Freudian Theory of Culture. *The Journal of Social Psychology* 87:189-195.

Purpose: To present a case study of Hopi initiation, thereby testing a key portion of Whiting's Freudian analysis of initiation that could not be tested cross-culturally (according to Whiting). *Hypothesis:* That Hopi initiation alters the behavior of initiates in exactly the way Whiting's theory predicts—i.e., that the rites help the initiates adjust to their society by "brainwashing" problem behavior which causes them to conflict with their systems, thus providing construct evidence of the validity of Freudian theory based on the assumption that culture serves the needs of individuals. *Method and Procedure:* Giving psychological tests to a group of Hopi boys before and after initiation, and to a control group who were similar in all variables except the experience of initiation. Measurements were of the levels of dependence an aggresion through performance on tasks, verbal TATs, and pictorial TATs. *Results:* The tests demonstrate that the newly initiated subjects forming the experimental group showed a marked change toward less aggression and more dependence after initiation than their control counterparts. *Conclusion:* The Hopi evidence supports the validity of Freudian theory, but should not be interpreted as a renunciation of the symbolic-interaction theory which sees initiation as an institution in the service of groups. The two theories are compatible and mutually supportive.

Granzberg, Gary, 1973, The Psychological Intergration of Culture: A Cross-Cultural Study of Hopi Type Initiation Rites. *The Journal of Social Psychology* 90:3-7.

Purpose: To explore the possibility that, in accordance with Whiting's theory on the subject of initiation, Hopi initiation and Hopi child training are integrated by virtue of the fact that the child rearing produces the disruptive aggression and independence in children which the initiation counteracts. *Hypothesis:* (a) The Hopi's discontinuous child-rearing pattern of indulgence followed by compliance training produces frustration in children which manifests itself in independence, aggresion, and recalcitrance, and (b) the use of masks and a disciplinary whipping in initiation symbolically communicates the need for impulse control and compliance, and helps, thereby, to reduce the aggressiveness and noncompliance of children. *Method:* Cross-cultural study of the two cultural elements in these hypotheses (child-rearing and initiation) from societies selected on the basis of linguistic and geographic separation from the population of societies that has been rated for the presence or absence of child-reaing factors and initiation factors by Whiting and Barry, Bacon and Child. Ratings on indulgence, compliance, and initiation were done by "naive" judges. *Results:* There exists a strong cross-cultural co-occurence of indulgence followed by compliance child training and group initiation rites featuring the use of masks and /or disciplinary whipping. *Conclusion:* "The study should be included among the many that provide evidence in support of the basic psychological anthropology premise that elements of culture can be integrated by underlying psychological processes."

Granzberg, Gary, 1973, Twin Infanticide—A Cross-Cultural Test of a Materialistic Explanation. *Ethos* 1:405.

Hypothesis: Twin infanticide is found in societies that provide insufficient facilities for a mother to properly rear two children at once while at the same time fulfilling her other responsibilities. *Method:* 1) Human Relations Area Files. (A slight overrepresentation of new world and African societies in the sample, and a maximum amount of linguistic and geographic separation has not always been attained). The Independent Variable: 1) The amount of help available to mothers as inferred from a) settlement pattern size, b) family size, 2) the degree to which mothers are free from work as measured by a) the extent to which she is free from subsistence production duties, b) the extent to which she is free from time-consuming child care tasks such as breast feeding the child and carrying it around with her, even when it is asleep. Summary Score: The score for each society was obtained by summing the scores on each variable. The Dependent Variable: A reliability check by an independent judge on one-third of the sample showed 95% agreement with the author's ratings. *Results:* Infanticide is correlated with ecological factors. Contrary to the common practice of treating infanticide as one monolithic institution, this study supports work by Whiting (1964), which shows that infanticide includes different practices, each aimed at solving different problems in society.

Grinder, Robert E. and Robert E. McMichael, 1963, Cultural Significance on Conscience Development: Resistance to Temptation and Quiet among Samoans and American Caucasians. *Journal of Abnormal and Social Psychology* 66(5):503-507.

In this study (a) the socialization effects of a shame and a guilt culture on conscience development are compared with Samoan and American Caucasian children, and (b) the relationships between resistance to temptation and guilt are investigated. Inferences about conscience strength were made from behavior in a real-life temptation situation and from responses to projective story completion items depicting transgressions. The results show that the Samoan *S*s were significantly less likely than the mainland *S*s to resist temptation and to show susceptibility toward remorse, confession, and restitution after transgression. The projective measures of guilt are shown to be highly interrelated but inconsistently related to temptation behavior. (JA)

Hare, A. Paul and Dean Peaboyd, 1971, Attitude Content and Agreement Set in Autonomy-Authoritarianism Items for United States, African, and Philippine University Students. *Journal of Social Psychology* 83:23-31.

Used cross-cultural data, including sets of autonomy and authoritarian items, to reexamine the importance of attitude content and agreement set in such items. Consistent results in this and other studies—the means, variability, reliability, and correlations for two types of items—suggest that content and set are normally both important components of the scores. External correlates of such scales may relate to either content or set. The social background characteristics of these cross-cultural samples seem more related to content. (JA)

Haritos-Fatouros, M. and Irving L. Child, 1977, Transcultural Similarity in Personal Significance of Esthetic Interests. *Journal of Cross-Cultural Psychology* 8(3):285-298.

A measure of esthetic interest in visual art—tendency to prefer art which experts consider esthetically better—was developed in the United States, but showed high internal consistency in Greece as well. Measures of self-characterizations correlated with esthetic interest and of active versus passive preferences in food and drink, originally developed in the United States, also showed internal consistency in Greece. The correlations among these measures found in the United States, moreover, were substantially replicated in Greece. The personal significance of esthetic interests is thus shown to have marked transcultural stability. In both countries, esthetic interest is positively related to liking for autonomy, variety, and challenge. (JA)

Hay, Thomas H., 1968, "Ojibwa Emotional Restraint and the Socialization Process." Ph. D. dissertation, Michigan State University.

This study focuses on the motivation of the extreme restraint characteristic of the typical Ojibwa Indian and on the learning process through which motivation for this restraint is developed. Hypotheses derived from two different theories of the motivation of the restraint and from two different theories of the development of extreme restraint are tested in this study. One of the theories of the motivation of restraint traces this restraint to an exaggerated fear of retaliation for openly aggressive behavior. The other theory traces restraint to an exaggerated fear of doing serious injury to others by openly aggressive behavior. The data to test the hypotheses derived from these theories was gathered through observations of the interaction of adults and children in nine Ojibwa households at Lac du Flambeau, Wisconsin, and four Ojibwa households at Berens River, Manitoba. The sample is definitely biased toward the more culturally conservative families. Observations recorded for twenty-nine adults tested the hypothesis derived from the motivational theories. The binomial test of goodness of fit was used to test the learning hypotheses for thirty-two children. The theory that Ojibwa restraint is motivated by fear of retaliation is not supported by the data. The theory that Ojibwa restraint is motivated by fear of doing serious injury to others is neither clearly supported nor contradicted by the data. There is, however, reason to believe that minor modifications of this theory would lead to deduction consistent with data.

Hay, Thomas J., 1971, The Windigo Psychosis. Psychodynamic Cultural and Social Factors in Aberrant Behavior. *American Anthropologist* 73:1.

Although windigo cannibalism is unique to the northern Algonquins, the psychodynamic factors which produce it are general. The differential occurrence of the disorder is explained in terms of the nothern Algonquin emphasis on following inner promptings, the absence of cultural alternatives, and in terms of the nature of interaction in the particular bands for which cannibalism was reported. (AA)

Hoffman, Martin L., 1971, Father Absence and Conscience Development. *Developmental Psychology* 4(3):400-406.

A father-absent and a father-present group—controlled for sex, IQ, and social class—were compared concerning seven moral attributes and overt aggression. All subjects were seventh-grade white children. The data were based on structured and semiprojective items and ratings by parents, teachers, and peers. Father-absent boys obtained lower scores for all the moral indices—significantly lower for internal moral judgment, maximum guilt following transgressions, acceptance of blame, moral values, and rule conformity. They were also rated by teachers as significantly more aggressive than father-present boys. No differences between father absence and father presence were obtained for girls. Evidence is presented that the effects of father absence on boys are similar but somewhat more pronounced than the effects of nonidentification with a father who is present which suggests that some but not all of the effects of father absence are attributable to the lack of paternal model. Evidence is also presented which suggests that the effects of father absence on boys may be partly mediated by the resulting changes in the mother's child-rearing practices. (JA)

Hsu, Francis L. K, 1971, Psychological Homeostasis and Jen: Conceptual Tools for Advancing Psychological Anthropology. *American Anthropologist* 73:23.

Personality is a Western concept rooted in individualism. The basic importance accorded it in psychological anthropology has obscured our understanding of how Western man lives in Western-society and culture, or how any man lives in any society and culture. What is missing is the central ingredient in the human mode of existence: man's relationship with his fellow man. Homeostasis describes the process whereby every human individual tends to seek certain kinds of affective involvement with some of his fellow humans. Jen refers to the internal and external limits of the individual's affective involvement. With the aid of five major hypotheses based on these concepts, a review is made of facts drawn from China, the United States and Japan. (AA)

Jackson, Gary B. and A. Kimball Romney, 1973, Historical Inference from Cross-Cultural Data: The Case of Dowry. *Ethos* 1:517.

Purpose: To show that dowry is a relatively recent cultural pattern and second, to show that the existence of dowry is dependent on a complex level of cultural development. *Data:* From Murdock's world ethnographic sample of 565 cultures. Arguments: (1) the geographical distribution of dowry is restricted in area indicating recent development. (2) dowry is dependent upon a high level of cultural complexity: that is, cultural complexity is a necessary though not sufficient condition for the appearance of the practice of dowry. *Findings:* Through statistics, (1) dowry is found in only two of the six major geographical regions. Seventy-five percent of all cases are located within the circum-Mediterranean area. (2) In, 21 out of 24 societies the assumption fits that cultural evolution moves from simple forms to more complex structures involving higher levels of political integration and technology.

Johnstone, John W. C., 1970, Age-Grade Consciousness. *Sociology of Education* 43:56.

Studies of generational phenomena are said not to have paid sufficient attention to the distinction between cohort and kinship aspects of generations. Using empirical measures of class consciousness as a model, consciousness of kind based on age is measured and related to theoretically relevant determinants and consequences. Age-grade consciousness is found among a sample of architecture students to be positively linked with familial value conflict and negatively linked with commitment to becoming a professional architect. A path model is presented to interpret the relationships.

Kiefer, Christie W., 1970, The Psychological Interdependence of Family, School and Bureaucracy in Japan. *American Anthropologist* 72:66.

The Japanese "examination hell" phenomenon is viewed as a series of crisis rites through which the child passes from family-centered to peer centered values in a "particularistic" society. It is held that this model has greater explanatory power than the "minimization of competition" model proposed by others and that it also helps to explain the phenomenon of student radicalism and centrifugal relationships in middle-class communities. (AA)

Kilbride, Janet E. and Matthew Yarczower, 1976, Recognition of Happy and Sad Facial Expressions among Baganda and U.S. Children. *Journal of Cross-Cultural Psychology* 7(2)181-194.

The recognition of happy and sad expressions by U.S. children and by Baganda children and adults was assessed using schematic drawings. Developmental and cultural differences and similarities in this ability were found. The happy expression was more easily identified by the young children than the sad expression. When stimuli potentially contradictory to the facial expression (e.g., red dress on a sad girl, tears on a happy face) were added to the drawings, many African and U.S. children changed their previous judgments. In several cases, only the Baganda children changed their judgments; the American children were unaffected. Socioeconomic factors and certain cultural values may have been responsible for yielding cross-cultural differences. (JA)

Klingelhafer, C. L., 1971, What Tanzanian Secondary School Students Plan to Teach Their Children. *Journal of Cross-Cultural Psychology* 2(2):189-195.

The responses of 3,457 Tanzanian secondary school students to the question "If you become a parent, what two things will you try to teach your children?" were analysed. While the overall distribution of responses was related to the sex and ethnic group membership (Asian or African) or the respondent, the subgroups did not differ in the striking frequency with which they named obedience or manners as the goal. The paper attempts to account for the heavy stress placed on this important traditional African element of child rearing by these elite groups and tries to explain the unexpectedly close agreement in the frequency with which the different sex-ethnic subgroups mention obedience as a primary goal of child training.

Krauss, Herbert H., 1970, Social Development and Suicide. *Journal of Cross-Cultural Psychology* 1:159-167.

Studied 58 societies to test the relationship between societal complexity and frequency of suicide. Suicide frequency was highest in the medium complexity cultures and lowest in the low complexity cultures. The highly complex cultures were divided between high and low suicide rates. "It is suggested that this result may eventually be understood in terms of the way in which societies bind their members into patterned social relations."(JA)

Legesse, Asmarom, 1973, The Controlled Cross-Cultural Test. *Ethos* 1:521.

Purpose: To examine the usefulness of the matching technique in assembling cross-cultural samples. The essential feature of the procedure proposed here is that the sample of cases consists of two segments: an experimental sample and a control sample.

Lem, S., 1969, A Model of Culture. *Voprosy Filosofii* 23:49-62.

Culture is viewed in terms of a "system of games." Within this context, the problems of "cultural codes" and "culture as a meta-game" are considered, and a "model of culture" is proposed. (JA)

Lester, David, 1970, Adolescent Suicide and Premarital Sexual Behavior. *Journal of Social Psychology* 82:131-132.

C. Kluckhohn's suggestion that adolescent suicide would occur more in societies where premarital sexual expression was severely punished was tested on a sample of 40 nonliterate societies. The hypothesis was not confirmed. (JA)

Lester, David, 1971, Suicide and Homicide Rates and the Society's Need for Affiliation. *Journal of Cross-Cultural Psychology* 2:405.

Two clusters are reported: murder, suicide and alcoholism formed one and ulcers and hypertension formed the second. These two groups of causes of death are related to the operation of aggressiveness in the societies: deaths due to aggressiveness or acting-out and deaths due to inhibition of aggression. The societal need to achieve (as assessed from children's tales in the society) would correlate with deaths from inhibition of aggression whereas the societal need for power would correlate with deaths from aggressiveness. The data from a sample of developed nations only partially supported his hypotheses. Need achievement (n Ach) was unrelated both to the suicide and the homicide rate while n Pow was significantly related only to the suicide rate.

Lester, Barry, Milton Kotelchuck, E. Spelke, Marthe Sellers and Robert Klein, 1974, Separation Protest in Guatemalan Infants: Cross-Cultural and Cognitive Findings. *Developmental Psychology* 10:79-85.

The purpose of this study was to investigate the onset and development of separation protest in a non-Western culture. Forty-two boys and girls distributed over the ages of nine, twelve, eighteen, and twenty-four months were assessed for reactions to arrival and departures of their mother, father and a stranger. The infants were also given a test of object permanence. The results showed that the pattern of separation protest was similar in Guatemala and the U.S. although the age of onset of separation protest was earlier in Guatemala. The results also gave tentative support for a relation between separation protest and object permanence.

Levin, Joseph, and Eliezer S. Karni, 1971, A Comparative Study of the CPI Femininity Scale: Validation in Israel. *Journal of Cross-Cultural Psychology* 2:387.

The 38-item Femininity Scale of the California Psychological Inventory has validly differentiated between males and females in seven countries, and the extension of these findings to other countries would help yield an instrument for further cross-cultural studies. A Hebrew translation of the scale was administered to a random sample of the Israeli population, consisting of 200 males and 200 females. The means were 16.36 and 22.02 respectively and the difference of 5.66 is highly significant (p less than .001). All the items, except one, differentiated in the proper direction, though several items showed low discriminating power. The validity in Israel is one of the highest among the countries for which studies are available, and is next to the results obtained in the U.S.

LeVine, R. A., 1966, *Dreams and Deeds.* Chicago: University of Chicago Press.

Purpose: To answer the question: for three ethnic groups in Nigeria "are the differential rates and patterns of advancement related to motivational differences between the culturally diverse populations? *Hypothesis:* Inasmuch as societies can be maintained only through the willing conformity of individuals to social norms, there must be some kind of "fit" between the personality characteristics (or behavioral dispositions) of individuals in a society and the social structures within which they function. Personality structures ought to be correlated with structural characteristics. *Method:* It was decided to use dreams for the comparison fof the three Nigerian groups on the grounds thay they would enable us to study the same aspects of personality as a TAT without the cultural contamination that the latter's pictures introduce. Dreams were collected from self-report of student *Ss. Conclusions:* (1) The amount of social incentive provided by a status mobility system for individual achieving behavior is positively related to the frequency of n Achievement in the population. (Frequency of achievement imagery in dream reports followed status-mobility hypothesis). (?) We cannot be certain that such factors as religion, population density, and colonial history are not accountable for variation in achievement and motivation along with the variable of ethnic difference. (3) It is quite plausible that population pressure is translated into economic achievement in Africa through the child training practices of anxious parents which produce higher levels of n Achievement in their children. (4) Associated with well known regional variations in levels of economic development and Western-ization in Nigeria are individual behavioral dispositions of a deep-seated nature which are probably resistant to change. They (the dispositions) are not randomly distributed, but cluster in the three major ethnic groups of Nigeria. (5) There is a consistent pattern of group differences revealed in unconscious imagery, explicit value-attitude formations, educational achievement, and economic and political behavior. The latter behaviors are the outcomes of culturally determined differences in the incidence of personality characteristics such as n Achievement and authoritarianism among the three ethnic groups.

Levine, Robert A, 1973, Patterns of Personality in Africa. *Ethos* 2:123.

This article is an attempt by a psychological anthropologist to extract from his experience of Africans preliminary answers to general questions that specialists rarely consider but "cannot afford to ignore": Are the distinctively African patterns of personality existing now? What differences are there in behavior and personality between Africans and Westerners? How do personality characteristics of Africans affect their social adaptation to changing conditions?

Levy, Robert, 1973, *The Tahitians.* Chicago: University of Chicago Press.

A good ethnography with much psychological and psychoanalytic interpretation.

Lindzey, Gardner, 1961, *Projective Techniques and Cross-cultural Research.* New York: Appleton-Century Crofts.

Written primarily for applications in anthropological research. Definitions, theoretical foundations, varieties, and the interpretive process of projective techniques are explored. (JA)

McKissack, Ian J., 1971, Conformity in Ghana. *British Journal of Social and Clinical Psychology* 10:87.

Discusses studies of African cultural patterns in which certain behavior measures of social processes should show cross-cultural variations. The testing of 26 Ghanaian college students is described and compared to other studies which consider the influence of social pressure on African *S*s that is exerted in face-to-face interaction situations.

Madsen, Millard., and Catherine Connor, 1973, Cooperative and Competitive Behavior of Retarded and Nonretarded Children at Two Ages. *Child Development* 44(1):175-178.

Assessed cooperative-competitive interaction between eighteen pairs of non-retarded children aged six to seven or eleven to twelve years in a situation in which competitive interaction was non-adaptive in terms of reward attainment. The retarded group, and the six to seven year old retarded group was more cooperative than the eleven to twelve year old retarded group. Results are discussed in relation to previous developmental studies of cooperation-competition and placed in the context of cognitive and reinforcement theories of social development. (JA)

Margetts, Edward L., 1968, African Ethnopsychiatry in the Field. *Canadian Psychiatric Association Journal* 13:521-538.

Discusses the need for a more intensified approach to psychiatry in Africa, emphasizing the interdependence of anthropology, psychology, and psychiatry in primitive African cultures. Two kinds of field ethnopsychiatry which could be applied in Africa are described: clinical and research oriented. The phenomena which should be investigated by a psychiatrist working in the African field include: the normal and the abnormal person (both according to local African standards); conceptions of magic; practitioners of magic or ritual experts; social hierarchy: religion; birth and child rearing; genital customs; education; death and burial customs; dreams and other symbolism; demonology; secret societies; politics; suicide, murder, and cannibalism; justice; alcohol and drugs; sex habits; stories and myths; dances and music; art; and artifacts. (JA)

Meadow, Arnold, and Louise Bronson, 1969, Religious Affiliation and Psychopathology in a Mexican American Population. *Journal of Abnormal Psychology* 74:117-180.

Studies 54 Protestant and 54 Catholic Mexican-American *S*s of similar levels of acculturation, education, and socioeconomic background. Evaluations of psychopathology were derived from the L-R sections of the Cornell Medical Index and behavioral observations. The lower rate of pathological responses by Protestant *S*s was attributed to the social support offered by the small, intimate congregations with their strong, paternal leadership and the Protestant doctrines of asceticism and individual responsibility which contribute to impulse control. (JA)

Mehta, Perin H., Pritim K. Rohila, Norman D. Sundberg and Leona E. Tyler, 1972, Future Time Perspectives of Adolescents in India and the United States. *Journal of Cross-Cultural Psychology* 3:293.

A review of event-listing research suggests that longer time perspective is associated with more favorable characteristics including higher socio-economic level. The major samples consisted of approximately 100 boys to 80 girls each in ninth grades in small towns in India and America. They did not show significant differences on median time attributed to seven expected life events, though Indian boys showed greater diversity. In smaller samples in large cities, high socio-economic groups had longer time spans, but again nationality and sex differences did not appear. Content analysis showed a greater American emphasis on leisure and one's own courtship, marriage, and children, while a greater Indian emphasis was placed on other's courtship, marriage, and children, other's deaths and health.

Merelman, Richard M., 1972, The Adolescence of Political Socialization. *Sociology of Education* 45:35.

This article assesses political socialization research in terms of its theoretical adequacy, descriptive findings, and methodology. Research in political socialization has uncovered much about the substance of childhood and adolescent political orientations and also has managed to link some agencies of socialization reliability to particular political attitudes. Major deficiencies include the lack of attention to socialization as a process, the divorce from useful psychological and social theory, and the reliance on restrictive and inadequate methodologies. However, if care is taken research in political socialization can aid educators in the design of curricula and teaching practices.

Meyer, A., 1968, Superstition and Magic in the Caribbean: Some Psychiatric Consequences: Preliminary Investigation. *Psychiatria, Neurologia, Neurochirurgia* 71:421-434.

Present examples of magical and superstitional beliefs in the Caribbean area. The similarity of these beliefs in these culturally, linguistically, and socioeconomically often so different territories is striking. Magic and superstition influence, in a far higher degree than is mostly assumed, not only inter-human relations but the thought content and behavior pattern of the individual as well. They form a psychic disposition that could be described as compulsive paranoic. An attempt is made to propose a theory which could explain the extremely high incidence of paranoid reactions among psychotics as a result of these superstitional beliefs; however, it is concluded that further exploration in this field and especially of its impact on mental health, is prerequisite. (JA)

Miller, Stephen, 1973, Ends, Means, and Galumphing: Some Leitmotifs of Play. *American Anthropologist* 75:87.

Two main questions are asked here about play. (1) Is it really a coherent category of activity in spite of the diversity of forms it takes in man and animals? (2) Does it make sense in terms of the evolution of behavior that play should have become so ubiquitous among our activities? These questions are approached by looking at play as a way of orchestrating the ends and means of action in which the means are the center of interest, in which the economic of survival are subordinated to combinatorial flexibility. (AA)

Minturn, Leigh, Martin Grosse and Santoah Haider, 1969, Cultural Patterning of Sexual Beliefs and Behavior. *Ethnology* 8:301-318.

Purpose: To investigate (1) the interrelationships among some forms of sexual behaviors and beliefs concerning sex, (2) methods used by societies to arrange and dissolve marriages and the degree of segregation of unmarried adolescents from opposite-sexual peers, (3) homosexual relatonships and rape as two kinds of sexual behavior which are considered to be deviant by many societies, (4) the use of aphrodisiacs and love charms and other beliefs and practices which are indicative of sex anxiety. *Method:* Sample: 135 societies drawn from HRAF—scaling according to frequency distributions of variables investigated. *Results:* (1) Segregation of adolescents from peers of opposite sex is *not* significantly related to any of the other variables. (2) Scales for marriage arrangement and ease of divorce are not significantly related to any of the scales of sex practices, with the exception that marriages tend to be arranged where homosexuality is accepted and frequent. (3) Societies in which homosexuality is relatively accepted form of behavior for men have a higher incidence of homosexuality and higher sexual anxiety. Homosexuality is more frequent and more accepted in societies with a low initial indulgence of sex in children and high severity of sex training. (4) There is low punishment for rape in societies with severe sex training, indicating that rape is not based on high anxiety. (5) Both rape and homosexuality show significant relationships with the custom of male genital mutilations during initiation ceremonies. (6) Rape and homosexuality scales show no relationships to Whiting's measure of the length of postpartum taboo. (7) Sex charms do occur in societies with long postpartum sex taboos.

Modan, B., I. Nissenkorn and S. R. Lewkowski, 1970, Suicide in a Heterogeneous Society. *British Journal of Psychiatry* 116:65-68.

Jewish suicides have shown an annual rate of 11.8/100,000 population, with incidence rising in males to age 35 vs. a steady age rise with females. European-born show the highest rates, and the methods are, as usual, sex-specific. A striking phenomenon is the high incidence of death by burning in females of African-Asian or Arab origin. Suicide peaks on Sunday which is the equivalent of the Western Monday. (JA)

Munroe, Robert L. and Ruth H. Munroe, 1972, Obedience among Children in an East African Society. *Journal of Cross-Cultural Psychology* 3:395.

Among the world's culture areas, African societies are rated the highest in socialization for compliance. The Kikuyu, a group with typically high compliance training, were tested experimentally for obedience. Eighteen children between five and nine year of age were given two tasks by their own mothers and the same two tasks by another child's mother. Overall obedience was very high, with ten children obeying fully on all tasks. The strongest contrast with previous findings was that, unlike American children, Kikuyu children did not disobey their own mothers more than another child's mother. The strong compliance emphasis was tentatively argued to be a concomitant of the child's participation in the household's economic activities.

Munroe, Robert L., Ruth Munroe and Sara Nerlove, 1973, Male Pregnancy Symptoms and Cross-Sex Identity: Two Replications. *Journal of Social Psychology* 89:147-148.

Hypothesis and Purpose: To report two attempts to replicate earlier work showing that males who manifest pregnancy-like symptoms during wife's pregnancy are, in contrast to nonsymptoms males, more likely to give female-like responses on covert measures of sex identity and hypermasculine responses on overt measures. The symptoms have been interpreted to indicate the presence of cross-sex indentity, with the hypermasculine responses thought to be indicative of attempts to deal with the syndrome. *Method:* Testing was based on Spearman's *rho* calculated for symptomatology scores and the measures. Eleven males from Nilotic speaking Luo of western Kenya were interviewed. Twenty-six males from the Gusii tribe of Kenya were also interviewed. Results: all reported one or more symptoms. For measures expected to yield female-like responses (a) symptomatoloty was associated with drinking, but not wife-beating or fighting (b) symptomatology was associated with semantic differential description of self as strong. Symptomatology among the Gusii was associated with nearness of self to father. *Conclusion:* Seven societies have been found so far in which male symptomatology has been shown to be related to one or more measures of sex identity.

Murray, John B., 1968, Learning in Homosexuality. *Psychological Reports* 23:659-662.

Distinguishing between sex in the biological sense and sex-role or sex-identity as a reflection of culture allows for research of psychology and psychiatrists on the subtle influences of learning in homosexuality. (JA)

Naroll, Raoull, 1970, What Have We Learned from Cross-Cultural Surveys. *American Anthropologist* 72:1227.

This is a review of cross-cultural surveys. The tasks and problems of such surveys are reviewed and a system of evaluating their validity is presented. Surveys of kinship have shown their validity of a developmental pattern in residence rules, descent rules and kin terms; much has been learned about kin avoidance and much suggested about inheritance, marriage and divorce patterns. Surveys of cultural evolution have established the validity of seven major elements of cultural evolution and firmily linked these to archeological findings; evolutionary links to several aspects of life style have also been shown or suggested. Many surveys have shown relationships between child training and adult behavior and between social settings and antisocial behavior, but the nature of the linkages remains largely unsettled. Unresolved too are most conflicts between rival modes of explanation of functional conundrums, such as puberty rites and unilateral cross-cousin marriage. Factor analysis of large trait matrices have shown the importance of at least five major factors.

Newton, Niles, 1970, The Effect of Psychological Environment on Childbirth: Combined Cross-Cultural and Experimental Approach. *Journal of Cross-Cultural Psychology* 1:85.

A cross-cultural survey of birth patterning revealed marked differences in the speed of labor and indicated extreme variations in the psychological environment during labor and delivery. Speedier, easier labors appear to be related to acceptance of birth as normal physiologic phenonmenon uncomplicated by sexual shame or fear-inducing rituals. The hypotheses development from cross-cultural surveys were then tested experimentally in mice. Disturbance applied during labor resulted in reduction of labor speed immediately after the disturbance. Mice continuously disturbed at term delivered first pups significantly later, and had a 54% higher pup mortality rate. When expectant mice were rotated between familiar environment with shelter and glass fish bowl imbued with cat odor, spending equal amounts of time in each, significantly fewer births took place in the latter. (JA)

Osofsky, Joy D. and Barbara Danzger, 1971, Relationships between Neonatal Characteristics and Mother-Infant Interaction. *Developmental Psychology* 10(1):124-130.

Studied fifty-one mothers and their newborn infants to evaluate the relationships between neonatal styles and the early mother-infant relationship. The procedure included an infant assessment with the Brazelton Neonatal Behavioral Assessment Scale, a mother-infant observation during feeding, and an interview concerning maternal attitudes and perceptions. Findings suggest that there are consistencies in infant state and behavioral measures across situations; e.g., the infant who was alert and responded to auditory cues during the Brazelton assessment looked at the mother a great deal during the feeding observation. Data also suggested consistent and interactive relationships between patterns of maternal stimulation and infant behavior in corresponding area, e.g., the attentive, sensitive mother tending to have a responsive baby and vice-versa. Findings provide additional information about the early development of the complex relationships between children and parents. (JA)

Pelicier, Yves, 1968, The Psychology of People and Psychiatry. *Revue de Psychologie des Peuples* 23:288-302.

Proposes that there are ethnocultural stereotypes in the expression of various psychiatric disease entities. Suicide is less frequent in Africa, whereas hyponchondria is prevalent. In Japan, Indonesia, North Africa, Alaska, and Siberia, there appears to be a prevalence of echolalia, echopraxia, and obsessive-compulsive neurosis. Additional examples of frequent manifestations of particular symptoms in certain cultures are provided. (JA)

Peterson, Donald R. and Guiseppe Migliorino, 1967, The Uses and Limitations of Factor Analysis in Cross-Cultural Research on Socialization. *International Journal of Psychology* 2:215-220.

Available evidence shows that highly complex multifactorial systems for describing parent and child behavior from culture do not meet the test of statistical invariance and structure stability which must be satisfied by any adequately general descriptive framework. Limiting the system to small sets of high variance factors yields acceptable stability and conceptual clarity. Besides factorial study, effective intercultural comparisons require specific behavioral analysis.

Phillips, Beeman N., Roy P. Martin and Leon Zorman, 1971, Factorial Structure of the Children's School Questionnaire in American and Slovenian Samples. *Journal of Cross-Cultural Psychology* 2:65.

In the present study, the factorial structure of the Children's School Questionnaire, and differences on common factors, were investigated in samples of American and Slovenian children. The majority of the evidence indicates that the test measures the same major attributes in both samples, with one factor, labeled school anxiety, over-shadowing all the others. In addition, on the five common factors—school anxiety, sex role (2), school aspirations, and feelings of inadequacy in school—nationality, social status, and sex differences were found. Sex differences were generally larger among Slovenian Ss, while social status differences were generally larger among American Ss. Socio-cultural differences between the two nationalities were discussed and these differences were used to account for the major findings, although the "explanations" were more or less hypothetical. (JA)

Plattner, Sunya and Leigh Minturn, 1975, A Comparative and Longitudinal Study of the Behavior of Communally Raised Children. *Ethos* 3(4):469.

Purpose: To gather child behavior observational data from a communal setting and compare these data with the same data gathered from the children of nuclear families. *Methods:* Interview of mothers on commune in Colorado as well as mothers of children in nuclear families in a preschool in town and in a Montessori preschool in same town. Observation of children for six ten-minute time periods each, scoring children according to categories of succorance, nurturance, responsibility, self-reliance, achievement, dominance, sociability, aggression, obedience, and attention-getting (five subjects in each group-commune, preschool). T-test computations were done in each category. *Results:* Commune preschoolers scored higher in "self-reliance" than town preschoolers from nuclear families. The latter scored higher in "achievement behavior" than the former. In longitudinal study, the only variable which showed change over one year was "succorance" which had become prevalent in the kindergarten (nuclear family) environment than in the commune preschool environment. *Conclusions:* The behavior of commune children does differ from that of children raised in isolated nuclear families; and these differences are stable over time even for young children.

Pretwich, Sheldon G., 1969, "The Influence of Two Counseling Methods on the Physical and Verbal Aggression of Pre-School Indian Children." Ph. D. dissertation, Arizona State University.

The purpose of this study was to: a) investigate the influence of anthropomorphic models as a therapeutic vehicle to facilitate five year old Indian children in learning to express and appropriately deal with aggressive impulses, and b) investigate the influence of group counseling with Indian mothers as it affects five year old Indian children's aggression.

Raina, T. N. and M. K. Raina, 1971, Perception of Teacher-Educators in India about the Ideal Pupil. *Journal of Educational Research* 64:303-306.

Attempted to a) determine what concepts teacher-educators in India have of the ideal student in terms of characteristics they believe should be encouraged and discouraged, and b) compare the results with concepts of teachers in the United States. Torrance's Ideal Pupil Checklist was administered to 100 teachers of education in teacher training colleges in Rajasthan. When the 62 characteristics of the Checklist were ranked, a rank-order coefficient of correlation of .76 was obtained between the ranks assigned by the Rajasthan teacher-educators and the United States teachers. In general, the Rajasthan *S*s emphasize the receptive nature of man and deemphasize man's self-acting nature more than United States teachers. (JA)

Roberts, J. M. and M. L. Forman, 1971, Riddles: Expressive Models of Interrogation. *Ethnology* 10:509.

This article attempts to present a comprehensive theory of riddles and riddling to account for uneven distribution of riddles in time and space in both cultural-historical and functional terms, for the structure and meaning of riddling patterns, the involvements of these patterns by individuals.

Rohner, Ronald P., Billie R. DeWalt and Robert C. Ness, 1973, Ethnographer Bias in Cross-Cultural Research: An Empirical Study. *Behavior Science Notes* 8:275.

We direct attention in this paper to the problem of ethnographer bias (i.e., systematic errors occurring in the ethnographic reporting process) in cross-cultural research, and therefore in ethnographic fieldwork itself. Using multiple regression and other multivariate statistics, we assess the influence of ethnographer bias on the correlation between traits in the cross-cultural survey component of Rohner's Rejection-Acceptance Project (RAP). These procedures suggest a systematic ethnographer error, "the bias of romanticism," in anthropological research. Overall, however, the relationships among substantive variables in this research cannot be explained by this bias or by other forms of systematic error plaguing cross-cultural research. Thus, in the absence of a successful competing theory, we conclude that all but one of the universal causal-functional relationships postulated in Rohner's theory are validated. (AA)

Rohner, Ronald R. and Leonard Katz, 1970, Testing for Validity and Reliability in Cross-Cultural Research. *American Anthropologist* 72:1068.

A set of procedures is offered for assessing interrater reliability and certain aspects of validity of codes in cross-cultural studies. The method assumes that at least two independent raters have coded more than one trait coded by a second, and all the codings by a single rater are intercorrelated with each other. The results are presented in a multitrait-multirater matrix. From this matrix it is possible to determine the interrater reliability and discriminant validity of traits in addition to a higher order concept based on pairs of traits. (AA)

Rohrl, Vivian J., 1970. A Nutritional Factor in Windigo Psychosis. *American Anthropologist* 72:97.

This paper reviews reports of windigo psychosis, in particular those cases that are "cured" before they are "full-blown," with a view to studying evidence of an organic factor related to the development of illness. Knowledge of biological factors related to ritual behavior in different cultures is reviewed in this context, together with examples of windigo cases and relevant information about nutrition. It is indicated that the traditional "cure" of windigo symptoms, which frequently induces the ingestion of fatty meat, particularly bear meat, indicates a positively reinforced—due to beneficial effect—curing method for this condition. (AA)

Rossi, Ino, 1973, The Unconscious in the Anthropology of Claude Levi-Strauss. *American Anthropologist* 75:20.

Levi-Strauss claims that the unconscious activity of the mind is more important than the conscious one for understanding social phenomena and that the unconscious consits of an aggregate of forms which are imposed on psychological and physical content. The real inspiration of Levi-Strauss' notion is the Kantian notion of mental constraints and the postulate of isomorphism of mental and physical laws. The methodological usefulness of the unconscious as a principle of intelligibility is placed in evidence. (AA)

Samuel, T. J., 1966, The Strengthening of the Motivation for Family Limitation in India. *Journal of Family Welfare* 13:1-16.

The main factors for low "motivation" for family limitation in India are tradition, religion, and fatalism. Education, economic incentives and disincentives may be helpful. Some of these are suggested. (JA)

Schlegel, Alice, 1973, The Adolescent Socialization of the Hopi Girl. *Ethnology* 12:449.

This socio-cultural study seeks to prove that a crisis of adolescence of the Hopi girl, which might be brought about by existing restrictions placed upon her by her mother and the need to find a husband, does not occur to the same extent as in Western culture, nor does the stage of adolescence lack moodiness, intergenerational conflict, or anxiety over sex and love as in Margaret Mead's Samoan studies. The explanation from this is that there are no conflicting standards or alternative choices leading to dilemmas, and the "crisis" of the Hopi girl is comprehensible within the context of the socialization process.

Shweder, Richard A., 1973, The Between and Within of Cross-Cultural Research. *Ethos* 1:531.

Purpose: An analysis of data that indicates a discrepancy between across unit and within unit findings and discusses the possibility that valid cross-cultural variables are intraculturally inappropriate. *Method and Data:* The structure of Rorschach test response categories and social behavior in small groups. *Conclusion:* By suggesting that under certain conditions cross-cultural and intra-cultural research are not mutually relevant. There are two modes of comparative cultural research: (1) cross-cultural population sample is selected and correlations across this sample of cultures are used to test hypotheses and discover universal dimensions of variations. (2) A comparative intra-cultural replication is performed and the correlations within each of a number of cultures are used to test hypotheses and discover universal dimensions or variation. For reasons other than "problems of measurement" all known cultures may not differ in the same ways. Valid indicators of a theoretical variable may be discovered within any of them, or may be discovered within each of all cultures without being discovered across them.

Siegmann, Aron W, 1966, Father Absence During Early Childhood and Anti-Social Behavior. *Journal of Abnormal Psychology* 71(1):71-74.

Parsons's suggestion that difficulties in achieving adequate sex-role identification is a significant source of male antisocial behavior leads to the hypothesis that father absence during early childhood will be related to antisocial acting out. A comparison of the responses of eighty-one "father-absent" male medical students to an anonymously administered antisocial behavior scale with those of eighty-nine comparable "father-present" students supports the hypothesis. (JA)

Skea, Susan, Juris G. Draguns and Leslie Phillips, 1969, Ethnic Characteristics of Psychiatric Symptomology within and across Regional Groupings: A Study of an Israeli Child Guidance Clinic Population. *Israel Annals of Psychiatry and Related Disciplines* 7:31-42.

Compared discrete manifestations and inclusive categories of symptomatology between socioeconomically and educationally matched groups of boys of Iraqi, Yeminite, German, and Polish parentage in a child guidance clinic. Attempts were also made to compare smaller, unmatched groups of girls. Results reveal differences in psychopathological expression among all the groups. Middle Eastern boys tended toward overtly expressed maladaptive and aggressive behavior, while ideational and self-directed symptomatology predominated among the European boys. Within each of the two regions, boys of Iraqi parentage differed from Yeminites in more direct and explicit expression of aggression, and boys of Polish extraction exceeded those of German background in avoidance of and withdrawal from social contact. Results obtained with girls were not parallel to those observed in boys and need fuller investigation. (JA)

Sommerlad, Elizabeth A. and W. P. Bellingham, 1972, Cooperation-Competition: A Comparison of Australian, European and Aboriginal School Children. *Journal of Cross-Cultural Psychology* 3:149.

Australian, European, and full-blood Aboriginal school children were assigned to groups of four individuals who performed a task in which cooperation maximized and competition minimized reward. The Aboriginal sample showed significantly more cooperative responses than the European sample, with individuals in the stream preparing for secondary education showing more competitive behavior than those continuing post-primary courses emphasizing manual training and domestic science. The role of kinship as a determinant of cooperation was investigated, but Aborigines from the same tribe with reciprocal kinship obligations failed to be more cooperative than those Aborigines from different tribes.

Stephens, William N., 1972, A Cross-Cultural Study of Modesty. *Behavior Science Notes* 7(1):1-28.

This cross-cultural survey of sex customs treats sexual modesty in clothing and speech, privacy for intercourse, ceremonial license, and joking and avoidance. Sexual modesty is found to be uncorrelated with a number of sex taboos but positively correlated with the attempt to confine sexual intercourse within marriage. This combination of sex restrictions, termed modesty-chastity, is very much the property of peasant societies, as opposed to primitive societies. The most sexually free cases in the sample tend to have a narrowly genital orientation to sex and to be preoccupied with sexual jokes and obscenity. The conclusion lists a full range of sex restrictions and sexual fears and proposes a germinal sex problem, best accounted for in Freudian terms. (JA)

Tanaka, Yasumasa, 1972, Values in the Subjective Culture: A Social Psychological View. *Journal of Cross-Cultural Psychology* 3:57.

Using POLDI (a variation of the semantic differential method) as a measuring instrument, evidence was shown that there is the subtle but real cultural uniqueness of evaluative criteria despite the overall consistency in the semantic frame of reference when Japanese and German *Ss* judged a set of nation concepts. Next, Evaluative Atlases of several critical concepts were constructed on the basis of data collected in 15 language/culture communities by means of multilingual semantic differentials, and comparisons were made among the 15 communities. Finally, a plan of intercultural cooperation was proposed, in that the responsibility of social and behavioral scientists is stressed for both making up and executing plans for the engineering of such intercultural cooperation.

Urbina, Susana and Alan Grey, 1975, Cultural and Sex Differences in the Sex Distribution of Dream Characters. *Journal of Cross-Cultural Psychology* 6(3):358-364.

The validity of previous reports regarding sex differences in ratio of male characters in dreams was investigated. Eight dreams were obtained for each of 192 college students in Lima, Peru, and New York City. Odd-even reliabilities for male dream characters ranged from .36 to .72. U.S. subjects had a higher percentage of male dream characters than the Peruvians (p less than .01). U.S. males had a greater percentage of men in their dreams than U.S. females; in Peru the sex difference was reversed. (p less than .01). These findings contradict previous reports of males universally dreaming more about men than do females, attributed by Hall to oedipal conflicts. Present results allow the conclusion that sex differences in the percentage of male characters in dreams are not universal. Differences in the sex ratio of dream characters more likely reflect sociocultural differences in contact between the sexes. (JA)

Watson, Lawrence C., 1972, Sexual Socialization in Guajiro Society. *Ethnology* 11:150.

In Guajiro society there is an apparent relationship between severe socialization of female sexual behavior and the demands made on a woman's behavior by the institution of marriage, the success of which has a bearing on the ability of her family to maintain its status in society and to contract useful political alliances. Severe socialization is functionally adapted to these demands because it produces negative fixation in the sexual system, which in turn acts as a psychic monitoring device to discourage the unmarried girl from experimenting sexually and thereby increases the likelihood that she will remain sexually chaste, marry well, and be potentially valuable to her lineage for cementing a political alliance.

Weigert, Andrew J. and Darwin L. Thomas, 1970, Socialization and Religiosity: A Cross-National Analysis of Catholic Adolescents. *Sociometry* 33:305-326.

Relates dimensions of religiosity (belief, experience, knowledge, and practice) to adolescents' perception of the control and support received from parents. A total of 740 *S*s were chosen from 4 urban male Catholic schools in the United States, Puerto Rico, and Mexico. Except for the Mexican sample and the knowledge dimension, the apriori hypothesis that adolescents perceiving a high (low) degree of control and support score highest (lowest) on religiosity is moderately verified, mainly because of a positive relationship between support and religiosity, although control is noticeably related in the Puerto Rican sample. For the Anglo samples, the usefulness of socialization variables in understanding religiosity is demonstrated, and the differences across samples point to the importance of reasons for religious behavior. (JA)

Whittaker, James O. and S. J. Whittaker, 1972, A Cross-Cultural Study of Geocentrism. *Journal of Cross-Cultural Psychology* 3:417.

College students in the United States, Argentina, Fiji, India, and New Zealand were asked to draw a map of the world in 10 minutes, putting in as much detail as possible. Maps were examined for number of countries, and other detials. Geocentrism seems to be reflected in the fact that one's own country is almost always disproportionately large, and it also seems to be reflected in the fact that neighboring countries always tend to be drawn on the map.

Whiting, John W.M., 1959, Sorcery, Sin and the Superego: A Cross-Cultural Study of Some Mechanisms of Social Control. *Nebraska Symposium on Motivation* 1959:174-194.

This article critically examines three essentially independent motivational systems found in societies over the world: (a) sorcery, the exaggerated and paranoid fear of retaliation from other humans, (b) sin, the sense of sin deriving from the projected dread of punishment by gods or ghosts, and (c) the superego, the sense of guilt and readiness to accept blame deriving from a sense of personal responsibility for one's actions.

Wittmer, Joe, 1970, Homogeneity of Personality Characters: A Comparison between Old Order Amish and Non-Amish. *American Anthropologist* 72:1063.

The purpose of this study was to compare the variability of measured personality characteristics of twenty-five Amish and twenty-five non-Amish male youth, between the ages of eighteen and twenty-one, from the same community. This study assumed that the homogeneous nature of the Amish culture would predetermine greater similarity of personality among the Amish youth. The findings indicate that the aspect of personality similarity was significantly greater for the Amish group on nine of sixteen measures of personality. The findings were discussed in light of the Amish culture.

Wohlford, Paul, John Sanstrock, Stephen Berger and David Liberman, 1971, Older Brothers' Influence on Sex-typed Aggressive and Dependent Behavior in Father-Absent Children. *Developmental Psychology* 4(2):124-134.

The role of the older male sibling as a potential surrogate male role model for father-absent children was explored using sixty-six impoverished black preschool boys and girls as subjects. The variables of masculinity-femininity, aggression, and dependency were assessed by two instruments, the doll-play interview and the maternal interview. Children with older male siblings were significantly more aggressive on the maternal interview aggression score, less frequently, and less intensely dependent on both dependency measures than children with no older male siblings. The presence or absence of older female siblings did not affect the older brother's influence. While there were also some significant main effects of sex, the sibling x sex interaction effects were nonsignificant.

ETHNICITY AND CULTURE CONTACT

Anant, Santokh S., 1970, Self- and Mutual-Perception of Salient Personality Traits of Different Caste Groups. *Journal of Cross-Cultural Psychology* 1:41.

As part of a project to study the changing inter-caste attitudes in India, 239 urban subjects, belonging to four traditional Hindu castes and Harijan castes (former "Untouchables"), checked five traits (from a list of 88) most characteristic of their own and other groups. A comparison of results with similar studies conducted earlier points to the fading of earlier sterotypes about castes. The picture of one's own caste was often similar to the perception of that caste by other castes, indicating a general acceptability of some of the caste-stereotypes. The higher castes still show resistance to relinquish age-old prejudices against the lower castes. (AA)

Averill, James R., Edward M. Option, Jr. and Richard Lazarus, 1969, Cross-Cultural Studies of Psychophysiological Responses During Stress and Emotion. *International Journal of Psychology* 4:82-102

Within a theoretical framework that considers emotions in terms of stimulus properties, appraisers and related sub-systems and response categories, experimental data on emotion can be fruitfully studied. Data gathered from Japanese and American *S*s who watched a sub-incision film yielded similar results, with the exception of differences in skin conductance, and the tendency of Japanese *S*s to respond physiologically at the same level throughout, in contrast to their American counterparts. Current investigations proceed along lines of exploring expressive reactions and interpersonal relations in stress and emotions. Similarities discovered between cultures deserve emphasis, "for ultimately it is only in terms of pancultural psychological processes that differences can be interpreted."

Baldauf, Richard B. and Harold I. Ayabe, 1977, Acculturation and Educational Achievement in American Samoan Adolescents. *Journal of Cross-Cultural Psychology* 8(2):241-256.

The relationship of educational achievement to overt (the directly observable) and covert (the psychological) measures of acculturation was explored for 190 high school seniors from American Samoa using canonical variate analysis. Three statistically significant and situationally interpretable relationships were found to exist between the overt and covert sets of variables, indicating that multiple acculturative approaches were operating simultaneously within Samoan adolescent culture. Educational achievement was found to be related mainly to the modern man approach to acculturation, the only approach to cross-validate. The study emphasized the probable multivariate nature of the acculturation process and the importance of verifying hypothesis through cross-validation. (JA)

Bergeron, Arthur P. and Mark P. Zanna, 1973, Group Membership and Belief Similarity as Determinants of Interpersonal Attraction in Peru. *Journal of Cross-Cultural Psychology* 4:397

College students in two universities in Arequipa, Peru rated target persons differing in terms of group membership and belief similarity on a series of scales designed to measure various aspects of interpersonal attraction. The results indicated that, whereas belief similarity was a reliable determinant of interpersonal attraction, group membership accounted for significantly more variance, even when interpersonal attraction was assessed on dimensions which imply low levels of intimacy. These results were contrasted with those obtained in the United States in connection with the so-called race versus belief controversy. The differences between the two sets of results were attributed to the strong group norms in economically less advanced countries.

Biller, Henry B., 1968, A Note on Father-Absence and Masculine Development in Lower-Class Negro and White Boys. *Child Development* 39(3):1003-1006.

Explores the relation of father absence and sociocultural background to masculine development. *S*s were twenty-nine six-year-old lower-class Negro and white boys. In terms of projective sex-role orientation (Brown's IT Scale), white father-present boys were the most masculine; there was no significant difference between white father-absent and Negro father-present boys; and Negro father-absent boys were the least masculine. No significant differences relating to either direct sex-role preference or teacher's rating of masculinity on a multidimensional scale were found. The results suggested that underlying sex-role orientation is more influenced by father availability and family background than are more manifest aspects of masculinity. (JA)

Carment, David W. and T. R. Paliwal, 1970, Correlates of Birth Control Practices in India. *Journal of Cross-Cultural Psychology* 4:111.

Scores on Rotter's I-E scale, attitudes regarding contraception, and other personal and familial data were obtained from vasectomized and nonvasectomized factory workers in urban North India. It was found that those in favor of contraception were more internal than those against. I-E scores did not differentiate between the vasectomiz-ed and nonvasectomized, but the vasectomized, as compared to the nonvasectomized, had more living children and more male than female children. There was some suggestion as well that those who had alone made the decision to be vasectomized were more likely to perceive the outcome as negative than were those who had made a joint decision with their wives. Finally, it was noted that a greater pro-portion of Sikhs than Hindus supported contraception.

Caudill, William, 1973, The Influence of Social Structure and Culture on Human Behavior in Modern Japan. *Ethos* 3:343.

This article presents some ideas on the effects of social and cultural change on psychological adjustment in Japan. It is based on a review of literature written in the last 100 years on Japanese national character, with special emphasis on the psychological and behavioral characteristics that seem to have persisted from the past and remain viable in modern Japanese life.

Chawla, Tilak R., 1970, Cultural Factors and Kahn Intelligence Test. *Indian Psychological Review* 6:77-79.

Examined the culture-free characteristics of the Kahn In-telligence Tests (KIT). The KIT was administered to 154 public school children in India—82 boys and 72 girls. Analysis of data using analysis of variance showed that groups of *S*s coming from different subcultures, i.e., rural vs. urban, socioeconomic levels, language groups, and sex, did not differ significantly in their IQ scores. The findings suggest that scores on the KIT are not influenced by cultural ecology. (JA)

Christozov, Christo, 1970, Schizophrenia in North Africa Examined from the Viewpoint of Transcultural Psychiatry. *Annales Medico-Psychologiques* 1:521-554.

Studies 260 male *S*s hospitalized in Morocco on individual, familial, and collective levels with respect to age, family status, number of offspring, occupation, residence characteristics, duration and number of hospitalizations, neurologic condition, and incidence of alcoholism, cannibalism, and syphilis to examine how ethnic, cultural, and religious peculiarities of North African society mark the clinical picture and dynamism of schizophrenia. Paranoia, followed in importance by catatonia, is the predominant form, doubtlessly representing a fundamental characteristic of North African psycho-pathology. Other clinical characteristics, as well as prognosis, are discussed in relation to their counterparts in European countries. (JA)

Cohen, Erick, 1968, "Social Images" in an Israeli Development Town. *Human Relations* 21:163-176.

Studied social images in an Israeli town to determine whether the dichotomy of higher class harmonious images and lower class conflicting images is valid. At least one further variable, the equalitarian image, should be added since not everyone perceives society hierarchically. A fourfold typology is proposed, based on a dual dichotomy: harmonious vs. conflicting and ascriptive vs. nonascriptive images. (JA)

Dawson, John L. M., William Ng and Wing Cheung, 1972, Effects of Parental Attitudes and Modern Exposure on Chinese Traditional-Modern Attitude Formation. *Journal of Cross-Cultural Psychology* 3:201.

Following recent Traditional-Modern attitude change regarding research, additional evidence to support traditional-modern attitude change hypotheses is presented, and is concerned with the relative effects of parental socialization and other modernizing influences on attitude change among groups of Hong Kong Chinese. Younger Hakka village children were found, as expected, to have significantly more traditional attitudes than other children, while their traditional-modern attitudes also correlated more highly with those of their parents. Two matched adolescent Anglo-Chinese and Chinese Secondary samples were also chosen to examine the relative effects of parental socialization and mass media on attitude change. Both parental T-M attitudes and exposure to mass media were relevant to the development of student's T-M attitudes at the Anglo-Chinese school but for the Chinese Middle school only parental T-M attitudes were relevant, not exposure to mass media. (JA)

Deshen, Shlomo, 1972, Ethnicity and Citizenship in the Ritual of an Israeli Synagogue. *Southwestern Journal of Anthropology* 28:69.

Tension between citizenship and ethnicity is expressed in an Israeli ethnic synagogue by changes in ritual and symbolism. The symbolic expression of these changes relates worshippers of the synagogue, who are recent immigrants to Israel, to their new heterogeneous environment. Analysis of the changes in symbols demonstrates that the referential aspects have expanded, consistent with alterations in traditional relationships. The reinterpreted symbols may be categorized in terms of a typology of religious change as instances of "innovation," in the sense that the experiential range to which the symbol applies has been changed. (AA)

Diop, A., 1968, Kinship and the Wolof Family. *Annales Medico Psychologiques* 2:398

Deals with developments in the traditional kinship structure of the Wolof people (Sudan and Senegal), from the matriarchal and bilateral to the patriarchal system, as a result of Islamic influence. Wolof family organization is also studied within the context of changes due to colonization and the expediency of a monetary economy, focusing on how the traditional family gradually breaks up to make way for couples, even in rural areas. (JA)

Douglas, Mary, 1968, The Relevance of Tribal Studies. *Journal of Psychosomatic Research* 12:21-28.

Insight into tribal rituals can be found by studying their social dimensions. The two main functions of tribal rituals are coercion in social situations and the expression of a vision of the essential nature of society. The central problem of interpretation of the ritual is the relation between individual psychological needs and public social needs. The public ritual expresses the latter public concern and not the former individual concern. Illustrations are provided by general reproductive rituals. (JA)

DuPeez, Peter and D. G. Ward, 1970, Personal Constructs of Modern and Traditional Xhosa. *Journal of Social Psychology* 82:149-160.

Based on data gathered from 40 working adults and 40 youths, several differences were found between modern and traditional Xhosa. Members of the modern group showed greater homogeneity in construing themselves, used more permeable constructs which covered wider ranges of events, and had the self and ideal self more closely related than in the traditional group. The greater diversity of self-constructs in the traditional group is taken to imply that it is falling apart, and that there is low agreement about how members ought to see themselves, a conclusion which is confirmed by the low self-ideal correlations in this group. (JA)

Edgerton, Robert, B., 1971, A Traditional African Psychiatrist, *Southwestern Journal of Anthropology* 27:259.

Accounts of African ethnopsychiatry have typically emphasized suggestion and the placebo effect. In this account of a Hehe traditional psychiatrist from Tanzania, these considerations are important, but of equal importance is his emphasis upon botanical and pharmacological empiricism. Despite the fact that his epistemology of mental illness is developed within a belief system that emphasizes witchcraft and moral magic, and although he has become expert in dealing with such supernatural considerations, he is primarily a pragmatic psychopharmacologist. His devotion to empiricism in botany and pharmacology, while unusual among his people, may nevertheless have historical antecedents among the Hehe and may be more common throughout African ethnopsychiatry than has yet been recognized. This African psychiatrist—like so many of the men who built Western psychiatry—serves to remind us that even within a supernatural belief system the beginnings of science may emerge. (AA)

Edgerton, Robert, B. and Marvin Karno, 1971, Mexican-American Bilingualism and the Perception of Mental Illness. *Archives of General Psychiatry* 24:286-290.

Presented a household survey interview to 444 Mexican-Americans and 224 Anglo-Americans on beliefs and perceptions of mental illness. The two groups did not differ significantly, but there were significant differences within the Mexican-American group. *Ss* who completed the interview in Spanish differed from those who took it in English in beliefs on (a) depression, (b) juvenile delinquency, (c) the inheritance of mental illness, (d) the effectiveness of prayer, and (e) the value of familistic orientation. Results suggest that the more commonly described cultural traits of the Mexican-American are most applicable to those who speak only or mostly Spanish. Findings indicate "the need for mental health professionals who possess both fluency in Spanish and sensitive understanding of the culture of the Mexican-American poor." (JA)

El-Islam, M. Fakhr and Samia A. Ahmed, 1971, Traditional Interpretation and Treatment of Mental Illness in an Arab Psychiatric Clinic. *Journal of Cross-Cultural Psychology* 2:301.

Traditional interpretations of beliefs commonly entertained and rituals commonly practiced among a sample of 153 Arab psychiatric patients were studied. Ritual practice associated significantly with illiteracy and with the presence of observable disorders of behavior. This interpretations-ritual relationship is not, however, of a one-to-one nature. The belief that general physical weakness is the cause of psychogenic symptoms is exposed and its implications for therapy are discussed from the traditional and medico-psychological angles. (JA)

Feaster, J. Gerald, 1968, Measurement and Determinants of Innovativeness among Primitive Agriculturists. *Rural Sociology* 33:339-348.

Investigated the innovativeness of "shifting cultivators," who were Mayan Indians in British Honduras. Attitude statements were used to construct both an innovation and a traditional scale. It was assumed that those favoring the statements in the innovation scale were implicitly expressing a willingness to internalize values demanded by a nontraditional agriculture, and those scoring positively in the traditionalism scale were apathetic toward changes in their way of life. In general, the shifting cultivators had favorable attitudes toward innovation. Results of multiple regression analyses show that age, education, level of living, contact with extension agents, and aspirations were significant variables related to the modification of traditional attitudes. (JA)

Feldman, David H. and Winston Markwalder, 1971, Systematic Scoring of Ranked Distractors for the Assessment of Piagetian Reasoning Levels. *Educational and Psychological Measurement* 31:347-362.

Attempted to determine if a map reading test could be used to assess both a child's map reading skill and his level of reasoning ability according to Piaget's theory of cognitive development. The latter would be assessed by the analysis of the child's choice of distractors. A new instrument for measuring spatial reasoning was designed and validated based on conceptual analysis of a geographic map. All 25 items were designed to induce responses indicative of the 4 reasoning levels suggested by Piaget. The sample included 270 5th, 7th and 9th graders evenly distributed across 3 different ethnic groups (Black, white, and Chinese). The results tend to indicate that the instrument devised may be capable of measuring reasoning stage levels as well as map achievement. Results also show that children of different ethnic backgrounds tend to go through the same set of developmental stages and that children of specific developmental levels tend to select distractor indications of that level. (JA)

Friedman, Neil, 1969, Africa and the Afro-American: The Changing Negro Identity. *Psychiatry* 32:127-136.

Advances the theory that the emergence of Africa on the international scene, as well as the interest in African history without the colonial veil, gives the American Negro a new positive identification. Previously the identity of blacks was characterized by negative images, but now it is becoming more positive because of an improved view of Africa and the position of the black man as a serious figure in the political world. (JA)

Garber, Malcolm, 1968, "Ethnicity and Measures of Educability: Differences among Navajo, Pueblo and Rural Spanish American First Graders on Measures of Learning Style, Hearing Vocabulary, Entry Skills, Motivation and Home Environment Processes." Ph.D. dissertation, University of Southern California.

A battery of psychological tests were given to 65 Navajo, 65 rural Spanish-American, and 75 Pueblo children including the following:

(1) The Illinois Test of Psycholinguistic Ability; (2) The Peabody Picture Vocabulary Test; (3) The Preschool Inventory; (4) A nonstandard entry skill scale; (5) A set of Motivation items related to self-esteem, mother-father identification, reward preference, locus of control and test/school anxiety. The parents of the children were interviewed with the Environmental Process Characteristics Questionnaire. The measures were selected on the basis that educationally relevant prescriptions could be generated. These prescriptions should assist in the facilitation of English language arts skills development for the culturally divergent groups of children studied. The major null hypothesis was that there would be no differences among the Navajo, Pueblo, and Rural Spanish first graders along the following general dimensions: Learning Style, English Language, Hearing Vocabulary, Entry Skills, Motivation, and Environmental Process Characteristics. Each one of these dimensions was measured using the above mentioned tests. There was enough similarity within each group studied to plan educational programs for each group as a class rather than for each individual in the group. However, each group was substantially different, suggesting separate curricular planning for each group as a class rather than for each individual in the group. (JA)

Gardiner, Harry W. and Dalad Lematawekul, 1970, Second-Generation Chinese in Thailand: A study of Ethnic Identification. *Journal of Cross-Cultural Psychology* 1:333.

This study investigated the ethnic identification of second-generation Chinese in Thailand. One hundred and seventy-six adolescents 14-18 years of age (92 males, 84 females) were separated into (1) those who used Chinese family names and those who used Thai family names and (2) those who had attended Chinese schools and those who had not attended such schools. The following measures were employed: Behavioral Differential Scale, Assimilation-Orientation Inventory, California Fascism Scale, Conformity Scale, and the Gough-Sanford Rigidity Scale. It was hypothesized that (1) second generation Chinese who used Chinese family names would have a higher degree of identification with Chinese than those who used Thai family names; (2) those who had attended Chinese schools would identify more closely with Chinese than those who had not attended such schools; and (3) scores on the F-scale, C-scale, and R-scale would be positively correlated with the degree of Chinese identification. Analysis of results indicates support for the first two hypotheses but not for the third. Possible areas of future research are suggested. (JA)

Goldschmidt, Walter, 1973, Guilt and Pollution in Sebei Mortuary Rituals. *Ethos* 1:75.

This analysis of Sebei death ceremonials deals directly with the interplay between the private motivations of the individual and the structural context within which they operate. The symbolic meaning of the rituals themselves is thus seen as mediating between the private and internal psychological tensions and the public demands that are made upon the persons.

Grey-Little, Bernadette, 1973, The Salience of Negative Information in Impression Formation Among Two Danish Samples. *Journal of Cross-Cultural Psychology* 4:193.

Two Danish samples were asked to rate an unknown other based on two descriptions, one containing praiseworthy and the other reproachable behaviors. With both samples, negative descriptions had a delayed disproportionate effect on the impression formed. The results for Danish subjects are similar to those found with Americans in spite of broad social and cultural differences which would seem to militate against this similarity. (AA)

Guthrie, George M., 1977, A Social-Psychological Analysis of Modernization in the Philippines. *Journal of Cross-Cultural Psychology* 8(2):177-206.

Four field studies of aspects of modernization in the Philippines are summarized: transitory ownership of space in a city, the development of the fishing industry in a provincial town, the practices of market vendors, and the development of modern attitudes. Processes of change and resistance are interpreted with reference to laboratory studies of cross-situational consistency, gaming strategies, avoidance learning, and operant conditioning. (JA)

Harrison, Robert H. and Edward H. Kass, 1968, MMPI Correlates of Negro Acculturation in a Northern City. *Journal of Personality and Social Psychology* 10:262-270.

Compared MMPI data from three groups of pregnant women living in a northern city: Negroes born in the south (SN), Negroes born in the north (NN), and whites born in the north (W). Five of sixteen MMPI scales, twenty of twenty race-sensitive factor scales, and 166 of the 550 MMPI items differentiated among groups at statistically significant levels. The NN group was halfway between the SN and W groups on the majority and items examined. Results are interpreted as reflecting a process of Negro acculturation to the predominantly white urban society.

Hess, Robert D. and Virginia C. Shipman, 1965, Early Experience and the Socialization of Cognitive Modes in Children. *Child Development* 36(4):869-886.

What is cultural deprivation and how does it act to shape and depress the resources of the human mind? The arguments presented are: (1) The behavior which leads to social, educational, and economic poverty is socialized in early childhood. (2) The central quality involved is a lack of cognitive meaning in the mother-child communication system. (3) The growth of cognitive processes is fostered in family control systems which offer a wide range of alternatives of action and thought; such growth is constricted by systems of control which offer predetermined solutions and few alternatives. Data on *Ss* studied—160 Negro mothers and their four-year-old children selected from four different social status levels—support the arguments. (JA)

Hetherington, E. Mavis, 1966, Effects of Paternal Absence on Sex-Typed Behaviors in Negro and White Pre-Adolescent Males. *Journal of Personality and Social Psychology* 4(1):87-91.

Investigates the effects of race, father-absence, and time of departure of the father on sex-typed behaviors of preadolescent males, if the father left after the age of five, sex-typed behaviors are similar to those of boys from homes in which the father is present; however, if the father left in the first four years of life, considerable disruption of these behaviors is found. Both groups of boys with fathers absent are significantly more dependent on their peers than father-present boys. The only racial difference obtained indicated that Negro boys participate more in competitive activities involving force than do white boys. (JA)

Hill, Clifford A., 1977, A Review of the Language Deficit Position: Some Sociolinguistic and Psycholinguistic Perspectives. *IRCD Bulletin* 12(4).

The author outlines Basil Bernstein's theory of restricted and elaborated speech codes and explains Bereiter and Engelmann's use of this theory to support their own language deficit position. He then proceeds to review the major criticisms of this position. The sociolinguistic criticisms question the use of norms of written discourse to judge oral response and a lack of knowledge concerning the actual verbal skills of the informants in everyday communication. The psycholinguistic criticisms challenge the assumption that nonstandard forms of language reflect deficient cognition and the use of an inadequately conceived theory of reference in evaluating language performance.

Hoffman, Michel, 1970, Toward a Typology of Attitudes and Aspirations of Young Africans Who are Faced with Modernization. *Revue Internationale de Sociologie* 6:147-159.

Interview Data Collected in 1968 from 1,000 fifteen to thirty year old young Africans were organized into a typology of attitudes toward modernization. Questions dealt with current social changes, transitional difficulties, traditional customs, and the modern nation. Based on descriptions of a "successful acquaintance," three types emerged: those with no such model (predominantly illiterate, rural and female), those with an agrarian village model (27%), and those with a modernized success model (43%). Within these types, subgroups were distinguished according to life satisfaction or discontent.(JA)

Hsu, Francis L. K., 1973, Prejudice and Its Intellectual Effect in American Anthropology: An Ethnographic Report. *American Anthropologist* 75:1.

This article deals with some deep forms of prejudice in American anthropology in terms of its dominant ideas and its products. The foundation of this prejudice seems to be Western individualism. It expresses itself by excluding contrary ideas from its public forums and by elaborating and escalating ideas in conformity with it. In spite of its cross-cultural protestations, American anthropology will become White American anthropology unless our fraternity consciously takes a more open-minded approach to other competing assumptions—rooted in other cultures—about man and what makes him run. There is a world of difference between a truly cross-cultural science of man and a White centered science of man with cross-cultural decorations. (AA)

Inkeles, Alex, 1977, Understanding and Misunderstanding Individual Modernity. *Journal of Cross-Cultural Psychology* 8(2):135-176.

A number of issues have arisen from the publication of *Becoming Modern* by Inkeles and Smith. This paper raises each issue in turn and attempts to support the major assertions of that sutdy. Included are the reasons for studying the individual, the role of personality characteristics, the personal features of modernity, the universality and empirical status of the concept, some sources of individual modernity, relationships between modernity, stress, and alienation, the contrast between modernity and traditionalism, and the consequences of individual modernity for one's society. (JA)

Iwai, Hiroshi and David K. Reynolds, 1970, Morita Therapy: The Views from the West. *American Journal of Psychiatry* 126:1031-1036.

Discusses various Western interpretations of Morita therapy, a Japanese method of treating neurosis. The divergences of opinion are approached through 5 topics, including the relationship of Morita therapy with Zen Buddhism and its emphasis on bed rest and work therapy. It is concluded that personal and social background and research setting influence differing understandings of Morita therapy. (JA)

Jamias, Maria F., Renato Y. Pablo and Donald M. Taylor, 1971, Ethnic Awareness in Filipino Children. *Journal of Social Psychology* 83:157-164.

Investigated Filipino children's self-perception in terms of ethnic identity and assessed how accurately they recognized sketches of persons representing two important out-groups, i.e., Americans and Chinese. Each of the 90 Tagalog male *S*s (6, 8, and 10 year old) was administered a picture identification test designed to assess *S*s ethnic affiliation. Results demonstrate that the frequency of identifying with an ethnic group increased with age and that children identified more often with their regional group than with the national group. *S*s were more accurate in recognizing Chinese pictures than those representing Americans, implying that accuracy of ethnic perception is related to the frequency of contact with the group. (JA)

Jayagopal, Rajabather, 1970, "Problem Solving Abilities and Psychomotor Skills of Navajo Indians, Spanish Americans and Anglos in Junior High School." Ph.D. dissertation, University of New Mexico.

The purpose of this study was to investigate the problem solving abilities of Navajo Indians, Spanish Americans and Anglos in two schools of Albuquerque, using WISC performance subtests as criterion measures and including the five psychomotor skills, perception, visual set, emotional set, physical set and fine motor acts as predictor variables at intra- and inter-ethnic levels.

Jones, Pauline A., 1977, The Validity of Traditional-Modern Attitude Measures. *Journal of Cross-Cultural Psychology* 8(2):207-239.

This paper presents findings of analyses of the intercorrelations of items from five traditional-modern (T-M) attitude scales, and of correlations of the items with background variables assumed to be indicators of modernism in values. It also reports findings relating T-M values to students' educational aspirations and achievement. In general, the findings demonstrate a closer association between modernism in values and educational achievement and aspirations than between modernism and community, parental and family background variables. The discussion points to the importance of using both the factorial analyses of the inter-item correlations and the "predictive validity" coefficients as complementary empirical evidence for moving toward both the refinement of a theoretical conception of modernity and the revision of measures of modern attitudes. (JA)

Kagan, Spencer and Millard C. Madsen, 1971, Co-operation and Competition of Mexican, Mexican-American, and Anglo-American Children of Two Ages under Four Instructional Sets. *Developmental Psychology* 5(1):32-39.

A game measuring cooperation and competition was played with pairs of four to five-year-old Anglo- and Mexican-Americans and with seven to nine-year-old, Anglo-Americans, Mexican-Americans, and Mexicans. Cooperative play allowed both pair members to receive rewards; competitive play was irrational, allowing no subject to reach his goal. The number of moves pairs took to reach a goal indicated that four to five-year-olds were more cooperative than the older subjects. Among the seven to nine-year-olds, Mexicans were most cooperative, Mexican-Americans next most, and Anglo-Americans least cooperative. Among the older children, instructional sets designed to create an "I" orientation increased competition, whereas sets stressing a "we" orientation increased cooperation. Qualitative differences between patterns of play were noted for the cultural and age groups. Sex differences were not found. (JA)

Kagitcibasi, Cigdem, 1973, Psychological Aspects of Modernization in Turkey. *Journal of Cross-Cultural Psychology* 4:157.

Attitudinal, aspirational, familial, and social structural variables were assessed among Turkish high school students. Two main personality types emerged. Type 1, the traditional, was characterized by core authoritarianism, anomia, pessimism about personal future, belief in external control of reinforcement, and religious orientation. Type 2, the modern, was characterized by optimism about personal future, belief in internal control of reinforcement, and achievement orientation. Type 2 was found to develop in a family atmosphere characterized by affection, whereas Type 1 was associated with family control. Family control, in turn, was found to be more characteristic of immobile, lower-SES homes. Thus, social structural variables affected attitudinal dispositions, and specifically modernity, through the mediating role of the family. Sex differences in modernity were also observed. (AA)

Kelly, Richard, Raymond Cazabon, Charles Fisher and Roger Laroque, 1970, Ethnic Origin and Psychiatric Disorders in a Hospitalized Population. *Canadian Psychiatric Association Journal* 15:177-182.

Explored the relationship between ethnic origin and the incidence of different types of psychiatric disorders within a hospitalized Canadian population. Results indicate differences in the distribution of patients among the major diagnostic classifications as a function of ethnic background. In the male population, *S*s of British origin showed a higher incidence of alcoholism and a lower incidence of psychosis than *S*s of French and other backgrounds. Among the males diagnosed as psychotic, *S*s of French and other backgrounds showed a larger percentage of schizophrenic reactions and smaller percentage of affective psychosis among the *S*s of other origins. Several tentative hypotheses are offered. It is felt that the major significance of the findings is the indication that the Canadian population offers potential for research into the relationship between cultural factors and mental illness. (JA)

Kennedy, John G., 1969, Psychosocial Dynamics of Witchcraft Systems. *International Journal of Social Psychiatry* 15:165-178.

Based on the arguments presented, "it no longer seems useful to perpetrate the anthropological notion of witchcraft as a 'positive philosphy' which functions to maintain social order and continuity." It is also argued that "witchcraft systems are forms of institutionalized patterns of psychopathology which tend to be pathogenic...and which create built-in self-perpetrating stress systems." An attempt is made "to indicate how witchcraft systems as a consequence of their inherent psycho-social dynamics tend to regularly generate the hate and aggression which they allegedly function to relieve...The modern witchfinding movements of Africa are concrete evidence of the intense psychosocial stress potentially inherent within witchcraft systems." (JA)

King, Michael and Johanna King, 1971, Some Correlates of University Performance in a Developing Country: The Case of Ethiopia. *Journal of Cross-Cultural Psychology* 2:293.

Language background, educational background, and scores on a variety of achievement and aptitude tests were examined for their relation to the first semester performance of 1,123 freshman students at the Haile Selassie I University in Ethiopia. Among the test data, proficiency in English language skills was most strongly related to university grades. Scores from tests requiring skill in the official Ethiopian language, Amharic, predicted poorly to university performance, and tests of mathematic-numerical ability showed moderate to weak predictive utility. The only language or educational background data related to performance was educational mobility, the students' tendency to move to areas of greater educational resources during their pre-university education. This mobility was interpreted as reflecting strong motiviation for education, a factor which deserves further research attention.

Kloskowska, Antonina, 1966, Symbolization Process and Social Interaction: Towards the Definition of the Sociology of Culture. *Polish Sociological Bulletin* 2:8–19.

Discusses the theoretical relationships between the spheres of social and cultural phenomena as a critical point in determining the object of a sociology of culture. This dichotomy is then reduced to the establishment of three models to describe the relations between social interaction and the symbolization process toward defining the sociology of communication. It is concluded that a definition of the sociology of culture requires the conceptualization of continual exchange between personal interaction on one hand, and genetic and communicative symbolization on the other. (JA).

Knight, George P. and Spencer Kagan, 1977, Acculturation of Prosocial and Competitive Behaviors among Second and Third Generation Mexican-American Children. *Journal of Cross-Cultural Psychology* 8(3):273-284.

To determine the direction of acculturation of prosocial and competitive behaviors among Mexican-American children, a behavioral choice card was administered to second- and third-generation Mexican-American children in a "traditional" Mexican-American community. Increasing generation level was associated with decreasing frequency of altruism/group enhancement and equality choices and increasing frequency of rivalry/superiority choices, supporting an acculturation to the majority rather than acculturation to the barrio model. (JA)

Kraemer, Alfred J., 1969, The Development of Cultural Self-Awareness: Design of a Program of Instruction. *HumRRO Professional Paper* 27-69.

Describes the design of a training process for developing cultural self-awareness, i.e., awareness of the cultural nature of one's own cognitions. Spontaneous interactions of Americans with foreigners in simulated on-the-job encounters are video-taped. Different behavioral manifestations of particular cognitions and their relation to American cultural premises and values are shown in sequences of video-taped excerpts used for training. The training is intended to enhance the effectiveness of United States personnel in overseas assignments. (JA)

Kraus, Robert F., 1968, Cross-Cultural Validation of Psychoanalytic Theories of Depression. *Pennsylvania Psychiatric Quarterly* 8:24-33.

Reviews a study on the Ashanti of central Ghana by M. J. Field, relating organic, social, and multiple cultural factors which produce psychological susceptibility to depression among Ashanti women. An overview of the culture emphasizing changes occasioned by the disruptive force of European and Christian influence producing an unstable social system is presented. Depression literature is reviewed in relation to the ethnographic data. (JA)

Kubany, Edward S., Ronald Gallimore and Judith Buell, 1970, The Effects of Extrinsic Factors on Achievement-Oriented Behavior: A Non-Western Case. *Journal of Cross-Cultural Psychology* 1:77.

It has been suggested that the Western conception of intrinsic motivation may be irrelevant among cultures which attach significance to group acceptance. To test this hypothesis, Filipino high school boys in Hawaii were asked to perform a task either in the presence of the experimenter or in anonymous privacy. Pretask instructions implied that striving to do well is highly desirable. As predicted, subjects in the public condition showed more achievement-oriented behavior (greater preference for a moderately difficult task). The results were discussed in terms of a distinction between intrinsic and extrinsic motivation and in terms of the effects of situational variables upon achievement-oriented behavior. (JA)

Lammers, Donald M., 1969, "Self-Concepts of American Indian Adolescents Having Segregated and Desegregated Elementary Backgrounds." Ed.D. dissertation, Syracuse University.

The Purpose of this study was to compare the self concepts and academic achievement of two select groups of Onondaga Indians (one group educated in a segregated elementary school and the other in a desegregated elementary school) and a select group of white students attending junior high school. In view of the findings of the study, the following conclusions can be stated: (1) There is evidence to indicate that significant differences in obtained elementary school grade point averages do exist among segregated Indian, desegregated Indian, and white students. In comparing the three groups, the median grade point average in order from lowest to highest was desegregated Indians, segregated Indians, and whites. (2) There is no significant evidence to indicate that, as measured by the Self-Social Symbols Tasks and Self-Concept of Ability Scale, differences exist in terms of self concept among segregated Indian, desegregated Indian, and white students. (3) There is evidence to indicate that significant differences in class ranking, as measured by a class ranking instrument, do exist among segregated Indian, desegregated Indian, and white students. The segregated Indians had the highest percentage above the class median in art and music. The desegregated Indians did not have the highest percentage in any of the five categories. (4) There is no significant evidence to indicate that, as measured by the Questionnaire on Attitudes Toward Different Testing Situations differences exist in terms of Test anxiety among segregated Indian, desegregated Indian, and white students. Certain aspects of the results of this study do support the popular notion that there are social and educational advantages to be derived by Indian students educated in predominantly white elementary school culture and environment. The amount of possible effect on the Indians by the whites appears to be dependent on how well the Indians' culture and expectations match that of the white society which surrounds them. (AA)

LeCompte, William and Guney K. LeCompte, 1970, Effects of Education and Intercultural Contact on Traditional Attitudes in Turkey. *Journal of Social Psychology* 80:11-21.

At two different high schools in Istanbul, Turkey, 152 girls from the first and third year rate their approval of 35 statements describing traditional and individualistic actions. The statements were weighted to yield scores for seven issues involving the person in relation to his family. A separate sample of 180 high school seniors from other towns in Turkey was used to validate the directions of the scales. Correlated sample tests with the latter sample indicated that fathers were rated as significantly more traditional on six of the seven issues. Analysis of variance results for the Istanbul data supported the hypothesis that scores would be less traditional with greater education and with attendance at a foreign school. The greatest differences occured in issues involving independence on career choice and relations between the sexes, while religious practices and respect for elders showed least change.

LeCompte, William and Guney K. LeCompte, 1973, Generational Attribution in Turkish and American Youth: A Study of Social Norms Involving the Family. *Journal of Cross-Cultural Psychology* 4:175.

One hundred seventy-four Turkish and 171 American adolescents rated their own and their father's approval of 35 statements describing traditional or individualistic actions. The statements were weighted to yield scores on seven family-related issues, and the latter scores were factor analyzed. Factor scores were submitted to analysis of variance to determine the effects of culture, sex, and generational attribution (self versus father-ratings). Predictions of greater approval of individualistic actions for American versus Turkish respondents, self versus father-ratings, and males versus females were all supported with the "Independence-in-Choice" factor (p. less than .01). On the "Traditional-Respect" factor, the mean for American self-ratings alone approved of independent actions, different from all other means (p. less than .01). The possibility of sequential stages of change in different attitude domains was discussed. (AA)

Lefley, Harriet P., 1972, Modal Personality in the Bahamas. *Journal of Cross-Cultural Psychology* 3:135.

Modal personality of a colonial people evolving toward independence was investigated. The research was presented as Phase I of a longitudinal study of behavioral adaptation to sociopolitical change. A questionnaire and 40-item Sentence Completion Test, tapping aggression, anxiety, authority relations, dependency, interpersonal attitudes, values and aspirations were administered to a representative sample of 160 Bahamian adults. Passivity, hostility/acquiescence toward authority, internalization of anger, lack of achievement orientation, and a strong emphasis on interpersonal relations and psychological equilibrium, with a concurrent de-emphasis of economics, were modal characteristics. Despite significant differences in percentage response, groups differentiated by age, sex, SES, education, and father-absence were alike in central tendency. Comparative data from Thailand and the Philippines were presented. The relationship of modal personality to historical factors, and its implications for sociocultural change, were also discussed. (JA)

Lieblich, Amia, Anat Ninio and Sol Kugelmass, 1972, Effects of Ethnic Origin and Parental SES on WPPSI Performance of Preschool Children in Israel. *Journal of Cross-Cultural Psychology* 3:159.

A Hebrew translation of the Wechsler Preschool Primary Scale of Intelligence was administered to 1072 Israeli-born children aging 4 to 6 1/2 years. Groups originating from Israel, East Europe, Middle East and North Africa, all subdivided into High vs. Low SES groups, were identified. The eight groups differed significantly in the *level* but usually not in the *pattern* of the subtests' scores. First generation Oriental children performed relatively lower, but the gap between second-generation Israeli children of Oriental and Western origin is notably diminished. (JA)

Lipton, Jack P. and Raymond T. Garza, 1977, Responsibility Attribution among Mexican-American, Black, and Anglo Adolescents and Adults. *Journal of Cross-Cultural Psychology* 8(3):259-272.

Although the literature dealing with attribution of responsibility (AR) is rather extensive, the cross-cultural perspectives have not been fully explored. This study investigates AR in a rigorous, factorial design involving ethnicity (Mexican-Americans, Blacks, Anglos), sex, age (adults, adolescents), Heider's levels of causality, outcome quality (positive, negative), and outcome intensity (mild, severe). The cultural factor was highly significant both as a main effect and in interaction with other combinations of variables. It is brought out that "classic" theories of AR do not always have universal applicability and in fact may only be valid among Anglos. Explanations for these strong findings are suggested in terms of different family structures among minority groups as well as their "subordinate" status within the United States. (JA)

Littig, Lawrence W., 1971, Motives of Negro Americans Who Aspire to Traditionally Open and Closed Occupations. *Journal of Cross-Cultural Psychology* 2:77.

The aspirations of Negro American college students to occupations which traditionally have been open or closed to them were examined as functions of (a) the predominantly middle or working class status of the college attended and (b) individual differences in achievement, affiliation, and power motivation. Among Negro students in a middle class Negro college aspiration of traditionally open occupations was associated with weak affiliation motivation. Among students attending a predominantly working class Negro college, strong achievement motivation and strong power motivation were related to aspiration to traditionally closed occupations. It was inferrred that the personality basis for occupational integration may differ as a function of the social class milieu in which the Negro student is functioning at the time he makes occupational decisions. Replication on minorities in other nations is suggested. (AA)

Longabaugh, Richard, 1973, Mother Behavior as a Variable Moderating the Effects of Father Absence. *Ethos* Vol. I No. 4:457-465

Purpose: To investigate empirically one aspect on the mediating process, the mother-son relationship in father-absent as compared with father-present homes. *Hypotheses:* (1) Father-absent boys will demonstrate a more feminine semantic style than will father-present boys. (2) The mother-son interaction pattern in father-absent homes will be characterized by a higher rate of interaction than will exist in father-present homes. No such difference will obtain for daughters. *Method:* Observation of mother-child interaction in 51 mother-child dyads from a black, "lower-class" community in Cambridge, Mass.—half were of Barbadian descent, half were American. All children were 5 to 12 years of age. Questionnaire of children's dreams given to mother, then mother-child interaction observed. *Osgood semantic differential* technique used to test degree of masculinity. *Results:*

Father presence vs. absence had no main effect on masculinity of child's semantic style, nor on interaction with the child's sex, nor on mother's behavior with child. FA mothers engage sons in higher rate of resource transaction—more frequently depriving them of resources, especially autonomy, give more support and seek information more often. Mother's behavior is significantly related to masculinity of son's semantic style; the more she interacts with him, the less masculine his semantic style. *Conclusion:* Mother behavior toward the son is a variable moderating the relationship between father absence and femininity of son's semantic style (supporting Whiting's hypothesis that father absence increases the mother's manipulation of affect in relation to her son).

Lystad, Mary H., 1970, Adolescent Social Attitudes in South Africa and Swaziland. *American Anthropologist* 72:1389.

A content analysis was undertaken of stories written by adolescents in urban townships in South Africa and in an urban setting in Swaziland. The findings concerning the nature of the actors and the relationships between actors in the stories suggest that South Africans in their early years encountered more elements of modernity than do the Swazis.

McKendry, James M., Margaret S. McKendry and George M. Guthrie, 1972, Inflated Expectations and Social Reinforcement in the Lowland Philippines. *Journal of Cross-Cultural Psychology* 3:83.

Two alternative hypotheses of the psychological impact of planned social change in the lowland Philippines were investigated. (1) Planned social change produces social reinforcement which leads to a more content population; or (2) it leads to a cycle of rising expectations which outstrip actual accomplishment, the result of which is dissatisfaction and hostility—especially among the young people. Results in general favored the social reinforcement hypothesis. Efforts aimed at increasing a community's level of development tend to produce more modern value systems and increased general contentment. However, they also tend to produce a greater emphasis upon the local government to continue to meet the needs of people.

Madsen, Millard C., 1967, Cooperative and Competitive Motivation of Children in three Mexican Sub-cultures. *Psychological Reports,* 20:1307-1320.

Large samples of children in southern Mexico, representative of the urban middle class, urban poor, and a rural Indian village, participated in four experiments. These were designed to assess cooperative and competitive motivation under the following condi tions: (1) simple altruism, (2) work output, (3) solution of a problem in which competition minimized individual reward. Significant differences between groups were obtained in experiments 3 and 4 with the urban middle-class children providing to be much more competitive than their urban poor and rural counterparts.

Madsen, Millard C., 1971, Developmental and Cross-Cultural Differences in the Cooperative and Competitive Behavior of Young Children. *Journal of Cross-Cultural Psychology* 2:365.

A two-person experimental task was developed for use in the study of age and cultural differences in the cooperative-competitive behavior of children in a small Mexican town and in California. The results indicate a higher level of cooperation among Mexican than among Anglo-American children and an increase in nonadaptive competition with age among the Anglo-American children. (JA)

Madsen, Millard C. and Ariella Shapira, 1970, Cooperative and Competitive Behavior of Urban Afro-American, Anglo-American, Mexican-American and Mexican Village Children. *Developmental Psychology,* 3:16-20.

In three experiments, 48 seven to nine year old children from each of three ethnic groups in the United States performed on the cooperation board developed by M. C. Madsen. In Experiment I, Mexican-American boys were less competitive than Mexican-American girls and Afro-and Anglo-Americans of both sexes. In experiment II, all three groups behaved in a highly competitive manner. In Experiment III, the three groups behaved in a nonadaptive competitive manner while 36 seven to nine year old village children in Mexico behaved cooperatively. (JA)

Marconi, Juan, 1969, Cultural Barriers in Communication which Affect the Growth of Programs for the Control and Prevention of Alcoholism. *Acts Psiquiatrica y Psicologica de America Latina* 15:351-355.

Describes problems in reaching Chile's three cultural types—an educated middle class guided by scientific theory, a large working class guided by folk medicine, and the aborigines who practice a medicinal ritual. A survey showed alcoholism to be a large problem among the lower classes, particularly the aborigines. Existing programs for alcoholism at the National Health Service and the University of Chile are reviewed and suggestions are made for a more effective program.

Marsella, Anthony, David Kinzie and Paul Gordon, 1973, Ethnic Variations in the Expression of Depression. *Journal of Cross-Cultural Psychology* 4:435

Samples of Americans of Japanese, Chinese, and European ancestry evidencing clinical levels of depression were administered a depression symptom checklist, and the results were submitted to a factor analysis. Groups differed with respect to the functional dimensions expressed by the patterns. In general, existential symptoms dominated the patterns of the Japanese and Caucasians, while somatic symptoms were more characteristic of the Chinese. In addition, the Japanese evidenced an interpersonal symptom pattern, and both oriental groups manifested a cognitive symptom pattern. A theory was proposed which suggested that symptoms are related to extensions of the self-conditioned via socialization experiences. The role of individual differences, stress, and cultural definitions of disorder in determining the expression of depression was also discussed. (JA)

Martinez, Joe L., Sergio R. Martinez, Esteban L. Olmedo and Roy D. Goldman, 1976, The Semantic Differential Technique—A Comparison of Chicano and Anglo High School Students. *Journal of Cross-Cultural Psychology* 7(3):325-334.

Osgood's semantic differential technique was used to investigate responses of Chicano and Anglo high school students on five concepts viewed as basic to the traditional Mexican family structure: (1) self, (2) male, (3) female, (4) father, and (5) mother. It was found that the Chicanos and Anglos differed significantly on the five concepts, suggesting that these concepts have different affective meanings for the cultural groups. The results also showed that the differences seem to be centered around the potency dimension. In addition, there were sex differences also centered around the potency dimension, as well as an ethnic by sex interaction. (JA)

Mason, Evelyn P., 1969, Cross Validation Study of Personality Characteristic of Junior High School Students from American Indian, Mexican, and Caucasian Ethnic Backgrounds. *Journal of Social Psychology* 77:15-24.

A cross-validation study of the responses of twenty-two American Indian, nine Mexican-American, and sixteen Caucasian adolescents to the CPI showed an overall significant ethnic difference ordered with Caucasian highest and Indian lowest. This ordering did not occur in the 1st study and resulted from the more negative response of the Mexican male and more positive response of the Mexican female in the 2nd study. The evidence of a generalized more negative response by females regardless of ethnic background was validated, however. Of greatest significance was the consistent, all pervasive negative responses of both male and female American Indians. (JA)

Masuda, Minoru, Gary H. Matsumoto and Gerald M. Meredith,
1970, Ethnic Identity in Three Generations of Japanese Americans.
Journal of Social Psychology 81:199-207.

Ethnic identification in three generations of Japanese Americans
in Seattle, Washington, was quantified with a 50-item Ethnic Identity
Questionnaire. The total ethnic identity scores were significantly different across generations in the hypothesized direction, 1st, 2nd, 3rd.
No difference was seen between sexes within generations. Acculturation of the immigrant, 1st generation was indicated by item score
analyses as was the presence of a considerable residual of Japanese
ethnic identity in the 3rd generation Japanese-American. Education
and socio-economic status were negatively associated with ethnic identification and Buddhist religion was not a significant factor.

Masuda, Minoru R., Shin Hasegawa and Gary Matsumoto, 1973,
The Ethnic Identity Questionnaire: A Comparison of Three Japanese
Age Groups in Tachikawa, Japan, Honolulu, and Seattle, *Journal of
Cross-Cultural Psychology* 4:229

Three generational age groups of Japanese in Tachikawa, Japan,
Honolulu, and Seattle were compared on their responses to the Ethnic
Identity Questionnaire. At all locations, there was an attenuation of
ethnic identification, here seen to be defined by the instrument as Mei-
ji Era Japaneseness. The elderly were cross-culturally consensual in
their attitudes. The Seattle and Honolulu second- and third generation Japanese-Americans were more similar to each other than to their
Tachikawa age counterparts. The lower Honolulu scores were attributed to their greater social, economic, and political power. In
Tachikawa, there was a continuity of Japanese pride, but increasingly
fragmented attitudes in family kinship and traditional behavior and
attitude. (AA)

Mead, Margaret, 1966, *New Lives for Old,* New York: William Mor-
row & Co.

Purpose: To investigate problems of continuity and change among
the Manus of the southwest Pacific. *Method:* Diachronic and syn-
chronic descriptions of child development, economic and social
development among the Manus. *Conclusions:* (1) Manus believe that
all men are brothers and that (2) rapid change is not only possible, but
may actually by very desirable. "Instead of advocating slow partial
changes, we should advocate that a people who choose to practice a
new technology or enter into drastically new kinds of economic relationships will do this more easily if they live in different houses, wear
different clothes, and eat different, or differently cooked, food." Par-

tial change promotes discord. Changes in political and social structures must occur at the same time as "congruent" changes.

Melamed, Leslie, 1968, Race Awareness in South African Children.
Journal of Social Psychology 76:3-8

The relative value of four physiognomic features which
distinguish between the races in South Africa was examined at age
levels, six, eight, and ten. No age differences were found and skin col-
or appeared to be the most dominant cue used when it was available.
Age differences in learning to discriminate between the other cues
were found. This suggests that age differences found in racial
awareness of children older than six could be an artifact of the test
situation. (JA)

Melamed, Leslie, 1970, Mac Crone's Race Attitudes Scale: Thirty
Years After. *Psychologia Africana* 13:202-208

Administered I.D. Mac Crone's scale of ethnic attitudes to 57
undergraduates. Results were compared with those obtained by Mac
Crone in 1937. Marked changes were observed in the scale and Q
values. The changes in scale values were partly explained by a change
in the method of scale value assessment and by changes in *S*s' perceptions of the items. Q value changes were possibly due to the smaller
sample and a nonuniform shift in ratings of items. It is concluded that
while the scale can still be used for ordering respondents on a continuum, it cannot be used to determine absolute position on the scale.
(JA)

Miller, Anthony G., 1972, Cooperation and Competition among
Blackfoot Indian and Urban Canadian Children. *Child Development*
43:1104-1110.

Blackfoot Indian and urban Canadian children played a game requiring cooperation under two reward conditions. Under a group
reward condition children from both cultural backgrounds cooperated
effectively. Later, when the children were rewarded individually, the
Blackfoot children continued to cooperate even more effectively than
under the group reward situation, while the urban group showed competitive behavior which grossly impaired their performance. In a second game, which placed a premium on the inhibition of competitive
responses for effective play, similar, although less striking, differences
were found.

Miller, A. G., 1973, Integration and Acculturation of Cooperative
Behavior Among Blackfoot Indian and Non-Indian Canadian
Children. *Journal of Cross-Cultural Psychology* 4:374.

Teams of boys from a integrated elementary school played a

game on the Madsen Cooperation Board which, while permitting either cooperative or competitive behavior, rewarded cooperative behavior. Indian teams, all-white teams, and integrated teams all showed a similar pattern of behavior on the games. This pattern was marked differently from the behavior patterns which have been demonstrated for either Blackfoot or white children from nonintegrated schools. The behavior of all the groups from the integrated schools was midway between that of nonintegrated white and Blackfoot children in terms of the frequency of cooperative responses. The data are discussed in terms of acculturation and the effects of integrated schooling. (JA)

Niehoff, Arthur H. and J. Charnel Anderson, 1968, The Primary Variables in Directed Cross-Cultural Change. *HumRRO Professional Paper* 26:36–68.

Compared 171 cases of cross-cultural change projects, and extracted factors that acted as sanctions or barriers in the introduction of innovations. Three types of behavior were noted: (a) techniques of the change agent, e.g., communication, demonstration, and flexibility; (b) motivation—in the form of felt need, practical economic benefit, novelty—for acceptance or rejection by the recipients; and (c) reaction produced by the traditional cultural patterns, e.g., leadership, theological beliefs and economic patterns. (JA)

Okana, Yukio and Bernard Spilka, 1971, Ethnic Identity, Alienation and Achievement Orientation in Japanese-American Families. *Journal of Cross-Cultural Psychology* 2:273

The need for a strong indentification with one's traditional heritage has been a chief tenet voiced in minority group movements. To test the hypothesis that ethnic identity counters the alienative feelings attributed to minority status and supports achievement values, samples of Japanese-American high school students and their mothers were evaluated. These subjects represented Sansei and Nisei Japanese Americans, respectively. They were selected from Buddhist and Christian churches in Denver, Colorado. Buddhist mothers were found to be more ethnically identified than Christian mothers, but their children did not differ in ethnic identity. Buddhist adolescents scored higher in both achievement orientation and alienation compared with Christian adolescents. These differences were discussed in their possible relation to differential home environments.

Orpen, Christopher, 1971, The Relationship Between Extroversion and Tough-mindedness in a "Tough Minded" Culture. *Journal of Psychology* 78:27-29

Tested the hypothesis that social attitudes are not closely related to deep-lying personality trends in cases where the social attitudes are culturally sanctioned. Ninety Afrikaans-speaking South African school children brought up in the relatively "tough-minded" Afrikaans cultural climate were given measures of tender-mindedness, extroversion, and social distance. *Ss* were given the Eysenck Personality Inventory, Eysenck's Tender-Mindedness scale, and the Bogardus social distance scale. The correlation between the personality dimension of extroversion and tender-minded attitude was negligible, supporting the hypothesis. This major finding and others are discussed in terms of the cultural determination of the relationship between extroversion and tough-minded attitudes. (AA)

Ortner, Shery B., 1973, Sherpa Purity. *American Anthropologist* 75:49.

This paper explores the relationship between explicit cultural forms ("symbols") and underlying cultural orientations. It assumes the position that the two are intimately interrelated, indeed inseparable, and further that it is the symbolic forms themselves which are the mechanisms linking underlying cultural orientations to observable modes of socio-cultural action. These points are elaborated through a detailed analysis of one such body of cultural forms, the set of phenomena considered polluting among the Sherpa of Nepal. (AA)

Osborne, Olive H., 1969, The Yoruba Village as a Therapeutic Community. *Journal of Health and Social Behavior* 10:187-200.

Among the Egba-Ebgado Yoruba peoples of Nigeria there are several village psychiatric treatment programs. Nigerian psychiatrists believe that such village programs have greater therapeutic and economic efficacy than treatment modalities and structures commonly found in Western society. The identification and assessment of social and cultural elements which enhance or detract from the therapeutic potential of the village treatment programs are discussed. Psychological, social and cultural data are utilized to suggest comparisons between Yoruba therapeutic communities and Western psychiatric communities. The potential of these programs and further refinement of the concept "therapeutic community" are also considered.

Peres, Yochanan and Zipporah Levy, 1969, Jews and Arabs: Ethnic Group Stereotypes in Israel. *Race* 10:479-492.

Discusses the concept stereotype and investigates "the stereotype which Arabs and Jews have of each other, and also the stereotyped image each group has of itself." Sixty Arab and Jewish undergraduates were interviewed. The image of centrality, inferiority, deprivation, interdependence, salience and visibility, and the political and spiritual attitudes of the minority and majority are discussed and compared. (JA)

Ramirez, M., C. Taylor and B. Petersen, 1971, Mexican-American Cultural Membership and Adjustment to School. *Developmental Psychology.* 4:141-148.

Mexican-American and Anglo-American junior high and high school students of the lower socioeconomic class were administered an attitudes-toward-education scale and a projective technique consisting of pictures for which they were asked to construct stories. The results showed that Mexican-Americans had expressed views toward education which were less positive than those of Anglo-Americans. On the projective technique, Mexican-Americans scored higher than on n Power and n Rejection and lower on n Achievement than Anglo-Americans. Mexican-American males scored higher on n Succorance toward females and on N Aggression toward females who were domineering than Anglo-American males. Mexican-American females scored higher on n Autonomy than Anglo-American females. These findings were interpreted as being the result of differences between the value orientations of the Mexican-American and Anglo-American ethnic groups. (JA)

Ramirez, Manuel and Douglass R. Price-Williams, 1976, Achievement Motivation in Children of Three Ethnic Groups in the United States. *Journal of Cross-Cultural Psychology.* 7(1):49-60.

Children of three ethnic groups in the United States—Anglos, Blacks, and Mexican Americans—were asked to tell a story about each of seven line drawings depicting persons in a setting related to education. Stories were scored for N achievement and family achievement (oriented toward achievement goals from which family would benefit or that would gain recognition from family members). The results showed that Mexican-American and Black children scored higher on family achievement than did Anglo children. Anglos however, scored higher on N achievement. On those cards depicting parental figures, however, Mexican-American and Black children tended to score higher on N achievement than did Anglo children. Females in all three ethnic groups scored lower on N achievement but higher on family achievement than males. It was concluded that contextual conditions are most important in expression of achievement motivation and that the particular form in which achievement is expressed is determined by the definition that culture gives to it. (AA)

Ramon, Shulamit, 1972, The Impact of Culture Change on Schizophrenia in Israel. *Journal of Cross-Cultural Psychology* 3:373.

This Israeli-based study considered the hypothesis that culture change, as a social process, can influence a family involved in this process to the point that one of its offspring exhibits schizophrenic behavior. The sample consisted of forty triads (parents and their young adult son) divided into four groups according to the variables of country of origin (Poland and Yemen) with and without a schizophrenic offspring. Interactions between cultural deviance and defects in communication was assumed. It was hypothesized that the group of families of schizophrenics expected to be higher on the cultural deviance score (Yemen) would be lower on defects in communication than the comparable group (Poland). Measures of the two interacting variables were derived from TAT stories given by each triad as a group. The findings confirm the hypothesis and thus allow the conclusion that, at present, defects in communication are conducive to cultural deviance in families of the Schizophrenic-Yemen group. (AA)

Resner, Gerald and Joseph Hartog, 1970, Concepts and Terminology of Mental Disorders Among Malays. *Journal of Cross-Cultural Psychology* 1:369.

This paper presents the concepts and terminology of mental disorder as they emerged spontaneously from Malays, both urban and rural, of West Malaysia during nearly 2 years of interviewing and examining patients and nonpatients. Translated into a Western framework and summarized, the concepts are: heredity, periodicity, congeniality, brain strain, stress (including interpersonal), susceptibility, infection, contagion, delayed onset, conditioning, and resistance. The parallelism between these folk and modern concepts suggest certain universal bases and clues to labeling and treatment of mental disorders. The study revealed existence of a skeletal community mental health program. (AA)

Rodgers, William B. and Richard E. Gardner, 1969, Linked Changes in Values and Behavior in the Out-Island Bahamas. *American Anthropologist* 71:21-35.

The relationships between observable changes in sociocultural behavior on the one hand and underlying value systems on the other is examined in two communities that stem from a single sociocultural tradition but that recently diverged because of differential exposure to economic development. Value preferences of individuals in each community were elicited by structured questionnaires, which allowed operational measurement of values and statistical testing of differences within and between the community samples. The findings are explained with reference to the nature of the behavioral responses of individuals to perceived modifications (related to economic development) in their environment. (AA)

Roll, Samuel and C. Brooks Brenneis, 1975, Chicano and Anglo Dreams of Death: A Replication. *Journal of Cross-Cultural Psychology* 6(3):377-383.

To replicate an earlier study in which Chicanos reported having more dreams of death than did their Anglo counterparts, we solicited dream reports from eighty Chicanos (forty males and forty females) and eighty Anglos (forty males and forty females). The dreams were scored for the presence of death-related dream content. Chi-Square tests revealed a statistically higher number of Chicano females reporting dreams of death (p less than .005), but the differences between Chicano males and Anglo males was not significant. The results were linked to the greater phenomenological emphasis on death in Chicano culture and greater tendency for Chicano women to carry the influences of the culture. (JA)

Ronch, Judah, Robert L. Cooper and Joshua A. Fishman, 1969, Word Naming and Usage Scores for a Sample of Yiddish-English Bilinguals. *Modern Language Journal* 53:232-235.

Reviewed the findings of a study using eight male, and seven female European-born Jewish adults who had used Yiddish as children and who continued in the United States for forty to sixty years. The societal domains measured were home, ethnic behavior, work, neighborhood, and Jewish cultural activities. A Word Naming Test in English and Yiddish was administered, and analysis of variance revealed that the "ratio of English to Yiddish words named varied as a function of domains." Ss rated themselves as using the most English in the home domain. Compared with analogous Puerto Ricans, the Yiddish-English bilinguals use more English in the home domain than do the Puerto Ricans. (JA)

Rosen, Bernard C., 1961, Family Structure and Achievement Motivation. *American Sociological Review.* 26:574-585.

The relationship of four demographic factors—family size, ordinal position, mother's age, and social class—to the socialization process and their impact upon the development of achievement motivation is examined in a study of two independent samples of young boys and their mothers. The data were obtained by means of projective test, personal interviews, and group-administered questionnaires. An analysis of the data indicates that these demographic variables are relevant to the development of achievement motivation, but their effects are complex, intricately inter-connected with one another, and difficult to assess individually. (JA)

Rothbart, Myron, 1970, Assessing the Likelihood of a Threatening Event: English Canadians' Evaluation of the Quebec Separatist Movement. *Journal of Personality and Social Psychology* 15:109-117.

Contrasted attitudes of 191 English Canadians living in Quebec with attitudes of a comparable, nonthreatened group living outside of French Canada. Measures were obtained of: (a) perceived causes of French Canadian dissatisfaction, (b) perceived strength of the separatist movement, (c) amount of information regarding separatism, (d) degree of opposition to separatism, and (e) estimated likelihood of Quebec's eventual separatism from Canada. On the basis of group differences and within-group multiple regression analysis, it was observed that estimated likelihood of separation varied inversely with strength of opposition to separation, and directly with knowledge of the separatist movement. It is proposed that a *S*s estimate of the likelihood of a threatening political event was the result of two competing factors: (a) his desire to minimize the prospect of an undesirable event, and (b) his awareness of the social conditions giving rise to that event. It is argued that fear motivates denial of a threat, but that the strength of the denial process could be sharply attenuated by the knowledge of the threatening event. (JA)

Roy, Chunilal, Ajit Choudhuri and Donald Irvine, 1970, The Prevalence of Mental Disorders among Saskatchewan Indians. *Journal of Cross-Cultural Psychology* 1:383.

Indian communities in Saskatchewan are undergoing social changes as a result of rapid growth in populations and a closer contact with the non-Indian communities. The effect of such changes may be reflected in the nature and extent of the mental health problems among the Indian populations. This paper is an attempt to understand such problems in Saskatchewan. Analysis of hospital first-admission statistics at the North Battleford psychiatric institution, for the period from 1961 to 1966, showed that the Indian sample contained significantly higher numbers of schizophrenics and epileptics. These findings prompted an active case-finding survey for the first time in Canada in an arbitrarily defined geographical area which contained 18 rural municipalities (non-Indian) and ten Indian reserves. Analysis of the data revealed that the prevalence of mental disorder was significantly higher in the Indian communities. Furthermore, the Indian sample contained significantly higher numbers of schizophrenics and mental retardates. Findings are discussed in terms of relevance to future cross-cultural psychiatric research and methodological problems. (AA)

Sanday, Peggy R., 1971, Analysis of the Psychological Reality of American-English Kin Terms in Urban Poverty Environment. *American Anthropologist* 73:555.

The purpose of this paper is (1) to describe and explain variation in the psychological reality of American-English kinship terms; and (2) to examine the relationship between results obtained in two approaches which have been used to find psychologically real definitions of American-English kinship terms. A general hypothesis is proposed which accounts for variation in psychological reality in terms of life cycle and certain social role variables, as well as the individual's experiential knowledge of the domain under study. This hypothesis was accepted after it was revised to include the mediating influence of the content of what is stored in memory. The data for this study were collected in a U.S. urban poverty environment. (AA)

Sanders, Mary, James P. Scholz and Spencer Kagan, 1976, Three Social Motives and Field Independence-Dependence in Anglo American and Mexican American Children. *Journal of Cross-Cultural Psychology*, 7(4):451-462.

Previous research has indicated that Mexican American children have higher N affiliation and are more field dependent than Anglo American children, who are more field independent and tend to have higher N achievement. The present study examines N achievement, N affiliation, N power, and field independence-field dependence among Anglo and Mexican American children. As predicted, Anglo American children were significantly more field independent, higher on N achievement and tended to be higher on N power; Mexican American children tended to be higher on N affiliation. Contrary to predictions, field independence-dependence was not related to N affiliation or N power; only the predicted positive relationship between field independence and N achievement was confirmed. Results are inconsistent with some previous conclusions that field dependence is related to the greater N affiliation of Mexican American compared to Anglo American children. (JA)

Sanjek, Roger, 1971, Brazilian Racial Terms: Some Aspects of Meaning and Learning. *American Anthropologist* 73:1126.

Harris notes that the New Ethnography has been characterized by a lack of quantitative methods. In a study of racial vocabulary in a Brazilian village, quantitative procedures are employed to show that, despite considerable ambiguity, a small portion of the corpus of 116 terms forms the cognitive map of most informants and organized the bulk of the domain. Data on how children acquire the vocabulary is used to demonstrate that skin color and hair form are the primary variables. (AA)

Sapir, J. David, 1970, Kujaama: Symbolic Separation among the Diola-Fogny. *American Anthropologist* 72:1330-1348.

The Diola-Fogny concept of "kujaama" represents a complex symbol that defines a set of pollution rules having to do mainly with blood and food avoidance between generations and between husband and wife at the death of one or the other. Analysis of the diverse manifestations of *Kujaama* shows that each represents bu one variant of a general principle, that is, the inauspiciousness of mixing separate categories. Further analysis places *kujaama* in the larger context of Fogny moral life and places the rituals associated with *kujaama* in the "grammar" of ritual acts and gestures. (AA)

Schwartz, Lola R., 1969, The Hierarchy of Resort in Curative Practices: The Admiralty Islands, Melanesia. *Journal of Health and Social Behavior* 10:201-209.

Relates the treatment of illness in the Admiralty Islands to the assignment of illness to one of four main categories: (a) interpersonal, soul damage by extrahuman agents, (b) interpersonal curing within group, (c) interpersonal sorcery outside of the group, and (d) impersonal organic damage by an imminent impersonal agent. The first two causal assignments persist as explanations for illness with implications for traditional cures in every instance. The third and fourth assignments vary inversely with one another in priority of resort to native or European curative practives. An analysis of factors in the allocation of cases between European (acculturative) and native (counter-acculturative) curative agents is presented.

Schwartz, Theodore, 1973, Cult and Context: The Paranoid Ethos in Melanesia. *Ethos* 2:153.

The cargo cult as a type-response to culture contact occurs in the context of an area-wide paranoid ethos that underlies Melanesian cultures. This article considers an aspect of cargo cults as a mode of psycho-cultural adjustment generated in the interaction between the deep, persisting stuctures of Melanesian and Western cultures.

Scribner, Sylvia and Michael Cole, 1973, Cognitive Consequences of Formal and Informal Education. *Science* 182:553-559.

Hypotheses: (a) That differences in the social organization of education promote differences in the organization of learning and thinking skills in the individual. (b) That school represents a specialized set of educational experiences which are discontinuous from those encountered in everyday life and that it requires and promotes ways of learning and thinking which often run counter to those nurtured in practical daily activities. *Method:* Cross culturally comparing evidence from various sources on education both in and out of school; in informal education, noninstitutional formal education, school learning, functional learning systems. *Conclusions:* The school's knowledge base, value system, and dominant learning situations, and the functional learning systems to which they give rise are all in conflict with those of the student's traditional culture. However, to expect massive changes in educational outcomes without a readiness to change the social organization of education is to invite cynicism and disillusionment.

Seda-Bonilla, Eduardo, 1969, Spiritualism, Psychoanalysis and Psychodrama. *American Anthropologist* 71:492.

The term "fluids" of spiritualism seems related to the libido concept in psychoanalysis. A mental breakdown explained as possession by spirits with whom the patient has been in contact in another existence (existential situation) seems to have affinity with a phenomenon similar to what psychoanalysts call a "flooding of the ego by a return of the repressed." When compared with psychotherapeutic practice, spiritualism reveals clear affinities with psychodrama.

Shapira, Ariella and Millard C. Madsen, 1969, Cooperative and Competitive Behavior of Kibbutz and Urban Children in Israel. *Child Development* 40(2):609-617.

Israeli children raised in either a kibbutz or urban setting participated in two experiments designed to assess the degree of cooperative versus competitive behavior. In Example I, both groups cooperated adaptively under group reward. With a change from group to individual reward, however, urban *S*s began to compete in a nonadaptive manner, while kibbutz *S*s continued to cooperate. Example II, in which competitive responding was more adaptive than in Experiment I, also showed kibbutz *S*s to be less competitive than urban *S*s, by a marginal level of significance. (JA)

Shapira, Ariella and Jacob Lomranz, 1972, Cooperative and Competitive Behavior of Rural Arab Children in Israel. *Journal of Cross-Cultural Psychology* 3:353.

Twenty groups of 9 to 11 year old boys and girls from an Arab village in Israel played a game which required cooperative interaction among them to attain prizes. Half of the groups consisted of children of the same "Hamula" (extended family) and half of children from different Hamulas. It was found that boys were more cooperative than girls. Hamula boys were less cooperative than non-Hamula boys, and Hamula girls were more cooperative than non-Hamula girls. These Arab village results were compared with cooperation-competition among subjects from rural communities in Mexico, the Canadian Indian population and Israeli kibbutzim. (JA)

Slogett, Barbara B., Ronald Gallimore and Edward S. Kubany, 1970, A Comparative Analysis of Fantasy Need Achievement among High and Low Achieving Male Hawaii-Americans. *Journal of Cross-Cultural Psychology* 1:53.

Fantasy need achievement scores were obtained from male high school students representing three ethnic groups: Filipino-Americans, Japanese-Americans, and indigenous Hawaiians who were further categorized into high-achieving and low-achieving groups. The only significant differences were between the Japanese and the two Hawaiian groups who had the lowest n Ach. These findings were interpreted as challenging the usefulness of the notion that Hawaiian children do well or poorly in school because they possess or lack n Ach.

Stanley, Gordon, 1969, Australian Students' Attitudes to Negroes and Aborigines on the Multifactor Racial Attitude Inventory (MRAI). *Journal of Social Psychology* 77:281-282.

The MRAI was administered to two groups of white Australian university students, one responding with the American Negro as target person (n = 76), the other with the Australian Aborigine as target person (n = 73). There were not significant differences between attitudes on these two groups and the cultural dissimilarity of the groups. The Australian students indicated a more favorable attitude to Negroes than American students.

Sundberg, Norman D., Pritam K. Rohila and Leona E. Tyler, 1970, Values of Indian and American Adolescents. *Journal of Personality and Social Psychology* 16:374-397.

Derived 17 hypotheses about Indian-American differences from a literature review. 9th grade Ss representing school populations in towns in Northern India (N = 48) and Western United States (N = 48) answered 90 Q-sort items. As expected, Indian Ss scored higher on deference and conformity, external control, extrinsic work values, and planning; Americans scored higher on sociability, sensuous enjoyment, and religiosity. Contrary to expectations, no differences were found in individuality, free will, and democratic values. When items were dichotomized into endorsement and rejection, the two groups showed four times as much communality in divergence. Similarity was greater between sexes within the cultures than across cultures. Findings imply more complexity than is suggested by the distinction between traditional and modern values. (JA)

Sydiaha, Daniel and Irving Rootman, 1969, Ethnic Groups within Communities: A Comparative Study of the Expression and Definition of Mental Illness. *Psychiatric Quarterly* 43:131-146.

Examined differences between French and non-French samples in two Canadian communities in an attempt to assess the importance of "traditional," "local," and "societal" cultural factors. Seventy percent of one community was French and thirteen per cent of the other. No evidence was found "for the importance of ethnic factors ('traditional culture') in the expression of mental illness or in community attitudes and conceptions about mental illness. . . .Minority groups in both communities tended to have a higher incidence of mental illness, and the non-French minority in the French community tended to be most uninformed in its attitudes and conceptions about mental illness." The pattern was considered an indirect ethnic influence. "Most of the statistically significant differences were obtained between towns, rather than within." (JA)

Szalay, Lorand B., Dale A. Lysne and Jean A. Bryson, 1972, Designing and Testing Cogent Communications. *Journal of Cross-Cultural Psychology* 3:247.

Experiments involving choice tasks were conducted to test the potential utility of word associations in constructing assertions and messages that are cogent in the sense that they actually bear on the interests and experiences of a particular audience. Similarity judgment tasks, which were based on verbal association data previously obtained from similar groups, were administered to U.S. and Korean student samples. The results supported the hypothesis that associations previously scoring higher by one cultural group would be judged "more similar," "more related," by a group from the same culture. In another experiment administered only to the Korean group, higher-scoring associations and their respective communication themes were combined into assertions. It was assumed that assertions based on strong associative linkages would be judged more meaningful by groups similar to the one on which the original data were obtained. The cogency of these association-based assertions constructed on the same themes by two cultural experts on Korea; the association-based assertions were found to be significantly more meaningful. (AA)

Tan, Mely G., 1968, "Social Mobility and Assimilation: The Chinese in the United States." Ph.D. Dissertation, University of California, Berkeley.

"This study proposes to examine the consequences of upward social mobility for racial or ethnic minority groups. Existing literature has shown that the question whether social mobility leads to structural assimilation, i.e., the disappearance of the group as a distinct entity, is problematic. The focus of this study is on the Chinese in the United States as a group which shows evidence of rapid social mobility and is recognizable as an ethnic minority group. . . . This attitude indicates an adherence to the idea of cultural pluralism. A crucial factor for the acceptance of this idea as the basic philosophy in race and ethnic relations is the attitude and social climate in the larger society. Undoubtedly, in this respect, there is and there will continue to be variation in time, by area, by degree of favorableness and by race or ethnic group involved. Today, the social climate in San Francisco seems favorable, at least towards the Orientals; witness the recent addition of the name in Chinese characters on the street signs in the Chinatown area and the rebuilding of Nihonmachi or Japan Town."

Taub, John M., 1971, The Sleep-Wakefulness Cycle in Mexican Adults. *Journal of Cross-Cultural Psychology* 2:353.

The sleep-wakefulness patterns of 257 Mexican males and females ranging in age from the 20s to 80s was studied using a questionnaire. The average duration of sleep exceeded that typically prescribed for other Western cultures (8 hours per 24), and significantly varied with age decreasing from the 20s to 50s, after which there was an increase. There was a significantly greater incidence of sleep disturbance in subjects over 50 compared to the other *S*s. The post-awakening mood of those with sleep disturbance and those over 50 was marked by a significantly greater frequency of negative affect. Significant age and sex differences were found for the frequency of dream recall. The duration and frequency of daytime naps in *S*s of all age groups revealed the presence of a polycyclic sleep-wakefulness cycle which has not been reported with such generality in other Western cultures. (JA)

Taylor, D. M., E. P. Dagot and R. C. Gardner, 1969, The Use of the Semantic Differential in Cross-Cultural Research. *Philippine Journal of Psychology* 2:43-51.

Two groups of English-Tagalog bilinguals rated each of eight ethnic group labels on the same forty-eight semantic diffential scales.

One hundred two responsed in English while a second group of 111 *Ss* was administered an identical form of the scales prepared in Tagalog by means of a back-translation procedure. Results indicate that there was moderate agreement between the factor structures of the ratings on both forms of the scales. In terms of responses on individual scales it seemed clear that the *Ss* who responded in their native language (Tagalog) were more willing to express thenselves evaluatively than those *Ss* who made their ratings on the English form. (JA)

Taylor, Donald M. and Lise M. Simrad, 1972, The Role of Bilingualism in Cross-Cutural Communication. *Journal of Cross-Cultural Psychology.* 3:101.

Mixed ethnic pairs of *Ss* (French/English) and same ethnic pairs (French/French and English/English) performed an experimental task designed to assess communicational efficiency. Following the communication tasks *Ss* completed a questionnaire which assessed their bilingual skills and attitudes about communicating with a member of a different ethnic group. The *Ss*, unlike previous studies, were French and English Canadian factory workers who daily interact with members of the other ethnic group. The results demonstrated that cross-cultural communication can be as efficient as within group communication. This efficiency seems to result because of a reciprocal bilingualism where members of each group have some degree of fluency in the language of the other. For the communication task both French and English were used almost equally and positive attitudes about communication were evidenced. (JA)

Termansen, Paul E. and Joan Ryan, 1970, Health and Disease in a British Columbian Indian Community. *Canadian Psychiatric Association Journal* 15:121-127.

Reviews previous studies on the type and incidence of physical and mental illness among the legal Indians in British Columbia. Data was gathered from responses of 51 doctors to a questionnaire and the provincial mental hospital charts and interviews. Results indicate a low incidence of mental disorder and raise questions as the the "manner in which Indian communities define and deal with mental illness." (JA)

Thompson, L. and J.A. Hostetler, 1970, The Hutterian Confession of Faith: A Documentary Analysis. *Alberta Journal of Educational Research* 16:29.

An experimental attempt is made to formulate the traditional character of the Hutterian Brethren from 16th century source documents. Original texts are analyzed in terms of 5 categories developed for purposes of cross-cultural comparison. The purpose of the analysis is to provide a basis for illuminating the problem of culture change in belief systems and to demonstrate a scientifically valid method of character analysis using historical sources. It is suggested that this model may be found useful for effective comparison of value systems of mankind on a worldwide scale. (JA)

Torrey, E. Fuller, 1970, Mental Health Services for American Indians and Eskimos. *Community Mental Health Journal* 6:455.

Surveys past and present mental health services for American Indians and Eskimos and finds them to be inadequate. A plan is outlined for the development of such services based upon a cooperative rather than a paternalistic venture with these minority groups. The plan is based upon the use of indigenous therapists for individual and group psychotherapy, the modification of etiological beliefs, and an emphasis upon primary prevention. The Alaskan Eskimo is used to illustrate how these principles could be into effect. The outcome would be a system of mental health services specifically adapted to the culture, realistically commensurate with available manpower, and compatible with dignity for the group.

Trible, Joseph Everett, 1969, "Psychosocial Characteristics of Employed and Unemployed Western Oklahoma Male American Indians." Ph.D. dissertation, the University of Oklahoma.

This study initially addresses itself to the problem of acculturation and, in particular, the problems of unemployment encountered by the Indian. More specifically, the main focus is an investigation inot some fo the psychosocial characteristics of the unemployed and employed Indian. Representing 19 different tribes living in western Oklahoma, 143 *S*s were presented with the California Psychological Inventory and a Labor Force Survey. The data, in the form of 69 variables on each *S* was analyzed by various multivariate statistical procedures. The findings from the analysis indicate that a set of *a priori* variables can serve as an index for discriminating between unemployed and employed Indians and that such a set of indices can serve to predict the probability of association for each *S* to one group or the other. Additional analyses were performed in the personality differences and several salient differences were found, particularly in the area of social and moral responsibilities, achievement potential, and certain other elements of the self concept. Additional nonparametric analyses were performed on certain sociological variables that constituted a modified "acculturation index" and several salient differences were found. Among those were the facts that the level of education and vocational training were unrelated to employment status. Finally, the study analyzed possible implications of the differences and suggested follow-up research on the predictive validity and the implementation of the indices to assist in a resolution of the unemployment problem among Indians. (JA)

Trujillo, Rupert, 1969, "Rural New Mexicans: Their Educational and Occupational Aspirations." Ed.D. dissertation, The University of New Mexico.

The purposes of this study were to investigate, within the framework of level of aspiration theory, the effects of an education-occupational program on (1) rural adults' educational and occupational aspirations and general areas of beliefs which tend to affect the individuals's ability to adapt to the conditions of urban economic life, and (2) rural students' educational and occupational aspirations, general areas of beliefs which tend to affect the individual's ability to adapt to the conditions of urban economic life, and school attitude. Results indicate that students have higher aspirations than their parents. A positive relation was found between attitudes toward change, mobility and adaptability and student's living in improved houses. Probably the most noteworthy finding was the fact that students living in improved houses attended school more often than students from houses which had not been improved.

Vogler, James Donald, 1968, "The Influence of Ethnicity and Socioeconomic Status on the Pictorial Test of Intelligence." Ed.D dissertation, University of Arizona.

Problem: This study sought to determine the influence of ethnicity and socioeconomic status on the Pictorial Test of Intelligence (PTI) by investigation the following questions: (1) Does Ethnicity of socioeconomic status effect differences in the distribution of IQ or individual subtest scores on the PTI? (2) Does ethnicity or socioeconomic status effect differences in the overall pattern of PTI subtest? (3) Are there items which are less culturally weighted then others? (4) Does ethnicity or socioeconomic status effect differences in predictive validity of the PTI? *Procedure:* Response to the PTI were obtained from 108 subjects representing samples of 27 subjects each selected from four different ethnic and socioeconomic status groups (upper Anglo, upper Mexican-American, lower Anglo, lower Mexican-American). In addition, their scores on the Metropolitan Readiness Test, Stanford Achievement Test, and their grades in reading and arithmetic were also obtained. *Findings and Conclusions:* One-way analyses of variance revealed significant differences (generally in favor of Anglo ethnic group membership and upper socioeconomic status) among the four groups in the study of all be the

Immediate Recall subtest. Factorial analyses of variance indicated that there was no significant interaction between ethnicity and socioeconomic status. It was also indicated that socio-economic status effected differences in six of the seven separate scores (total and six subtests) while ethnicity effected differences in only three of these. Thus, it was concluded that socio-economic status contributed more to the group differences in PTI scores than did ethnic group membership. The separate subtest scores for the four groups in the study were converted to normalized standard scores and, through analysis of variance, significant differences among the overall patterns were found to exist. The chi-square test was applied to the differences among the number of subjects in each of the four groups passing a particular item. With the exception of those items which could not be tested because of low excepted frequencies, all of the items on the Immediate Recall subtest failed to discriminate at or beyond the .10 level of significance and thus were determined to be "culture fair." It was noted that the predictive validity of the Immediate Recall subtest, scores, was only .09. The remaining subtests, by comparison, ranged from .40 to .59. Thus, it was concluded that removing the "cultural differentials" from a test may reduce its validity for the prediction of a culturally loaded criterion such as educational achievement test scores. No significant differences were found to exist among the four groups in the study in correlations of IQ scores on the PTI with Stanford Achievement Test scores or grades in reading and arithmetic. Significant differences did exist, however, in correlation with the Metropolitan Readiness Test. On the basis of the findings of the study, it was concluded that the PTI tends to discriminate against children from the Mexican-American and lower socio-economic status cultures in much the same fashion as the majority of the existing intelligence tests. (JA)

Werner, Emmy, E. and Rajalakshmi Muralidharan, 1970, Nutrition, Cognitive Status and Achievement Motivation of New Delhi Nursey School Children. *Journal of Cross-Cultural Psychology* 1:271.

Significant differences in head circumferences and growth rate, the Draw-A-Man IQ and measures of visual-motor development were found between 24 inadequately and 16 adequately nourished New Delhi nursery school children from lower-middle class homes. No differences were found on measures of language development when parental income, occupation and nursery school attendance were controlled. Results of achievement motivation tests varied with the sex of the child. On most measures, inadequately nourished children showed greater variability than the adequately nourished, and inadequately nourished girls had lower mean scores than inadequately nourished boys.

Weston, Peter J. and Martha T. Mednick, 1970, Race, Social Class and the Motive to Avoid Success in Women. *Journal of Cross-Cultural Psychology* 1:283.

This study sought to examine race and social class differences in the expression of fear of success in women. This concept, termed the Motive to Avoid Success (M-s), was developed and utilized by Horner (1968) to explain sex differences in achievement motivation. In our study, M-s imagery expressed in response to TAT-verbal cues was compared for black and white college women and two social class levels. The hypothesis that black women would show less M-s than white women was supported. The findings held for subjects at two schools and for two verbal cues. Social class differences were not found. Several interpretations and suggestions for follow-up studies are given.

Williams, Trevor H., 1972, Educational Aspirations: Longitudinal Evidence on Their Development in Canadian Youth. *Sociology of Education* 45:107.

The development of educational aspirations in high school students is represented in a casual model developed from the point of view of reference group theory and including measures of the influence of various causes specified is central to the investigation. The model is quantified via path analytic procedures separately for males and females using data on 3,687 Canadian students. The data suggest that the influence of referents changes over time, that parents exert the greatest influence, and that sex differences in this decision-making process are manifest.

Wolman, Carol, 1970, Group Therapy in Two Languages, English and Navajo. *American Journal of Psychotherapy* 24:677-685.

Reviews those social factors which lead many Navajo reservation Indians to alcohol abuse. Group therapy sessions are described where the Navajo language was employed and translated to the therapist by an interpreter. Guidelines for future groups of this nature are suggested. (JA)

Young, Virginia Heyer, 1970, Family and Childhood in a Southern Negro Community, *American Anthropologist* 72:269-288.

The American Negro family is generally interpreted, ethnocentrically, as an impoverished version of the American white family, in which deprivation has induced pathogenic and dysfunctional features. This concept of the family is assumed in studies of Negro personality formation, which furthermore have relied entirely on clinical methods of research. Fieldwork among Negro town-dwellers in the Southeastern United States plus a reassessment of the literature yield a sharply contrasting portrait and interpretation of the American Negro family in which organization strength and functionality are found. Observations of parent-child relations show highly distinctive behavioral styles, some of which have remained undiscovered by psychoanalytically oriented studies and others of which differ markedly from the extrapolations of clinical research. These forms and styles are viewed as aspects of an indigenous culture is argued as a corrective to the common viewpoint of deprivation as the prime cause of Negro behavior. (AA)

Za'rour, George I., 1972, Superstitions among Certain Groups of Lebanese Arab Students in Beirut. *Journal of Cross-Cultural Psychology* 3:273.

This study is partly exploratory to assess the extent to which superstitious beliefs and behavior are common among different groups of high school and university Lebanese Arab students in Beirut. Class level, sex, high school science achievement, and academic major were the main variables that were investigated as to their relevance to superstitiousness. More than 600 students in the 8th and 11th high school grades and university sophmores answered 59 items relating to superstitions with respect to acquaintance, belief in, and influence on behavior. It was found that superstitiousness significantly decreased with increasing level of education. Among the other variables investigated, the major findings were that among the university sophomore students, females and arts students were respectively more superstitious than males and science students. (AA)

Ziegler, Michael, Michael King, Johanna M. King and Suzanne M. Ziegler, 1972, Tribal Stereotypes Among Ethiopian Students. *Journal of Cross-Cultural Psychology* 3:193.

Ethnic stereotyping by Ethiopian students of four important ethnolinguistic groups (the Amhara, Tigre, Galla, and Gurage) was investigated. The method used was a modification of the Katz and Braly technique for assessing generality of stereotypes. The tendency to stereotype both one's own and other groups was quite marked, and there was considerable overlap between in-group and out-group description. Where there were discrepancies, the in-group evaluation was more positive and the out-group evaluation more negative. Individuals showed consistent differences in tendency to stereotype. Some of the stereotypic adjectives used support earlier, European descriptions; others indicate that Ethiopian students' attitudes reflect the country's movement towards modernization and Westernization.

Index

Index